Digital Business Discourse

Digital Business Discourse

Edited by

Erika Darics
Aston University, UK

First published 2015 by
PALGRAVE MACMILLAN

Palgrave Macmillan in the UK is an imprint of Macmillan Publishers Limited,
registered in England, company number 785998, of Houndmills, Basingstoke,
Hampshire RG21 6XS.

Palgrave Macmillan in the US is a division of St Martin's Press LLC,
175 Fifth Avenue, New York, NY 10010.

Palgrave Macmillan is a global academic imprint of the above companies and
has companies and representatives throughout the world.

Palgrave® and Macmillan® are registered trademarks in the United States,
the United Kingdom, Europe and other countries.

ISBN 978–1–137–40556–2

This book is printed on paper suitable for recycling and made from fully
managed and sustained forest sources. Logging, pulping and manufacturing
processes are expected to conform to the environmental regulations of the
country of origin.

A catalogue record for this book is available from the British Library.

A catalog record for this book is available from the Library of Congress.

Typeset by MPS Limited, Chennai, India.

Contents

List of Figures and Tables

Figures

Tables

Foreword

There is something intellectually stimulating in satisfying the child-like curiosity of uncovering the worlds hidden in a word. One of the reasons I agreed to write a foreword for this volume is because the title contains two words that have dominated my research life, "business" and "discourse," and are now increasingly appearing in association with "digital" in academic and professional literatures.

The *Oxford English Dictionary* reminds us that the more recent definition of "digital" refers to the sequence of discrete digits used by the new generation of computers (Holden, 2014). Since the 1980s, "digital" has come to be applied to large and small entities alike, from art and economy to shopping carts and ink. Few areas of human activity are unaffected by progressive and pervasive "digitization," a transformation greatly aided not only by the sophisticated products of ubiquitous computing but also, and especially, by the capillary presence of email, IM (instant messaging), and social media.

This volume is witness to this life-changing development: "Business Discourse" is now history (albeit very recent history), as new research developments inexorably push toward the new frontier of Digital Business Discourse (DBD). Business discourse as a multidisciplinary endeavor dates back to the 1990s, which makes it a contemporary of the growth of Internet in the West, but the speed of development and spread of digital business is a phenomenon that has taken both practitioners and researchers by surprise.

In a discussion on the ethics of commercial computing, IM is described as "essentially the CB radio of the Internet generation. ... one of the 'killer apps' in the land of Internet" (https://ethics.csc.ncsu.edu/commerce/anticompetitive/instant/study.php; accessed on November 12, 2014). As the studies of IM in organizational settings included in this volume show, IM can generate contradictory perceptions and reactions in its users, ranging from the pressure of continuous availability to increased social distance between interlocutors; the latter appears to provide an interactional environment where interpersonal conflict in the workplace can be negotiated without the pressures of face-to-face contact.

There is also a darker side to IM in the workplace: to what extent has IM become a tool for employee monitoring, and how concerned should both users and DBD researchers be about this development? While instantaneous connectivity supports multitasking and perhaps, ultimately, increases business effectiveness, studies of IM usage in organizations also raise disturbing issues engendered by digitization's erosion of the thin and highly penetrable boundary between public–personal spheres.

If IM is not intentionally public, the use of Twitter in business is unashamedly self-presentational and self-promotional, allegedly "democratic" in outlook but highly controlled and controlling in its operation. Similarly, Twitter deploys a 1,800-strong contingent of engineers to support the "public performance" of its users, CEOs included, which leads Girginova (this volume) to conclude that we are in the presence of "an important actor – not just a neutral container."

The studies in the present volume collectively represent a robust body of empirical research on technology use in and for organizational communication; some authors also suggest that a holistic, existential approach to digital business discourse could open up new vistas. For example, *communicology* (Maier and Deluliis, this volume), unveils the layers of meanings accessible through an exploration of the existential nature of communication, "the unique sense of being-in-the-workplace" generated by the "experience of using technology to communicate."

This, more philosophical approach to the relationship between the human and the digital enables us to ask impertinent questions about the forced (hyper)sociality of synchronous mediated communication. What is the personal cost of uninterrupted availability? Is "sociability" measurable in terms of the devices that keep us permanently connected? Under what circumstances are employees allowed to be "anti-social" by logging off from their IM/email and not answering work-related telephone calls out of hours?

The ubiquity of technology at and for work has created a social environment where social actors operate through mobile phones, tablets, and computers, as if these were additional, essential extensions of human bodies, organically integrated with the other physical limbs. We can surmise that the dependence of the social body on technology created by digitalization is potentially responsible for altering the experiential quality of being-in-the-world.

For Maurice Merleau-Ponty (1962), the great phenomenologist of perception, the body is the concrete expression of our being in the world and the foundation of a haptic epistemology. The body is the "nexus of living meanings" (p. 151), the centre of perceptual life so that "external perception and the perception of one's body vary in conjunction because they are two facets of one and the same act" (p. 205). If "perception opens up the horizons within which all knowledge takes place" (p. 207), how does digitalization enhance (or otherwise) the experiential reach of the social body in the workplace?

The current volume is instrumental in decisively and uniquely moving the field on, from BD (Business Discourse) to Digital Business Discourse (DBD): an obligatory step in the exploration of the social implications of the forthcoming DbD (Digital-by-Default) world.

Francesca Bargiela-Chiappini
University of Warwick

References

Holden, Richard (2014) "digital". http://public.oed.com/aspects-of-english/word-stories/digital/. Accessed on November 10, 2014.

Merleau-Ponty, Maurice (1962) *Phenomenology of Perception*. New York: Routledge & Kegan Paul.

NC State University (n.d.) "Ethics in Computing". https://ethics.csc.ncsu.edu/commerce/anticompetitive/instant/study.php. Accessed on November 12, 2014.

Acknowledgments

I am extremely grateful to all the colleagues who agreed to contribute to this volume and who volunteered their time and knowledge to review each other's work. I am particularly grateful to the contributors for their willingness to step out of their "disciplinary" comfort zones, for their engagement in interdisciplinary discussions, and perhaps most importantly, for their willingness to take on a multi- (or at times perhaps, trans-) disciplinary stance in their work. The enthusiasm and open-mindedness of the contributing authors made the editorial process truly enjoyable and a great opportunity for me to widen my horizons both academically and culturally.

I would also like to offer a special thanks to the anonymous reviewers who spoke so highly of the proposal of this book, assuring me of the timeliness of the publication, and to the numerous authors who kindly submitted a proposal for my initial call. Finalizing the line-up of chapters and informing the authors of the decision was one of the hardest tasks I had to do, and I hope that in the future I will have a chance to work with all the authors whose proposals did not fit the scope of this particular volume.

I reserve special thanks for Francesca Bargiela-Chiappini, who kindly agreed to write a Foreword to the book. Professor Bargiela-Chiappini's contribution to the field of business and intercultural discourse research is incomparable. Her *Business Discourse* (together with Catherine Nickerson and Brigitte Planken (Bargiela-Chiappini et al., 2007) and her *Handbook of Business Discourse* (Bargiela-Chiappini, 2009a) are now seminal works for anyone interested in professional and business discourse studies. To our great sadness, Professor Bargiela-Chiappini is now considering leaving academia; it is therefore a true honor to have her among the contributors to this volume. I would like to dedicate this book to her.

Notes on Contributors

Kristy Beers Fägersten is Associate Professor of English Linguistics at Södertörn University, Sweden. She has researched computer-mediated communication in the classroom and on message boards, and video-mediated communication. Beers Fägersten's main area of research is on swear word usage, and she is the author of *Who's Swearing Now?* (2012). Currently she is heading a project on the usage of English in Swedish, focusing in Swedish-language newspaper comic strips.

María Luisa Carrió-Pastor is Senior Lecturer of English Language at Universitat Politècnica de València, and head of the Applied Linguistics Department. Her research areas are corpus linguistics, pragmatics, and the study of academic and professional discourse.

Valerie Creelman is Associate Professor of Communications at Saint Mary's University, Canada. Her research examines the interplay between language, power, and identity formation in modern and historical forms of corporate communication. Her current research projects examine social interaction in online webcare. Her published work has appeared in *Business and Professional Communication Quarterly, English Studies in Canada,* and *Parergon.*

Erika Darics holds a PhD from Loughborough University, UK. Her research has examined the linguistic and discursive features of digital discourse, with particular emphasis on professional and workplace settings. Her published work has appeared in the *Journal of Politeness Research, Discourse, Context and Media,* and *International Journal of Business Communication.* She is interested in digitally mediated business communication, and currently works for the Centre of Interdisciplinary Research into Language and Diversity at Aston University, UK. @LinguaDigitalis

David Deluliis is a Ph.D. candidate and Visiting Instructor in the Department of Communication and Rhetorical Studies at Duquesne University. His research interests include Communication Theory and Research Methodology and Philosophy of Communication, particularly the philosophy and aesthetics of Marcel Proust.

Steven A. Edelson holds a PhD from Temple University and currently teaches at Walsh University in North Canton, Ohio. He teaches a variety of courses at the undergraduate and MBA level including in the areas of communications, organizational behavior, creativity and innovation, and entrepreneurship. His research focuses mainly on the intersection of entrepreneurship and organizational behavior. @ProfEdelson

Katerina Girginova is a PhD student at the Annenberg School for Communication where she researches questions of media and innovation. She has experience in several international media companies including IMG, Taylor & Francis, and the National Geographic Channel, and has obtained a BA in Communication Studies at The George Washington University and a MA in Communication, Culture & Technology at Georgetown University.

Philip Kim teaches at Walsh University in North Canton, Ohio. He received his MS and DSc from Robert Morris University, and he teaches a variety of undergraduate and MBA courses concentrating on management information systems, social media, and mobile technologies. @Ideapath

Carmen Lee is Associate Professor in the Department of English at The Chinese University of Hong Kong. She has published and carried out research projects on social aspects of language and literacy, linguistic practices on the internet, and multilingual practices in digital communication. She is the co-author of *Language Online* (2013).

Nives Lenassi has a PhD in Linguistics from the University of Ljubljana, Slovenia. She teaches business Italian at the Faculty of Economics in Ljubljana where she designed and developed various advanced-level Italian courses for university-level economics students as well as coauthored four textbooks for business Italian that are used to teach future business people in Slovenia. Her main research areas are selected linguistic features typical of general Italian and those characteristic of business Italian, with special attention to business correspondence and how to teach it effectively.

Craig T. Maier is a member of the Department of Communication & Rhetorical Studies at Duquesne University in Pittsburgh, Pennsylvania, where he teaches courses in rhetoric, corporate communication, and integrated marketing communication. His scholarly work takes rhetorical and philosophical approaches to applied communication problems, with a special interest in nonprofit organizations and religious institutions.

Bernie Chun Nam Mak graduated from the University of Hong Kong and moved to The Chinese University of Hong Kong, where he completed a PhD in Applied English Linguistics. He has been working and publishing on workplace discourse (including computer-mediated discourse in organizational settings) with regard to humor, small talk, code-switching, expletives, and jargon. Currently he is also interested in adult learning and lifelong education in relation to workplace communication.

Kris M. Markman holds a PhD in Communication Studies from the University of Texas at Austin. Her research has examined discourse structure in computer-mediated communication (CMC), with particular emphasis on turn construction in collaborative, task-based CMC settings. Her work on online conversation has appeared in the *Journal of Business Discourse* and the *Journal of Language & Social Psychology*, as well as several edited volumes. She is currently the Online Learning Librarian at Harvard University, where she is interested in how conversation structure affects learning in online workplace and educational environments.

Ron Scott, teaches at Walsh University in North Canton, Ohio. As a member of the English Department, he teaches professional writing and writing for digital culture. His scholarly work mostly focuses on games and gamification in both popular and professional cultures.

Karianne Skovholt is an associate professor at Buskerud and Vestfold University College, Norway. Her research interests are conversation analysis (CA), discourse analysis, organizational communication, classroom interaction and computer-mediated interaction. Her most recent publication is "The Communicative Functions of Emoticons in Workplace E-mails: :-)", *Journal of Computer-Mediated Communication* (2014).

Julie M. Szendrey teaches at Walsh University in North Canton, Ohio. She received her DBA from Anderson University, and she teaches both undergraduate and MBA marketing and research methods courses.

Camilla Vásquez is Associate Professor in the Department of World Languages at the University of South Florida. Her research centers on discourse and identity in various social, professional, and online domains. Her work on online language has appeared in *Discourse Context & Media*, *Journal of Pragmatics*, and *Narrative Inquiry*. She is the author of *The Discourse of Online Consumer Reviews* (2014).

Introduction: Business Communication in the Digital Age – Fresh Perspectives

Erika Darics

Although text-based, digitally mediated communication has been around for more than 60 years, the communicative environment and the digital genres that came into existence in this environment are still new and unsettled. The reason for this "novelty" is twofold.

First, the evolving media and emerging new communication technologies create new social and business contexts and thus novel communicative situations, continuously shaping interactions, meanings, discourse, and language. One recent example of this emerging context is the use of social media for corporate communication: the new media enables and fosters interactivity between corporations and businesses and their customers, which means that this new business environment and the resulting communicative situation has led to a change of paradigm in the ways businesses address and respond to their audiences. Perfectly crafted corporate messages – manifestos, reports, newsletters – have given way to instantaneous and often spontaneous interactions, with no time and opportunity for revisions or withdrawal of messages. The corporate world has had to respond flexibly to the requirements of this new social context and the resulting new communicative situation in order to avoid mistakes – which can be very costly, and at times lead to damaged reputations, destroyed brand images or loss of trust.

Second, the way in which people use language to communicate via these evolving communicative technologies is also in a state of flux. Computer-mediated discourse is still an emerging phenomenon and "has not yet had time (nor attained the requisite social status) to become formalised in 'rules;' but rather, varies according to the technological and social contexts online" (Herring, 2012, p. 2338; see also Androutsopoulos, 2006). Email, for example, has become the most important technology for business communication in recent years (Radicati & Levenstein, 2013), leading to new norms in business interactions, such as the use of less formal language in professional settings. The development of a new, informal register, emerging discursive strategies, and email-specific communicative practices have also been found to reach beyond emails, affecting already existing discursive practices in the workplace such as for example, making professional face-to-face communication "more informal and personalised" (Gimenez, 2000).

Language use and communication norms are in a constant state of change, reflecting and responding to the status of emerging social contexts, which are constantly changing themselves as a result of developing communicative technologies and the new communicative environments these technologies create. This leads to a *reciprocally emerging communicative situation*, which, for businesses and organizations, is very hard to manage, particularly since much communication within and originating from companies has become digitized. Previously centralized channels of marketing, PR, and corporate communication have now become decentralized through professional and personal blogs, official and half-official Twitter accounts, or community-initiated fan pages – channels that reach beyond the control of organizations. Internal and external organizational interactions have become less formal, more social; previously well-established communication channels and practices, such as complaint letters, published company manifestos, or reports are now becoming redundant. The new communicative channels, contexts and situations, and resulting discursive practices have drawn heightened attention to new competencies and digital language use.

In spite of these rapid developments, and the very pressing need for organizations and communication professionals to understand digitally mediated communication practices, research addressing digital business communication is still fragmented. Although recent publications on business communication and discourse acknowledge the importance of, and provide a brief overview of, electronic media in professional communication (see, for example, Breeze, 2013; Goodman & Hirsch, 2014; Schnurr, 2013), much more work is needed to map out precisely how digitally mediated channels are changing the landscape of professional and corporate communication. This is particularly true for communication training: on the one hand, popular literature addressing digital communication tends to base its claims on over-generalized observations or netiquettes, and training material is often based on authors' personal values, not reflecting the actual usage and functions of digital practices (see critique in Skovholt et al., 2014). On the other hand, empirically based research tends to be fragmented and dispersed in specialist outlets that are often inaccessible for representatives of other disciplines (see, for example, Fagan and Desai's article in the *Reference Librarian* (2003), or Haas et al.'s comprehensive article in a TESOL publication (Haas et al., 2011)).

The representation of digitally mediated professional genres is also problematic in higher education curricula, as pointed out by Kathpalia and Swit (2014), who speculate that the gap might be a result of the newness and unfamiliarity of digital modes of communication. The lack of representation of digital business discourse in training curricula as well as the scarcity of empirical, data-driven research and training publications, explains why students (and more worryingly, perhaps, employees in communication-critical positions) lack the awareness of how language works in digitally mediated professional contexts (Weninger & Kan, 2013). It is not surprising therefore that students, trainees, and communication professionals often only rely on *in situ* trial and error methods, rather than academic research findings (see Goodman & Hirsch, 2014).

This volume aims to attend to the above-described scarcity by offering an overview of the most recent research that addresses emerging communication practices in digitally mediated professional genres. The multi-disciplinary focus of the volume – digital/mediated, professional/ business, communication/discourse – provides a platform to represent several distinct interests, including business and organizational aspects, discourse and language studies, as well as a focus on computer-mediated communication and social media. This volume brings together scholars from a wide range of disciplinary backgrounds, from all over the world, with very differing research or teaching foci – but all equally interested in digitally mediated professional communication.

The diversity of the authors in this volume is well represented by their academic affiliations: some come from business schools, others from language departments, and some from departments of communication and rhetorical studies. During the review process, these disciplinary differences, unsurprisingly, led to heated debates and stark criticism in the discussions between authors. By crossing disciplinary boundaries, we not only questioned each other's methodologies, but the fundamental viewpoints represented, and the theoretical approaches taken by each chapter. I was in the privileged position of overseeing these discussions – and witnessing the onset of the much-needed dialogue(s) between scholars of various disciplines. I was also very positively surprised by the open-mindedness of the authors and their willingness to reformulate their arguments in order to accommodate academic and theoretical as well as professional and practical viewpoints.

The resulting volume is thus a unique collection of chapters that contribute to a fuller understanding of how computer-mediated communication technologies interact with institutional discourse practices. All the chapters take an articulated language and discourse-centered approach, drawing on empirical data from real life, and demonstrating how the findings can be applied in professional practice.

On the title

My struggles resulting from the multidisciplinary nature of the volume and the diversity of the book's prospective audience were also present during the process of finalizing the title of the volume. This has not been an easy decision: not only because the title has to function as a good and clear indication of what is to be expected, but also because its terms have multiple interpretations within the various disciplines and carry their own embedded controversies.

For example, until recently, academic scholarship addressing communication and discourse mediated via digital tools fell under the broad umbrella term of computer-mediated communication (or CMC for short). As several of the chapters in this volume attest, this more established term is still preferred among communication scholars. However, as Herring et al. also pointed out recently, "one might question whether the term is still appropriate to characterise the overall scope of the phenomenon" (2013, p. 5). Unsurprisingly, alternative terms to indicate a more precise focus have sprung up in the latest scholarship, such as "internet-mediated communication" to define the nature of mediation (Yus, 2011) or "digital discourse" (Thurlow & Mroczek, 2011) to broaden the technological aspect but clarify the focus on language and its use.

My choice to use the word "digital" in the title of the current volume is motivated by current technological developments in business contexts. The spread and popularity of cloud services and the multiplication of smartphones and other mobile communication devices have now transcended "computers" in the traditional sense of the word, leading to an almost-permanent digital connectedness and enabling people and organizations to communicate using a wide range of communication technologies via diverse channels.

The label of "business" with reference to communication in professional contexts has also been well-contested, alongside similar, at times overlapping, terms, such as professional, workplace, or institutional communication and discourse: for extensive deliberation over the terminology, see Bargiela-Chiappini and Nickerson (1999b), Bargiela-Chiappini et al. (2007),

Bargiela-Chiappini (2009b), Koester (2006), and Schnurr (2013). These publications tend to treat "business discourse" as one type of workplace discourse, which focuses exclusively on how people communicate in commercial organizations. This focus is particularly clear when contrasted with that of professional discourse. The latter is characterized by the involvement of a "lay" person, whereas "business discourse is dominated by talk and writing between individuals whose main work activities and interests are in the domain of business and who come together for the purpose of doing business" (Bargiela-Chiappini & Nickerson, 1999a, p. 2).

However, as several of the chapters in the present volume attest, what might have been a clear distinction between organizational/institutional players and the lay audience has been blurred in recent years – not least owing to the spread of social media and the resulting increased interactivity between organizations and a range of other stakeholders. The contributions from Vásquez (Chapter 1), Girginova (Chapter 2), Creelman (Chapter 8), and Edelson et al. (Chapter 9) in this volume provide a good example of the tension between what counts as public/private and personal/professional (see also Jameson, 2014), whereas Mak and Lee (Chapter 6) and Beers Fägertsen (Chapter 7) discuss interactional practices that might not traditionally be classified as "doing business." These contributions, however, confirm that the examination of social and not strictly task-related interactions has a rightful place within scholarship on business discourse as they form an organic part of the communication ecology of today's organizations and workplaces.

In this volume, therefore, our interpretation of the label "business" is a broad one: business communication takes place during formal or informal encounters when a message (or a succession of messages in an interaction) is communicated by or addressed to an organizational or individual entity engaged in work-related activity (compare with Schmisseur et al., 2009).

As for the final element of the title, there is little question about the highly contested and multidimensional nature of the term "discourse," whether we interpret it as *d*iscourse referring to language in use, or *D*iscourse viewed as a social practice, focusing on the interplay between language, society, and thought (on the *d*/*D*iscourse distinction, see, for example, Gee, 2013). The situation is even more complicated if we consider the complex relationship between business communication and business discourse (see, for example, Jian et al., 2008; Louhiala-Salminen, 2009; Schmisseur et al., 2009). As pointed out by Bhatia (2014), the disciplinary areas drawing on communication theory – traditionally falling under the umbrella term of business communication – and language/

discourse-centered approaches – traditionally referring to organizational discourse studies – started their "convergence" when stimulated by the "linguistic turn." The "linguistic turn" refers to a recent direction in social sciences, and is based on the understanding that "proper understanding of societies, social institutions, identities, and even cultures may be viewed as discursively constructed" (Alvesson & Kärreman, 2000, p. 137). This turn thus prompted social psychologists, cultural anthropologists, and communication scholars, among others, to adopt a linguistic/discourse analytic point of view in their research, leading to a convergence between discourse studies and academic fields with a social focus. This convergence makes the distinction between business discourse and business communication even harder to define. Jian et al. (2008) attest that "organizational actors operate *in* communication, *through* discourse," and it is *"through discourse* that language and communication meet" (p. 314). I have therefore chosen to represent "discourse" in the title, as it is specifically this pronounced focus on language and linguistic-interactional practices that this volume embraces. However, I have to point out that the individual chapters interpret the meaning of the term discourse as well as the relationship between business communication and business discourse differently, at times treating the last two as synonymous.

From the point of view of the "technological mediation," the individual contributions cover a wide range of communication channels and technologies, from smartphones and social media to corporate blogs and internal message boards, including the various levels of synchronicity (from instant messaging to email and fora), or various levels of privacy (personal emails to public Twitter accounts). In terms of "business," the chapters discuss what could be considered traditional business communication types (such as corporate communication or internal communication), as well as genres that blur the boundaries of business and private, such as consumer reviews or corporate blog comments. The discourse perspective also covers a range of interpretations of "discourse": chapters range from analyses focusing on linguistic–pragmatic phenomena of texts, to approaches that view *D*iscourse constituting the subjectivities of organizational stakeholders and producing organizational reality.

The structure of the book

The volume is divided into three sections: the first is entitled *New technologies – new modes of communication*, and aims to provide an overview of the language- and discourse-related issues representative of the digitally mediated communication modes. The second section, *New modes of communication – new conventions*, includes chapters addressing how the new communication technologies affect communication conventions. The final section is entitled *Theoretical and methodological approaches to digital business discourse*, and includes chapters with strong theoretical/methodological orientation.

The chapters in the first section, *New technologies – new modes of communication* focus on the introduction and presentation of emergent or previously established but not yet conventionalized online communicative genres, and discuss the language- and discourse-related issues representative of the various modes discussed.

Chapters 1 and 2 address what we could label as the newest communication practices of Web 2.0 – user-generated content and social media – practices that came into existence as a result of the most recent developments in communication technology. Both Vásquez and Girginova give a fascinating snapshot of the intense conversation that takes place between organizations and external stakeholders: Vásquez focuses on the discourse of consumers through the analysis of consumer reviews, while Girginova explores the interaction between CEOs and the public via Twitter.

Drawing on the Bakhtinian concept of "addressivity" (Bakhtin, 1986), in Chapter 1 Camilla Vásquez explores the discursive construction of "conversational" consumer reviews. Her close analysis of reviews from a range of popular consumer websites results in a well-defined repertoire of discursive resources, which, she points out, might not be essential for the communication of the propositional content of the messages, but play a crucial part in relational communication, "forging a bond between online writer and online reader," and thus affecting perceived helpfulness and the possible economic impact of reviews.

In Chapter 2, Katerina Girginova asks very important questions about the blurring boundaries between public and private communication and, through close analysis of CEOs' tweeting practices, she details the role these tweets take on in the communicative construction of organizations as well as the identities of the leaders. One of Girginova's most important findings is the realization that Twitter opens up a new communication channel, enabling employees and consumers to interact with CEOs, simultaneously extending and blurring the traditional notion of "organization." Her findings thus provide further evidence for the discursively constructed nature of organizations and provide empirical support for the theorization that "organizations exist only in so far as their members create them through discourse" (Mumby & Clair, 1997, p. 181).

In Chapters 3 and 4 we revisit genres that have traditionally been viewed as the earliest digitally mediated communication tools: instant messaging and email. However, as Markman and Lenassi respectively demonstrate, in spite of a 60-year history, the conventions and practices are far from established and conventionalized.

Although a range of other communication channels are now available for workplace communication, the popularity of instant messaging (or IM) continues to grow (Radicati & Levenstein, 2013). Kris Markman, in Chapter 3, provides a thorough overview of the constraints and affordances of IM, and reviews its role and position within the communication ecology of workplaces. Her conversation-analytic approach sheds light on the unique interactional practices users of IM employ, in particular when they would like to maintain coherence in the absence of audio-visual signals (see Berglund, 2009). Her case study on utterance chunking in IM conversations demonstrates the crucial role of the technique during interaction management in task-based interactions. The ability to manage interactions unobtrusively at work is a fine craft, but Markman's findings can equip communicators with strategies that enable them to achieve the delicate balance between getting work done and at the same time demonstrating a concern for the feelings and face of communication partners.

Nives Lenassi's work on emails in Chapter 4 provides a fascinating insight into Italian professional interactional practices in email. She reminds the reader about the issues non-native speakers of Italian might face when communicating via the digital medium of email (see also Incelli, 2013). Her study addressing a corpus of 275 Italian business emails yields surprisingly generalizable results, however. For instance, the important function of the formality of openings and closings in setting the tone, or – quite the contrary – the blurring of formal/informal registers is often expected in business correspondence. One key insight of the chapter points in the direction that, although now considered the oldest computer-mediated communication technology, email still constitutes a relatively "new" communication mode with interactional norms that are not yet conventionalized. As Lenassi notes, in professional contexts there is still a tension between the perceived (and often expected) formality of business and professional encounters, and the importance of conveying personal, emotional, and relational information in a medium that is noted for its lack of ability to transmit audio and visual information.

The second section of the volume is entitled *New modes of communication – new conventions*. The focus of this section is *Discourse in organizational* contexts: that is, its role in constituting the social reality of the organization, in particular power and professional and organizational identities. The four chapters presented in this section provide an interesting overview of a range of *Discourses* (leadership, employee, and corporate *Discourse*) and by applying language/discourse-centered analytical methodologies, they go on aptly to demonstrate Jian et al.'s point that "*Discourses constitute social actors as both objects to be examined and subjects to be disciplined*" (2008, p. 305).

Karianne Skovholt's study in Chapter 5 fits with the line of research that views leadership as a discursive construct (see Fairhurst, 2009), but furthers previous scholarship by exploring the interactional practices of a virtual leader. Skovholt points out the lack of leadership studies that draw on naturally occurring interactional data, and criticizes organizational disciplines for their theoretical and normative approach to leadership in computer-mediated contexts. Her discourse-analytic approach and close analysis of approximately 700 emails collected in a Norwegian distributed work team enables her to pinpoint a range of discourse strategies that contribute to the creation of trust, the promotion of in-group solidarity, and the positioning of the leader *vis-à-vis* subordinates. Her study thus provides empirically grounded evidence for theorizations about virtual leadership originating in organizational disciplines, but equally importantly, well-defined strategies to be considered by trainers and practitioners in leadership-communication training.

From Norway we travel to Hong Kong: in Chapter 6, Bernie Chun Nam Mak and Carmen Lee explore how two Hong Kong trading firms communicate via IM. In particular, the chapter explores the multiple functions of swearing in digitally mediated professional encounters, drawing our attention to the possible pitfalls of normative approaches in professional communication training. As demonstrated in the close analysis of the excerpts of naturally occurring IM conversations and follow-up interviews with the participants, phenomena labeled as "risky" or "taboo" in professional communication are, in fact, widely used in real workplaces. Mak and Lee identify a wide range of linguistic and discursive functions of swearing practices, shedding light on the subtle intra- and interpersonal effects these might have during interactions. From an applied perspective, Chapter 6 provides an excellent case for the importance of empirical, data-based research in business communication: unlike in face-to-face situations, swearing in digital communication requires a conscious input, and, as the excerpts attest, is used strategically in a range of denotative functions. As a result of its potentially damaging nature if used wrongly, however, they argue that it is essential to develop a thorough understanding of the phenomenon, including the contextual and cultural aspects of swearing. Mak and Lee's chapter provides an important step in this direction.

Chapter 7 explores the unfolding discourse of conflicting interests between employees and a corporation on a Swedish intranet message board. Kristy Beers-Fägersten's study is a fine example of how a potential crisis empowered stakeholders to review and change their interactional patterns, and of the role discourse played in how the possible threat was asserted and/or challenged – officially and among the employees. On the level of communicative practices, Beers-Fägersten shows that employees strategically used a range of linguistic and discursive practices to mitigate their conflicting views, but also to demonstrate their allegiance with the supporting or opposing sides. One of the most important realizations of the study concerns the changing nature of internal communication: the company intranet enabled employees to interact intensely with a corporation, which led to questioning and problematization of the corporate vision and goals, as well as the institution's moral accountability. The author thus suggests that intranets should be utilized more widely for pre-meeting purposes, to enable employees to find information about relevant issues, and for them to have sufficient time to "read, consider, deliberate, and formulate responses."

Furthering the theme of corporate crisis, Valerie Creelman's chapter examines an instance of external corporate communication. The focus of Chapter 8 is the customer comments posted as a response to an apology letter published on a corporate blog. The findings from Creelman's analysis of the original corporate apology provide empirical evidence for a range of crisis communication strategies (e.g., Coombs, 1995, 1998), and her analysis of the customer feedback shows that the company's inappropriate and ineffective communication efforts affected the company's reputation equally – if not more – than the actual product flaws. As Creelman puts it, this case "vividly illustrates the pivotal and precarious way the language present in a message designed to repair a company's image can potentially do further damage to it if its intended audience chooses to use elements of it to bolster a negative responsive reaction to it." The case study in Chapter 8 is thus a strong argument for the necessity for companies to understand the changing nature of their audiences, especially the fact that people are not only *able* but *keen* to engage in a discussion with an organization.

The third section is entitled *Theoretical and methodological approaches to digital business discourse*, and as the title suggests, the chapters in this section have a strong theoretical/methodological orientation. The aim of the last section is ambitious in its attempt to set new directions in digital business discourse research: Chapters 9 and 10, for example, introduce new concepts such as "digital emotional literacy" and "communicology," while Chapters 11 and 12, on the other hand, explore how previously established analytical frameworks can be adapted to digitally mediated communication settings. However, in spite of its theoretical nature, the chapters of the final section also maintain the overall aim of the volume by arguing for the use of empirical data and case studies.

In Chapter 9, Steven Edelson, Ron Scott, Phil Kim, and July Szendrey outline the possible pitfalls of open, immediate corporate communication, and argue that the concept of "digital emotional literacy" enables organizations to gain a deeper understanding of the current communication environment, and hence prosper in today's economy. Their proposed concept is the combination of "digital literacy" (see Buckingham, 2006) and "emotional intelligence" (see Gardner, 1985). The authors review the literature that addresses emotional intelligence (EI) in professional contexts, demonstrating the highly important nature of EI in professional interpersonal encounters. The case they provide for the need to transfer such intelligence to digitally mediated contexts is strong: they argue that "the challenge in organizations is no longer technological adoption or proficiency, but rather combining that technical skillset with emotional intelligence, enabling business communicators to go beyond use of technology to effective mastery of technological tools for effective corporate communications." This insight echoes the observations originating in business and marketing research, which point to the need for a "young, motivated demographic who understand both the digital world of social media and have the language skills needed to use it" (Hulme, 2014, p. 5). Edelson et al. thus provide a solution to nurture such a demographic, through the targeted development of digital emotional literacy skills.

In Chapter 10 Craig Maier and David Deluliis take a critical stance on permanent connectivity, arguing that we need a much deeper understanding of the effects of constant connectedness, the blurring line between private and public, and the availability of a wide range of technologies that enable multi-communication at work, calling for a new dimension in applied scholarship. In particular they urge academics and practitioners to "look beyond the 'how' of digital business discourse and think more critically about 'what' they are doing with their technologies and 'why' they are doing it." Maier and Deluliis introduce the concept of *communicology*, which, they argue, offers a way to refocus our attention on digital communication as a *human practice*, or more specifically on our own communicative experiences. Drawing on the conceptual framework of communicology, the chapter proposes a three-step method as a research and training tool in workplace settings, with the aim of raising awareness of the ways in which technology is changing the experience of business communication.

In Chapter 11 we leave behind the more theoretical/philosophical approaches of the previous two chapters, in order to explore the applicability of genre and rhetorical moves analysis in digital business discourse. We revisit email communication, exchanged between users of Business English as Lingua Franca (BELF). In Chapter 11 Carrió-Pastor highlights the lack of empirical data in business communication training, and argues that more research should be done to explore non-native use of English in digital business settings. Of particular interest is the cultural aspect of the discourse produced. As the author points out, such research can expose whether or to what extent non-native speakers are influenced by the conventions of their mother tongue. The findings of Carrió-Pastor's research into the corpus of business emails written by Indian professionals whose first language is not English show that the emails produced by speakers of English who acquired the language in school contained more rhetorical moves than traditional letters written by native speakers (Bhatia, 2004), with a proliferation of moves taking on relational functions, such as the expression of politeness or positive feedback. With their focus on intercultural issues, these findings can thus further not only the scholarship on digital discourse research, but also scholarship and training addressing intercultural aspects of business communication.

Finally, in the last chapter, I propose a framework (Deconstruction–Analysis–Explanation, or deanex for short) that could be used for both research and training in digital business communication. Through analysis of extracts from IM conversations the chapter demonstrates the usefulness of an interactional sociolinguistic approach for analysis and description of "written contextualization cues," which are used for the signaling of relational intent and the ways the content of messages should be understood in a text-based computer-mediated communicative environment. I draw on the theoretical framework of interactional sociolinguistics to illustrate that the subtle interactional roles of written non-verbal cues can be uncovered and identified by following the three stages of the deanex method. In a sense Chapter 12 synthesizes the points made by the chapters in the third section: it implies that to be able to encode and interpret the complexities of non-verbal signaling in writing, communicators need a special skills set as set forth by Edelson et al. in Chapter 10. Through the observation of natural data samples, the proposed interpretive method enables communicators to reflect on and revisit their own digital communicative practices (see Maier and Deluiis above), enabling both learners of a "lingua franca" language, and learners of electronic communication to improve the effectiveness of their communication (see Carrió-Pastor in Chapter 11).

Conclusion

Although diverse in their conceptual and methodological approaches, the chapters of this volume are all concerned with digitally mediated discourse in business settings, and share a fundamental point. This point refers to the data used as the basis for theorization. As noted by Vaara et al., "[natural] languages have received very little attention in organization and management studies. This is unfortunate since natural languages are the basic means of communication in organization" (2005, p. 595). Other researchers have urged empirical research to "move out of laboratory settings and into the field in order to advance the literature through asking and answering of questions that cannot be adequately tested in a laboratory setting" (p. 823). This is particularly important if further research aims to examine and understand the complex communicative ecology of contemporary workplaces, such as the effect of the blurred line between internal and external organizational communication (Jameson, 2014), or multi-communication practices (when interactants hold multiple, face-to-face, and electronically mediated interactions at the same time) (Gimenez, 2014).

I consider that the current volume makes a very strong case for such discourse-focused research, both within academic disciplines and for teaching and training in digital business communication. It successfully gathers together interdisciplinary scholarship that addresses the various forms of digitally mediated business-related communication genres, providing a comprehensive snapshot of the current state of digital communication practices of today's organizations.

References

Alvesson, M., & Kärreman, D. (2000). Taking the linguistic turn in organizational research: Challenges, responses, consequences. *Journal of Applied Behavioral Science, 36* (2), 136–158.

Androutsopoulos, J. (2006). Introduction: Sociolinguistics and computer-mediated communication. *Journal of Sociolinguistics, 10* (4), 419–438.

Bakhtin, M. M., Imerson C., & Holquist M. (1986), *Speech Genres and Other Late Essays* (trans. V. W. McGee) (1st edition). Austin, TX: University of Texas Press. doi: 9780292792562.

Bargiela-Chiappini, F. (Ed.) (2009a). *The Handbook of Business Discourse*. Edinburgh: Edinburgh University Press.

Bargiela-Chiappini, F. (2009b). Introduction: Business discourse. In F. Bargiela-Chiappini (Ed.), *The Handbook of Business Discourse* (pp. 1–17). Edinburgh: Edinburgh University Press.

Bargiela-Chiappini, F., & Nickerson, C. (1999a). Business writing as social action. In F. Bargiela-Chiappini, & C. Nickerson (Eds), *Writing Business: Genres, Media and Discourses* (pp. 1–34). Harlow: Pearson Education.

Bargiela-Chiappini, F., & Nickerson, C. (Eds) (1999b). *Writing Business: Genres, Media and Discourses*. Harlow: Pearson Education.

Bargiela-Chiappini, F., Nickerson, C., & Planken, B. (2007). *Business Discourse*. Basingstoke: Palgrave Macmillan.

Berglund, T. Ö. (2009). Disrupted turn adjacency and coherence maintenance in instant messaging conversations. *Language@internet, (6)*, 2010.10.30. Retrieved from http://www.languageatinternet.org/articles/2009/2106/?searchterm=ber glund.

Bhatia, V. (2004). *Worlds of Written Discourse: A Genre-Based View*. London and New York: Continuum International.

Bhatia, V. (2014). Analysing discourse variation in professional contexts. In V. Bhatia & S. Bremner (Eds), *The Routledge Handbook of Language and Professional Communication* (pp. 3–12). London and New York: Routledge.

Breeze, R. (2013). *Corporate Discourse*. London and New York: Bloomsbury.

Buckingham, D. (2006). Defining digital literacy – what do young people need to know about digital media?, *Digital Kompetanse, 4* (3), 122–134.

Coombs, W. T. (1995). Choosing the right words: The development of guidelines for the selection of the "appropriate" crisis-response strategies. *Management Communication Quarterly, 8* (4), 447–476.

Coombs, W. T. (1998). An analytic framework for crisis situations: Better responses from a better understanding of the situation. *Journal of Public Relations Research, 10* (3), 177–191.

Fagan, J. C., & Desai, C. M. (2003). Communication strategies for instant messaging and chat reference services. *The Reference Librarian, 38* (79–80), 121–155.

Fairhurst, G. T. (2009). Considering context in discursive leadership research. *Human Relations, 62* (11), 1607–1633. doi: 10.1177/0018726709346379.

Gardner, H. (1985). *Frames of Mind: The Theory of Multiple Intelligences*. New York: Basic Books.

Gee, J. P. (2013). *An Introduction to Discourse Analysis: Theory and Method* (3rd edition). New York and London: Routledge.

Ghose, A., & Ipeirotis, P. G. (2011). Estimating the helpfulness and economic impact of product reviews: Mining text and reviewer characteristics. *IEEE Transactions on Knowledge and Data Engineering, 23* (10), 1498–1512.

Gimenez, J. (2000). Business e-mail communication: Some emerging tendencies in register. *English for Specific Purposes, 19* (3), 237–251.

Gimenez, J. (2014). Multi-communication and the business English class: Research meets pedagogy. *English for Specific Purposes, 35*, 1–16. doi: http://dx.doi.org/10.1016/j.esp.2013.11.002.

Goodman, M. B., & Hirsch, P. B. (2014). Electronic media in professional communication. In V. Bhatia, & S. Bremner (Eds), *The Routledge Handbook of Language and Professional Communication* (pp. 129–146). London and New York: Routledge.

Haas, C., Takayoshi, P., Carr, B., Hudson, K., & Pollock, R. (2011). Young people's everyday literacies: The language features of instant messaging. *Research in the Teaching of English, 45* (4), 378–404.

Herring, S. C. (2012). Grammar and electronic communication. In C. A. Chapelle (Ed.), *Encyclopedia of Applied Linguistics*. Hoboken, NJ: Wiley/Blackwell. doi: 10.1002/9781405198431.wbeal0466.

Herring, S. C., Stein, D., & Virtanen, T. (Eds). (2013). *Pragmatics of Computer-Mediated Communication*. Berlin and Boston: Mouton De Gruyter.

Holmes, J. (2006). Workplace narratives, professional identity and relational practice. In A. De Fina, D. Schiffrin, & M. Bamberg (Eds), *Discourse and Identity* (pp. 166–187). Cambridge: Cambridge University Press.

Hulme, M. (2014). The rise of the linguarati. *Education First*. Retrieved from http://www.linguarati.com.

Incelli, E. (2013). Managing discourse in intercultural business email interactions: A case study of a British and Italian business transaction. *Journal of Multilingual and Multicultural Development, 34* (6), 515–532.

Jameson, D. A. (2014). Crossing public–private and personal–professional boundaries: How changes in technology may affect CEOs' communication. *Business and Professional Communication Quarterly, 77* (1), 7–30. doi: 10.1177/2329490613517133.

Jian, G., Schmisseur, A. M., & Fairhurst, G. T. (2008). Organizational discourse and communication: The progeny of Proteus. *Discourse & Communication, 2* (3), 299–320.

Kathpalia, S. S., & Ling, K. S. (2014). The changing landscape of business communication. In V. Bhatia, & S. Bremner (Eds), *The Routledge Handbook of Language and Professional Communication* (pp. 274–286). London and New York: Routledge.

Koester, A. (2006). *Investigating Workplace Discourse*. London and New York: Routledge.

Louhiala-Salminen, L. (2009). Business communication. In F. Bargiela-Chiappini (Ed.), *The Handbook of Business Discourse* (pp. 305–316). Edinburgh: Edinburgh University Press.

Martins, L. L., Gilson, L. L., & Maynard, M. T. (2004). Virtual teams: What do we know and where do we go from here? *Journal of Management, 30* (6), 805–835.

Mumby, D. K., & Clair, R. P. (1997). Organizational discourse. In T. A. van Dijk (Ed.), *Discourse as Structure and Process* (pp. 181–205). London: Sage.

Radicati, S., & Levenstein, J. (2013). *Email Statistics Report, 2013–2017*. Palo Alto, CA: The Radicati Group, Inc.

Schmisseur, A. M., Jian, G., & Fairhurst, G. T. (2009). Organisational communication. In F. Bargiela-Chiappini (Ed.), *The Handbook of Business Discourse* (pp. 256–268). Edinburgh: Edinburgh University Press.

Schnurr, S. (2013). *Exploring Professional Communication: Language in Action*. Abingdon: Routledge.

Skovholt, K., Grønning, A., & Kankaanranta, A. (2014). The communicative functions of emoticons in workplace emails::-). *Journal of Computer-Mediated Communication, 19* (4), 780–797. doi: 10.1111/jcc4.12063.

Thurlow, C., & Mroczek, K. (Eds) (2011). *Digital Discourse*. New York: Oxford University Press.

Vaara, E., Tienari, J., Piekkari, R., & Säntti, R. (2005). Language and the circuits of power in a merging multinational corporation. *Journal of Management Studies, 42* (3), 595–623.

Weninger, C., & Kan, K. H. (2013). (Critical) language awareness in business communication. *English for Specific Purposes, 32* (2), 59–71. doi: http://dx.doi.org/10.1016/j.esp.2012.09.002.

Yus, F. (2011). *Cyberpragmatics: Internet-Mediated Communication in Context*. Amsterdam and Philadelphia: John Benjamins Publishing.

Part I
New Technologies: New Modes of Communication

1

"Don't Even Get Me Started…": Interactive Metadiscourse in Online Consumer Reviews

Camilla Vásquez

Introduction

Online reviews enable any consumer with internet connectivity to access dozens, hundreds, and sometimes even thousands, of first-hand accounts of personal experience with a particular product, service, or business. Online consumer reviews have impacted consumer behavior in unprecedented ways. Whereas previously, as consumers, we relied on the word of mouth of members of our immediate social circles (friends, family, and acquaintances) – or on the opinions of a handful of experts (for example, travel writers, film reviewers, restaurant critics) – today our access to the opinions of millions of other consumers, on virtually any product or service, is just a few clicks away. Our access to such information, and the more widely distributed nature of online expertise in general, has a number of broader social implications, including a demonstrated impact on consumer purchasing (Forman et al., 2008).

What remains less clearly understood, however, is how readers make sense of all the review information available to them (Otterbacher, 2011). It has been suggested that users tend to process online reviews heuristically rather systematically: in other words, when we read reviews, we tend to use "salient and easily comprehended cues to activate judgment shortcuts or everyday decision rules called heuristics" rather than relying on systematic processing, which requires "deep levels of engagement with the information, careful attention, analysis and reasoning" (Sparks et al., 2013, p. 2). However, not much has been written about which discourse features make for an engaging online review, or what makes a particular review stand out from dozens of reviews discussing the same product, or what features of language might capture our attention more than others. In prior work, I have discussed various forms of involvement in online review discourse. For example, in a study of reviewer identities I noted that intertextual references to popular culture sources and humor can serve as discursive strategies for establishing a bond between review writers and their readers (Vásquez, 2014a). In another study, I examined how "story prefaces" and other devices used in conversational narratives were sometimes transferred to this digital genre, and exploited by online reviewers to engage readers of review texts (Vásquez, 2012). In this chapter, I advance the inquiry into interactivity in online reviews even further, by focusing on explicit forms of addressivity. Specifically, I explore several different types of interactive strategies that writers exploit to include readers as active participants in their discourse. I argue that, in this context, such forms of addressivity function as relational work in which reviewers attempt to recruit, and/or maintain, readers' attention and interest amid a vast field of online opinions. In some instances, these same features also serve to assert, or emphasize, an author's credibility or authority on a given topic. Showing how reviewers use language to accomplish this can provide insights into the types of linguistic resources that go into creating an engaging online text.

In the following pages, I first define online reviews as a genre of asynchronous computer-mediated communication (CMC), as well as a type of social media. I then discuss the notion of "addressivity" in discourse. This is followed by a description of the dataset of 1,000 online consumer reviews from which the subsequent examples were drawn.

Online reviews

Online customer reviews are "peer-generated product evaluations posted on company or third party websites" (Mudambi & Schuff, 2010, p. 186). Scholars in the international marketing community sometimes use the term "eWOM" (short for electronic-word-of-mouth) to refer to internet-based consumer reviews. eWOM has been defined as:

> Any positive or negative statement made by potential, actual, or former customers about a product or company, which is made available to a multitude of people and institutions via the Internet. (Hennig-Thurau et al., 2004, p. 39)

eWOM is perhaps the most pervasive form of user-generated business discourse today. In a world characterized by unprecedented mobility and growing interconnectivity, it has become common to rely on the eWOM of strangers, which can be freely and easily accessed on websites comprised of enormous user-generated databases. For instance, *TripAdvisor*, currently the most popular travel website, features over 150 million reviews. Our access to such an enormous amount of first-hand, user-generated information was unthinkable only two decades ago.

Electronic-word-of-mouth differs from more traditional forms of word-of-mouth in a number of important ways. First, traditional word-of-mouth is usually spoken, not written, and therefore reaches a much smaller, and more local, audience. In contrast, eWOM is characterized by both scalability and speed of diffusion. In other words, "information technologies enable opinions of a single individual to instantly reach thousands, or even millions of consumers" (Dellarocas et al., 2004, p. 3). Furthermore, traditional word-of-mouth is ephemeral, whereas eWOM usually leaves some type of lasting digital record. eWOM can also be considered a quintessentially "late modern" form of interaction, in that it centers on practices of consumption (Benwell & Stokoe, 2006), and it takes place in a technologically mediated form, between an author and a potentially vast audience, both of whom are – and will most likely remain – unknown to one another in an offline sense.

At the present time, online consumer reviews are a predominantly text-based[1] asynchronous (and often, anonymous) genre of computer-mediated communication, or CMC. Although they can be considered a form of "social media" (possessing the defining characteristics of Web 2.0 genres, such as being participatory, collaborative, user-generated, dynamic, and rich in information), a *Yelp* executive recently described online reviews as "the underdog" of social media, in the sense that they are often overlooked and taken for granted. Attention to online reviews in both the popular imagination as well as in scholarly work has been nowhere near as prominent as has been the focus on social networking and microblogging sites, such as *Facebook* or *Twitter*, for example. Certainly, as far as discourse analytic treatments of CMC are concerned, online reviews have received minimal attention. Existing publications include analyses of the discursive construction of reviewers' expertise (Mackiewicz, 2010a) and reviewer credibility (Mackiewicz, 2010b), the formulation of complaints (Vásquez, 2011) – and, more recently, features of involvement and narrativity (Vásquez, 2012), engagement resources (Tian, 2013), and generic structures associated with highly ranked reviews (Skalicky, 2013).

As a form of social media, online consumer reviews are comprised of digital, user-generated content. Yet, they differ from other popular forms of social media, because the social ties among participants tend to be weaker on review sites than on social networking sites, for example. In this respect, online reviews are best described as a "public" rather than "private" mode of computer-mediated discourse (Androutsopoulos, 2013), and most online review sites can be characterized as more "information-focused," rather than "relationally-driven," communities (according to the dimensions of online communities proposed by Kozinets, 2010). However, the relational aspect is not absent from online reviews. On the contrary, even anonymous reviewers use discourse in ways that forge personal connections with their readers. Therefore, in this chapter, I use the notion of addressivity to explain some of the specific ways in which online reviewers use language to carry out relational work with their potentially vast, though simultaneously indeterminate, readership. Understanding how anonymous authors create an "interaction" with their unknown audience can be useful for business communication educators and practitioners, who might be interested in extending these findings to other genres of business communication.

Addressivity

The notion of "audience" in CMC – and in social media more specifically – varies widely according to the genre in question (Seargeant et al., 2012). Although the authors of online reviews do not typically "know" their audience, they can nevertheless design their texts in a way that signals not only an interpersonal connection between reviewer and reader, but also an unfolding dialogue between both participants. The Bakhtinian notion of addressivity is useful in understanding how this works. According to Bakhtin (1986), addressivity refers to the way that "the speaker talks with an expectation of a response, agreement, sympathy, objection [...] and so forth" (p. 69). In other words, as speakers, writers, and CMC authors produce texts, they take into account the possible responses and reactions of the recipients of their texts. This anticipated, or imagined, interaction between writer and reader – and the ways in which that interaction is discursively constructed in online reviews – is the focus of the following analysis. Guidelines for business communication often recommend that authors of online texts should aim to be "conversational" in their style. This chapter offers some insights into the specific linguistic devices that are used by writers to achieve "conversational voice" when composing online texts.

Prior studies of addressivity in CMC (for example, Seargeant et al., 2012) have considered different forms of audience design among transnational, multilingual users interacting on *Facebook*, a semi-private site – in other words, how *Facebook* users indicate that a particular post was intended for a specific individual, or for a specific group. In contrast, my focus here is on addressivity in a more public form of CMC (that is, online reviews), where audiences are less clearly defined. More recently, Tian (2013) compared the "engagement systems" found in a set of online hotel reviews written in Chinese and English. Tian's work is relevant to my discussion here because the notion of engagement systems (from Systemic Functional Linguistics) also has its origins in Bakhtin's work on dialogism. Specifically, Tian explored the extent to which reviews from the two contexts could be characterized as "monogloss" (presenting a proposition as though it is "self-evidently right," or the only possible alternative) or "heterogloss" (acknowledging other alternative positions or interpretations). However, in my own discussion below, I consider a more specific form of dialogism – that is, reader addressivity – by which I mean those instances in which *the reader's* voice or presence is somehow brought into, or made relevant to, the review text.

Methods

The data in this study come from a corpus of 1,000 online reviews, sampled from five different websites. The dataset includes reviews of reviews of "search goods" (for example, appliances and other tangible objects), "experience goods" (for example, films), services (for example, hotels, restaurants), as well as reviews of a more intangible type of "product" (that is, recipes). Over 160 different types of products are represented, and the size of the dataset is around 150,000 words. I assume that each review was written by a unique author – although this is impossible to verify. Table 1.1 provides more specific details about the dataset, including the total number of reviews taken from each website, and the average number of words per review on each site.

The composition of this dataset reflects my evolving interest in the genre of online reviews. I first began researching online complaints with a small set of 100 hotel reviews from *TripAdvisor*, collected from the featured "Rants" section, which showcased "the worst of the worst" reviews on that site. For the project that followed, in order to balance the "Rants" with more mainstream reviews, I identified a corresponding five-star (positive) review for the same 100 hotels, as well as a corresponding one-star (negative) review, which was not highlighted in the "Rants" section. Next, in order to learn more about the genre of reviews more generally, I decided to collect reviews from four other popular websites known for featuring

Table 1.1   Descriptive information for the dataset, by website

Site	Product type*	Total number of reviews	Total number of words	Average # of words/review
TripAdvisor	Hotels (100)	300	59,811	199
Amazon	Various consumer goods (24)	200	36,198	181
Netflix	Movies (5)	100	11,408	114
Epicurious	Recipes (22)	300	17,518	58
Yelp	Restaurants (10)	100	18,432	184
TOTALS	161	1,000	143,367	147

* The number in parenthesis indicates the number of unique products for which reviews were collected. Multiple reviews were collected for each product.

reviews. I semi-randomly sampled 100 or more reviews from *Amazon* (reviews from products of different price categories were included: high-speed blenders, yoga mats, diaper bags, and tea), *Epicurious* (reviews of recipes of different types of dishes were included, for example: Salads, Meats, Pasta, Desserts, Appetizers), *Netflix* (reviews of films representing five popular genres were included: Action, Romantic Comedy, Documentary, Foreign, and Stand-Up Comedy), and *Yelp* (reviews of different restaurant types were sampled from two major cities in different regions in the U.S.).[2] As the final column in Table 1.1 shows, review sites vary considerably in terms of average length of review text. Although I have included data from all five sites in the discussion that follows, readers may notice that there a slightly more examples from the two of sites that tend to have some of the longer reviews, *TripAdvisor* and *Amazon*.

The present analysis contributes to a larger examination of "involvement strategies" in online review discourse. However, in contrast to earlier work, here I focus specifically on addressivity. The selection and analysis of representative excerpts below is the result of iterative readings and coding of the data for a variety of features conventionally associated with involvement (Besnier, 1994; Chafe, 1982; Tannen, 1985) and engagement (Hyland, 2005) in discourse. More specifically, I sought to identify those features in online reviews that are most typically associated with dialogue and conversational interaction.

Analysis

I begin this section with a brief overview of some common ways in which authors of online reviews signal the "give and take" of conversation. I then turn to more explicit examples of addressivity, in which review writers use language to orient to an imagined or anticipated reaction by the audience.

Discourse markers

One rather obvious way by which online writers can involve readers in their text is through the use of discourse markers, which are discourse features typically associated with conversation and other types of spoken interaction. Some of the discourse markers that commonly appear in online reviews include *you know, oh,* and *well.* The discourse marker *you know* has a highly interactional function, because it explicitly indexes a connection between speaker and addressee. Excerpt 1 illustrates the first few lines of a restaurant review. Appearing at the very onset of the review text, the discourse marker *you know* signals the start of a narrative of personal experience, and at the same time, conveys a sense of casualness.

Excerpt 1

You know, I've always sort of overlooked [*restaurant name*] and the first couple of times I'd gone, I was fairly judgmental. But on Wednesday, I definitely changed my tune. [*Yelp*]

Discourse markers are multifunctional in spoken discourse (Biber et al., 1999). Besides serving an interactional function, discourse markers can, for example, help speakers hold the floor, as they plan what they will say next. Their use in online review texts is therefore quite interesting, because writers of reviews do not face the same planning and production constraints as speakers do. In other words, review writers have more time to draft, compose, and revise their texts than speakers do when they participate in a typical conversational interaction. Therefore, the interpersonal function of this discourse marker seems to be especially salient in this asynchronous CMC context.

Another discourse marker that appears even more frequently than *you know* in online reviews is *well.* Most instances of *well* are sentence-initial, and *well* is often used at the very beginning of a review text, as seen in a recipe review and a hotel review, Excerpts 2 and 3, respectively.

Excerpt 2

Well, this is definitely labor intensive and I agree that the quality of the ingredients matter tremendously. [*Epicurious*]

Excerpt 3

Well, What I can say. My husband and I had recently got engaged and this was my treat to him on our anniversary of two years. [*TripAdvisor*]

Well is considered to be a "response marker" (Schiffrin, 1987), and as such, its use in these online reviews helps to create a sense of dialogicality in what is otherwise a monologic text. An interesting characteristic shared by Excerpt 3 and Excerpt 4 (below) is that in both instances the discourse marker *well* precedes a rhetorical question (*what can I say*, and *where do I begin*). These rhetorical questions serve as metalingustic markers, signaling the beginning of a narrative of personal experience. In Excerpt 4, the discourse marker *well* is preceded by another discourse marker, *oh*, which is often used to indicate an emotional state (Paltridge, 2012). In addition to the two discourse markers in the example below, the sense of audience involvement is further underscored by the two instances of second-person pronominal address.

> Excerpt 4
> oh <u>well</u>, where do I begin. ... If complimentary means 5 USD a day to you, then you will enjoy the wi-fi. [*TripAdvisor*]

In spoken discourse, *well* often appears in response to a question. In conversation analytic terms, discourse marker *well* tends to appear at the beginning of a second utterance in an adjacency pair. In this way, when using *well* to start a review, the review writer indexes the give-and-take nature of spoken interaction. This two-part exchange structure is even more explicitly constructed in the next example, where *well* appears at the beginning of a response to a question posed by the reviewer.

> Excerpt 5
> I have been on the "Holy Grail", shall we say, of finding the perfect yoga mat. What is the perfect yoga mat, you ask? <u>Well</u>, in my perfect yoga mat world, my dream mat would be longer so you are always on the mat. [*Amazon*]

In the question (*What is the perfect yoga mat, you ask?*), the reader is addressed directly and is also imagined by the reviewer as being the source of the question. In other words, the question is posed from the point of view of a reader; it is as though the reviewer imagines what kind of question a reader might ask following the initial remark about the quest for *finding the perfect yoga mat*. The reviewer then goes on to answer this question. The question–answer sequence embedded in this text serves as a device for allowing the reviewer to briefly digress from the evaluation of the focal product, and instead to describe her fantasy of an ideal product.

In Excerpt 6, taken from the beginning of a review of a high-speed blender, *well* serves as a marker of response again. In this example, the reviewer makes an intertextual reference to a prior review, and engages in a dialogue with the author of that review.

Excerpt 6
Someone named Laura wrote a review saying her [*product name*] quit after 10 smoothies, and that she guessed this was a fluke. <u>Well</u>, you're not the only one. [*Amazon*]

This time however, rather than the reviewer imagining how he would respond to a future reader, he responds directly to the comments of a previous reviewer – referring to her by name (*Laura*), and then addressing her directly with the second-person pronoun, *you*.

Discourse markers are a "non-essential" part of the clause – meaning that they are not syntactically necessary, nor do they add any new propositional or semantic meaning to the text (Brinton, 1996). Discourse analysts (Jucker, 1993; Schiffrin, 1987) argue that discourse markers serve a primarily relational function between participants in discourse. In spoken interaction, *well* often occurs in a response to a question, and as such, is found at the beginning of the second pair part of an adjacency pair. Therefore, it is especially interesting to consider the function(s) of this "response marker" in the genre of online reviews, which – unlike conversation – are asynchronous and monologic. The use of discourse markers in these texts helps review writers to create a sense of interaction. More specifically, the use of *well*, especially when it occurs at the very beginning of a text or immediately following a question, makes it seem as though the reviewer were responding to some real or imagined interlocutor.

Second-person address forms and metadiscourse

According to Hyland (2005), engagement markers, such as second-person address forms, also serve an interactional function in written discourse, as they "involve readers by allowing them to respond to the unfolding text" (p. 49). These types of metadiscourse, in Hyland's words, function not only in expressing solidarity, but also in "anticipating objectives and responding to an imagined dialogue with others. [...] reveal[ing] the extent to which the writer works to jointly construct the text with readers" (p. 50). In online reviews, second-person address is often realized through formulaic or idiomatic constructions that include imperatives. These are even more explicit markers of addressivity than the discourse markers discussed previously.

In Excerpt 7, which appears in the middle of a hotel review, the imperative *Wait!* is used to recruit, or hold, the reader's attention. In spoken interaction, the imperative *Wait!* can serve as a floor-holding mechanism, which – strictly speaking – is not needed in an asynchronous environment, where there is no threat of imminent interruption by another interlocutor. In spoken discourse, the construction *Wait! There's more* indicates to a hearer that a speaker has more to say about a topic. However, with a CMC text, the reader can immediately see onscreen that the text continues, so an explicit indication to the reader that "more on the topic is coming" clearly serves a more interactive rather than informational purpose. Thus, the use of *Wait! There's more* in an online review is a way for the writer to index the virtual presence and participation of the reader, and is a means for entreating the reader to remain with the text and to continue reading.

Excerpt 7
A one-speed ceiling fan was the only ventilation. Don't plan on sleeping. <u>Wait! There's more</u>: There was no iron in the room. I asked for one at the front desk. [*TripAdvisor*]

Other formulaic constructions typically associated with spoken discourse, such as *don't even get me started* may be used by a reviewer to draw readers' attention to a particular topic. In spoken discourse, the metadiscursive construction *don't even get me started* can function as a response signaling the speaker's preference to avoid elaborating on a particular topic that has been raised. However, in online reviews, the reviewer chooses which topics to bring up. In the context of online reviews, this expression associated with spoken discourse takes on a different function – that is, directing a reader's attention to a new topic. Excerpt 8 appears in the middle of a review of a hotel, as the reviewer shifts topic from issues of cleanliness to complaining about the food quality.

Excerpt 8
So disgusting, I still itch thinking about this horrible excuse for a hotel. <u>Don't even get me started</u> on the so called breakfast buffet, Totally gross!! [*TripAdvisor*]

The next example also occurs in the middle of a review, in this case, in a product review of a high-speed blender. Once again, the same device helps to shift topics from the preceding evaluation of the blender's motor, to the material that the blender carafe is made of. Here, the expression *don't even get me started* is preceded by discourse marker *oh*.

Excerpt 9
I may burn out a $50 [*brandname*] every 12–18 months, but at least those damn things don't quit on me in the middle of every single frozen drink task. <u>Oh, and don't even get me started</u> on the polycarbonate containers ... they sure do look pretty when you take them out of the box but, 8 months later after using them 2 or 3 times a week, they have a glazed/frosted appearance throughout the interior surface. [*Amazon*]

Often these forms of metadiscourse are combined with second-person pronouns, as can be seen in the next example. Excerpt 10 is from the opening lines of a hotel review. In this example, the expression *let me tell you* serves a strictly interactional function, because its deletion would result in no loss of propositional content. In other words, it does not contribute any descriptive or evaluative information about the hotel; instead, its primary function is to signal a connection between reviewer and reader.

Excerpt 10
We just returned from a 2 night stay and <u>let me tell you</u>. At first glance the place looks like nice villa. Upon closer inspection you will see. [*TripAdvisor*]

Not surprisingly, beyond the forms of metadiscourse highlighted in the preceding discussion, Excerpts 7, 9, and 10 also include instances of second-person pronouns and imperatives, for example: *Upon closer inspection <u>you</u> will see, they sure do look pretty when <u>you</u> take them out of the box*, and *<u>Don't</u> plan on sleeping*. Some of these expressions appear at the beginning of a review, while others appear in the middle of the text. This variable position within the text indicates that review writers can deploy them as a resource to either attract the audience's attention at the onset of the text, or as a device to maintain a reader's interest midway through the text.

Questions

As mentioned earlier, the use of questions in a review text can create a kind of dialogue between writer and reader. Even though online reviews are asynchronous and monologic texts, by sharing some of the processes of meaning-making with their readers through the asking of questions, reviewers position readers as active participants in the discourse. In some cases, as illustrated below, questions appear to be posed in anticipation of the reactions or responses of readers. As examples, Excerpts 11 and 12 illustrate the phenomenon of "imagined" questions, in which the reviewer simulates a dialogue by anticipating, and actually articulating, a follow-up inquiry that some curious reader might legitimately ask the reviewer. In both of these cases, the reviewers take on the "imagined" voices of other "imagined" participants involved in the interaction.

Excerpt 11
All said and done, <u>would we stay here again?</u> My husband says "never". I might if I was low on cash, it was late and I needed a place to crash for a single night. [*TripAdvisor*]

Excerpt 12
So, with all this, <u>why 4 vs 5 stars?</u> I have to wish for a sleeker, more modern decor. [*Yelp*]

In Excerpt 11, the question (*would we stay here again?*) – posed by an imagined reader – appears near the review's conclusion and serves as a frame for providing a final assessment of the overall experience. Interestingly, the first response to the question is provided from the point of view of the reviewer's husband, which is then followed by her own, slightly different response. This is an example of a heteroglossic text, in which several different "voices" are represented: the voice of the reader, who is indirectly positioned as the asker of the question, the reviewer's husband voice, and the reviewer's herself. Excerpt 12 appears at the end of a restaurant review, following the discussion of a mostly positive gastronomic experience. In this case, the question posed by an imagined reader serves as a device, which prompts the reviewer to explain that the less-than-perfect overall star rating (that is, *4 vs 5 stars*) was based on the restaurant's ambiance rather than on its food. In both examples the reviewers' use of questions and answers simulate a conversation, and they also function to represent the reviewer as a thoughtful, reasonable person, who has considered various perspectives and possibilities. This discursive construction of a "reasonable self" contributes to the identity of a credible reviewer (Vásquez, 2014a).

Other questions found in online reviews – especially those that include second-person pronouns – address readers more directly. In Excerpt 13, which appears in the middle of a hotel review, the rhetorical question directed at the reader (in combination with the repetition of *NEITHER room had*, as well as repeated orthographic emphasis, or all caps) communicates a sense of incredulity at the poor conditions of the hotel rooms.

Excerpt 13
NEITHER room had toilet paper. NEITHER room had TV remotes that was usable. The suite had a remote that was TAPED up holding it together. <u>Can you believe that?</u> The other room didn't even have a remote. [*TripAdvisor*]

Earlier, in Excerpts 5, 11 and 12, the imagined readers were positioned as the "question askers," directing their questions to the reviewer. However, in Excerpt 13, this participant structure is reversed. In Excerpt 12, the reviewer takes on the role of "question asker," addressing the question to her readers. This shows that it is possible for a reviewer to take up multiple discourse roles within a review text. To explain this phenomenon in terms of Goffman's (1981) production format: the reviewer/writer is sometimes simultaneously the "author" and the "animator" of a particular utterance, whereas other times, the reviewer is presented as only the "animator" of thoughts (or utterances), which are "imagined" as having some other "author." These examples illustrate the ways in which authors of some reviews are able to shift perspective and to construct reviews by writing from various points of view.

Questions and answers

Reviewers not only pose questions to their readers, but they also, on occasion, provide the responses to their own questions. In this way, the reviewer assumes the positions of multiple participants engaged in a single interaction. For example, in Excerpt 14, the author of a review of a high-speed blender poses a question to the reader, using two second-person pronouns (*Would <u>you</u>, <u>your</u> $40 blender*). She then immediately provides the response to her own question (*No*). Through this sequence, as the reviewer occupies the discourse roles of both question-asker and question-answerer (speaking "for" her readers, in a sense), she creates a sense of alignment, or shared perspective, between herself and her readers.

Excerpt 14
Would you toss whole strawberries, tops and all, into your $40 blender? <u>No</u>. With the [*product name*] you don't have to core your apples, just quarter them. [*Amazon*]

Similarly, the author of the film review in Excerpt 15 provides the response to a question posed about the film's ending (*so ya think* [...]? *Yup*).

Excerpt 15
And then comes the big collision that totals the movie [...] Thats right, so ya think someones gonna die? Yup. Let the suffering begin, as the camera refuses to move off the actors so that what were once convincing performances look like self-indulgent histrionics. [*Netflix*]

Simulating conversational interaction, the reviewer's question (*ya think someone's gonna die?*) is preceded by another marker of involvement: an expression of affirmation (*Thats right*). The question sequence actually begins with another discourse marker (*so*), and both the question's second-person pronoun subject and its verb are expressed as phonological reductions: *ya* instead of *you*, and *gonna* instead of *going to*. These linguistic choices also contribute to the sense of orality or conversation in Excerpt 15. In these highly "interactive" examples of addressivity, it is as though the writer is having a conversation with the reader. That they typically appear in the middle of reviews suggests that one of their functions is to maintain a reader's interest and involvement in what is otherwise a static, monologic text.

Anticipating reader responses

In other cases, only one side of an "imagined interaction" is presented by the reviewer, and readers are left to work out the other side on their own. In the following examples, reviewers only provide responses; and, unlike the examples in the preceding section, the questions, or statements, to which reviewers are ostensibly responding are *not* included in the review text. In Excerpt 16, the author makes a very strong evaluative claim, followed by an explicitly stated objection anticipated from an imagined segment of the review's readership (*all you Cali people*).

Excerpt 16
Healthy it is not, but a better burrito you will never ever consume. [...] And yes, I've lived on the west coast so all you Cali people that claim ordering a burrito in English is a recipe for failure ... well normally I'd agree with you but this time you're just wrong. [Restaurant name] is freakin' outstanding. [*Yelp*]

In Excerpt 16, the reviewer states a likely objection that people from California might have: which is that *ordering a burrito in English is a recipe for failure* (in other words, that Mexican food outside of a Spanish-speaking context is inauthentic, and cannot possibly be any good). He further aligns with this imagined audience, by indicating he is a former resident of the same region (*I've lived on the west coast*). This larger counter-claim is preceded by the affirmation *and yes,* which indexes an anticipatory response to any number of imagined – and presumably relevant – *yes–no* questions (for example, "Have you ever eaten Mexican food outside of your home state?" "Do you know good Mexican food?" "Have you ever had authentic Mexican food?"). In this example, as the reviewer anticipates objections, aligns with that segment of his readership who he considers to be experts on the given topic, and engages with this audience directly, he demonstrates that he is a credible source on the topic and that he knows what he is writing about. In this example, a strong connection between addressivity and an appeal to ethos is forged: this signals to readers that they should continue reading, and should not dismiss his review as uninformed.

In Excerpt 17, from a recipe review, the reviewer responds similarly to an imagined, or anticipated, *yes–no* question from a reader, and begins with the same *and yes,* construction.

Excerpt 17
Also check the crust at 7 minutes. I found the temp to be too high, <u>and yes</u>, I always use an oven thermometer. [*Epicurious*]

The construction *and yes* is used to signal a conversational response to an imagined dialogue; specifically, it serves to preface a response to particular a line of questioning. Here the imagined question, which is inferable only from the surrounding linguistic context, is probably something along the lines of "Did you use an oven thermometer to check the heat of the oven?" Once again, this can be considered an appeal to ethos, as the reviewer demonstrates her expertise as a cook who knows that she always needs to use an oven thermometer, even when she is following a recipe.

In Excerpt 18, the product reviewer uses repetition (*melt*), preceded by an affirmative response (*Yes*) and a speech act verb (*I said*), to simulate a dialogue, as though she were having a conversation with a reader. In doing so, this reviewer provides her own follow-up to an imagined reaction of incredulity in response to her claim about a piece of the expensive appliance actually melting during use.

Excerpt18
Meanwhile, the black plastic seal below the blade would fall apart – shredding and melt with use. <u>Yes I said melt</u>. [*Amazon*]

Here, metadiscourse is used to confirm to the reader that there is no error in interpretation of the reviewer's account of what happened. The way in which this metadiscourse is packaged does not refer to the written, text-based form of the review (for example, *Yes, I wrote/meant/* etc.) but rather, it is expressed as though it were spoken (that is, *Yes, I <u>said</u> melt*), further alluding to the give-and-take interaction of a conversation. This is similar to the example of metadiscourse, *what can I <u>say</u>* in Excerpt 3. Earlier studies of metadiscourse in other digital media, such as instant messaging, found that the metalinguistic terms deployed by users in these media do tend to rely on the metalanguage of speech (Jones & Schieffelin, 2009; Jones et al., 2011).

Excerpt 19 is taken from a longer review text. In the original text, this segment is parenthetically set off from the rest of the surrounding review. The reviewer's second-person address of the reader through the use of an imperative (*Now, don't tell me...*) imagines a response from her audience, as she anticipates possible critiques from others about the carelessness of her actions in overfilling her blender. This example begins with *Now*, another discourse marker, which in this instance, draws attention to an upcoming idea, and once again indexes a spoken interaction.

Excerpt 19
(<u>Now, don't tell me about</u> the directions and that I was careless. <u>I understand</u>. My point is that you can overfill the [competitor brand] and not have an accident. <u>and what good is a carafe you can only fill to the three quarter mark?</u>) [*Amazon*]

Here, the reviewer begins her parenthetical aside by reacting to an imagined response of how others might perceive her and how they might characterize her behavior. This is followed by a short sentence, *I understand*, which represents her own response to the imagined interlocutor(s). This text has what we might think of as dialogic overtones, or several intertextual allusions to the negotiation that takes place between speaker and hearer – or, in this case, between reader and writer. In this instance the dialogicality is accomplished through the reviewer's "arguing against" some imagined objections of the reader. Her parenthetical digression concludes as she poses a rhetorical question to her reader(s), in order to recruit support for her position (that is, *what good is a carafe [...]?*). As a marker of stance, rhetorical questions often serve to align writer and reader as having shared values (Myers, 2010).

Summary and conclusion

In the previous section, I have illustrated and discussed several forms of addressivity, or the ways in which an anticipated, or imagined, interaction between writer and reader is discursively constructed in online reviews. The forms I have identified, illustrated, and discussed have ranged from discourse markers and other conversational devices, to direct audience address through second-person pronouns and imperatives. In other examples, reviewers engaged an audience by posing a question, or by providing a response to an imagined question. These final examples are perhaps the most compelling because they simulate a dialogue, and allow the review writer to take on multiple discourse roles within what is otherwise a monologic text. In this mode of communication, where authors and audience are unknown to one another in an offline sense, these discourse features serve as resources for reviewers to engage and connect with their unknown audiences. These discourse features, which all have a relational function in online reviews, are summarized in Table 1.2.

Table 1.2 Summary of discourse features related to relational strategies

Discourse features	Examples	Functions
Discourse markers	*Well, You know, Now, Oh*	Mark interactivity; mark text as "speech like"
Imperatives and second-person pronouns	*Don't plan on sleeping. Upon closer inspection you will see.*	Address readers directly
Interactive metadiscourse	*What can I say Let me tell you*	Appeal for readers' continued interest and participation in reading the text; mark text as "speech like"
Questions	*Can you believe that? would we stay here again?*	Simulate give-and-take of conversation; elicit some type of overall evaluation of experience
Answers	*and yes, I always use an oven thermometer*	Simulate give-and-take of conversation; demonstrate a reviewer's credibility/ethos
Questions and answers (simulated dialogue)	*Would you toss whole strawberries [...] into your $40 blender? No. so ya think someones gonna die? Yup.*	Simulate give-and-take of conversation; alignment, shared perspective

Forms of addressivity can occur in various sections of a review text. Discourse markers, such as *you know* or *well*, with an interactive function, typically appear at the beginning of a review text and often initiate a highly narrative review. They also often precede a response to an imagined question. Other times, metalinguistic expressions such as *let me tell you, wait there's more*, and *don't even get me started* appear in the middle of review text, and here, these forms not only address readers more directly, but they also serve as appeals for readers' continued interest and participation in reading the text. Finally, questions posed toward the end of a review (whether they are addressed from the review writer to the reader, or whether they are "imagined questions" being metaphorically addressed from an imagined reader to a review writer) often function to elicit some type of overall evaluation of experience. That several of these features tend to cluster together in a particular segment of text – as seen in several of the examples discussed throughout this chapter – suggests that they are mutually reinforcing, in terms of their role in addressing the audience, and in creating a sense of reader involvement and interaction.

Authors of business communication textbooks and manuals often encourage students and practitioners to "be conversational" in their writing (for example, Guffey & Loewy, 2013; Shwom & Snyder, 2011). Similarly, commonsense advice for writers of online content consists of messages such as "write like you speak." Authors of blogs and other forms of online content are often exhorted to imagine a particular person as they craft their prose. As one popular blog for producers of online content explains: "We write for our audience, and if you can imagine a *single person* in your audience who you're writing to, your ideas and writing are going to flow much better" (Flynn, n.d.). Similarly, another blog with tips for fellow blog writers stresses that: "Good writing is like a conversation between the writer and the reader" (Zanelli, n.d.). Whether by observation, imitation, or intuition, writers of engaging reviews seem to have grasped this principle: by drawing on a range of interactive discursive resources, these reviewers have created texts that "speak to" their readers in various ways. Business communication professionals may find it useful to consider how the specific discursive resources illustrated in this chapter are deployed by writers in the creation of texts that can be described as "conversational."

Finally, it is important to point out that none of the discourse features discussed here – strictly speaking – are necessary, or required, for writing an informative consumer review. The descriptive and evaluative propositional content of these texts is not reliant on any of these linguistics resources. However, that does not mean they are insignificant textual elements. On the contrary, they serve an extremely important relational function, by indexing the relationship that is instantly created, as the text forges a bond between an online writer and an online reader: individuals who may have little else in common beyond that shared text.

Notes

1. Many review sites now offer users the opportunity to add multi-modal information (images, video) to their reviews. However, at this point in time, most of the evaluative information about the product or service being reviewed remains encoded at the textual level.
2. A more detailed discussion of the data sources and sampling procedures can be found in Vásquez, 2014b.

References

Androutsopoulos, J. (2013). Online data collection. In C. Mallinson, B. Childs & G. V. Herk (Eds), *Data collection in sociolinguistics: Methods and applications* (pp. 237–249). London: Continuum.

Bakhtin, M. (1986). *Speech genres and other late essays* (tr. V. W. McGee). Austin, TX: University of Texas Press.

Benwell, B., & Stokoe, E. (2006), *Discourse and identity*. Edinburgh: Edinburgh University Press.

Besnier, N. (1994). Involvement in linguistic practice: An ethnographic appraisal. *Journal of Pragmatics, 22*, 279–299.

Biber, D., Johansson, S., Leech, G., Conrad, S., & Finnegan, E. (1999). *Longman grammar of spoken and written English*. London: Pearson.

Brinton, L. (1996). *Pragmatic markers in English: Grammaticalization and discourse functions*. Berlin: Mouton de Gruyter.

Chafe, W. (1982). Integration and involvement in speaking, writing, and oral literature. In D. Tannen (Ed.), *Spoken and written language: Exploring orality and literacy* (pp. 35–53). Norwood, NJ: Ablex.

Dellarocas, C., Awad, N., & Zhang, X. (2004). Exploring the value of online reviews to organizations: Implications for revenue forecasting and planning. Working paper, Retrieved from: http://ssrn.com/abstract=620821.

Flynn, P. (n.d.). Smart passive income. Retrieved from: http://www.smartpassive income.com/blog-writing-tips/.

Forman, C., Ghose, A., & Wiesenfeld, B. (2008). Examining the relationship between reviews and sales: The role of reviewer identity disclosure in electronic markets. *Information Systems Research, 19*, 291–313.

Goffman, E. (1981). *Forms of talk*. Philadelphia, PA: University of Pennsylvania Press.

Guffey, M. E., & Loewy, D. (2013). *Business communication: Process and product* (7th Ed.). Mason, OH: Southwestern Cengage Learning.

Hennig-Thurau, T., Qwinner, K. P., Walsh, G., & Gremler, D. D. (2004). Electronic word-of-mouth via consumer-opinion platforms: What motivates consumers to articulate themselves on the Internet? *Journal of Interactive Marketing, 18* (1), 38–52.

Hyland, K. (2005). *Metadiscourse.* London: Continuum.

Jones, G. M., & Schieffelin, B. (2009). Enquoting voices, accomplishing talk: *"be+like"* in instant messaging. *Language and Communication, 29* (1), 77–113.

Jones, G. M., Schieffelin, B., & Smith, R. (2011). When friends who talk together stalk together: Online gossip as metacommunication. In C. Thurlow & K. Mroczek (Eds), *Digital discourse: Language in the new media* (pp. 26–47). Oxford: Oxford University Press.

Jucker, A. (1993). The discourse marker *well*: A relevance theoretic account. *Journal of Pragmatics, 19*, 435–452.

Kozinets, R. V. (2010). *Netnography.* London: Sage.

Mackiewicz, J. (2010a). Assertions of expertise in online product reviews. *Journal of Business and Technical Communication, 24* (1), 3–28.

Mackiewicz, J. (2010b). The co-construction of credibility in online product reviews. *Technical Communication Quarterly, 19* (4), 403–426.

Mudambi, S., & Schuff, D. (2010). What makes a helpful online review? A study of consumer reviews on Amazon.com. *MIS Quarterly, 34* (1), 185–200.

Myers, G. (2010). *The discourse of blogs and wikis.* London: Continuum.

Otterbacher, J. (2011). Being heard in review communities: Communication tactics and review prominence. *Journal of Computer-Mediated Communication, 16*, 424–444.

Paltridge, B. (2012). *Discourse Analysis* (2nd Ed.). London: Bloomsbury

Schiffrin, D. (1987). *Discourse markers.* Cambridge: Cambridge University Press.

Seargeant, P., Tagg, C., & Ngampramuan, W. (2012). Language choice and addressivity strategies in Thai–English social network interactions. *Journal of Sociolinguistics, 16* (4), 510–531.

Shwom, B., & Snyder, L. G. (2011). *Business communication: Polishing your professional presence.* Boston, MA: Prentice-Hall.

Skalicky, S. (2013). Was this analysis helpful? A genre analysis of the Amazon. com discourse community and its "most helpful" product reviews. *Discourse, Context & Media, 2* (2), 84–93.

Sparks, B., Perkins, H., & Buckley, R. (2013). Online travel reviews as persuasive communication: The effects of content type, source, and certification logos on consumer behavior. *Tourism Management, 39*, 1–9.

Tannen, D. (1985). Relative focus on involvement in oral and written discourse. In D. Olson, N. Torrance & A. Hildyard (Eds), *Literacy, language, and learning: The nature and consequences of reading and writing* (pp. 124–147). Cambridge: Cambridge University Press.

Tian, Y. (2013). Engagement in online hotel reviews: A comparative study. *Discourse, Context & Media, 2* (3), 184–191.

Vásquez, C. (2011). Complaints online: The case of TripAdvisor. *Journal of Pragmatics, 43*, 1707–1717.

Vásquez, C. (2012). Narrativity and involvement in online consumer reviews: The case of TripAdvisor. *Narrative Inquiry, 22* (1), 105–121.

Vásquez, C. (2014a). "Usually not one to complain but...": Constructing identities in online reviews. In C. Tagg & P. Seargeant (Eds), *The language of social media: Community and identity on the internet* (pp. 65–90). London: Palgrave Macmillan.

Vásquez, C. (2014b). *The discourse of online consumer reviews*. London: Bloomsbury Press.

Zanelli, L. (n.d.). Copyblogger. Retrieved from: http://www.copyblogger.com/authentic-writer/

Sources of online review data

Amazon (www.amazon.com)
Epicurious (www.epicurious.com)
Netflix (www.netflix.com)
TripAdvisor (www.tripadvisor.com)
Yelp (www.yelp.com)

2
Social CEOs: Tweeting as a Constitutive Form of Organizational Communication

Katerina Girginova

Introduction

We need not dig very deep into popular business literature today to find conflicting advice on organizational leaders and their social media practices. Publications tell us that a majority of CEOs state social business as a top organizational and personal priority,[1] and that customers are 82% more likely to trust and 77% more likely to buy from companies whose leaders personally engage with social media.[2] Yet, only 32% of the Fortune 500 CEOs actually have a social platform presence themselves.[3] Further, warnings that one wrong Tweet can have dire consequences[4] for those in the public eye abound and experts question whether there is even a need for CEOs to be personally involved in every aspect of organizational communication.[5]

What is missing from this often over-hyped and quantitative spectrum of literature is any sustained analysis of social media use from the perspective of the CEOs themselves. Take, for example, the growth of Twitter and tweeting leaders in the workplace. Tweeting CEOs present at once an enigmatic space of personal *and* professional media use, which can be understood simultaneously as a blurring and an extension of the traditional organization. Still, while there exists ample literature with prescriptive practices about how CEOs *ought* to Tweet there is a scarcity of descriptive research detailing how they *actually* Tweet.

This chapter begins to address this gap through personal interviews and Twitter feed analyses of a diverse group of ten CEOs. Moreover, by asking the question "what is the role of CEOs' personal tweeting practices[6] in the communicative constitution of organizations (CCO)?" this chapter contributes to a growing body of scholarship housed under the term CCO.

This research attempts to unravel the DNA of organizations and their leaders by analyzing communicative episodes as their building blocks. In turn, the study presents a rich milieu of observed Twitter practices, with the hope that they are instructive for academics and practitioners alike.

Digitizing CEOs

The new media landscape requires practical and conceptual reforms in the way we understand CEOs and their organizations (Norris & Porter, 2011). As Nyström (2009) notes, it is rare to see the emergence and enactment of a professional identity because this identity is "often the result of a dynamic relationship between different life spheres" (p. 1). Further, these life spheres often play out behind closed doors to the general public. Similarly, it is quite rare to be able to see the establishment of an organization and the different communicative activities that constitute it. Twitter, albeit in a curated way, affords us the unique opportunity to glimpse behind the scenes at these processes.

Unlike its predecessors the memo, conference call, meeting, or press release, Twitter offers an easily accessible, disseminated and supposedly unfiltered public access to CEOs. The microblogging service, which allows users to post 140 character parcels of digital content onto the web, launched in 2006 and has since grown to handle over a billion Tweets per couple of days. This equates to nearly 6,000 Tweets per second (Ingram, 2012). Dick Costollo, CEO of Twitter, describes the service as "the pulse of the planet" (Ingram, 2012, n.p.); a network for the zeitgeist. According to Costollo, Twitter levels the playing field for those in the public eye, such as celebrities and CEOs, by allowing them to engage directly with their audiences without the filters or constraints of publicists and other media outlets.

It is worth highlighting that this is an example of the frequently encountered democratizing rhetoric about the advantages of social media. While in theory CEOs may be free to post whatever content they wish on Twitter, in practice there remain plenty of professional constraints. Moreover, a layperson's access to a CEO's Twitter feed certainly does not equate with access to that CEO. Therefore, it is important to be able to recognize instances of this type of discourse in order to be able to interrogate them and to explore critically the practices dis/enabled by this platform.

Nevertheless, tweeting CEOs present an interesting case from a communicative standpoint because, as Melewar (2003) provocatively suggests, quite literally everything that can be linked to an organization – and this certainly includes a CEO's personal Tweets – shapes our understanding of it and makes up its image. Further, research indicates that many founding entrepreneurs, who comprise the majority of this study's sample, "view their businesses as a direct form of self-expression" (Shaywitz, 2012, n.p.). On the one hand, this poses the threat of an over-extension of the type of communicative practices constituting an organization and begs the question of where to draw the line. On the other hand, it allows us to take seriously CEOs' tweeting practices; their personal Tweets, however seemingly banal at times, shape and reinforce their professional identities as well as aid in the social construction of their organizations.

CEOs on Twitter: what we know

One of the biggest challenges for CEOs in the digital environment is the creation of an e-version(s) of themselves, which can "convey polysemic content to audiences, actual and imagined, without compromising one's own sense of self" (Papacharissi, 2012, p. 1989). For instance, a CEO who uses Twitter for personal purposes is potentially faced with reconciling many diverse aspects of his or her private and professional life under the use of one medium. This task can be challenging as "elements of one repertoire may be quite inappropriate, incomprehensible or even offensive in another community" (Wenger, 1998, p. 160).

Marwick and boyd (2010) suggest that this conflict is due to a blurring phenomenon called the context collapse. "Like much social media, Twitter creates a 'context collapse' (boyd, 2008) in which multiple audiences, usually thought of as separate, co-exist in a single social context" (p. 145). One strategy the authors discover on Twitter for tackling this challenge is explained by the theory of the "lowest common denominator"; a philosophy of sharing, which "limits users to topics that are safe for all possible readers" (p. 126).

Yet another way to frame the behaviors of a digitized CEOs is through Hogan's (2010) concept of an "exhibition." This is defined as a pre-composed act of self-disclosure, which can be viewed by anonymous audiences at asynchronous intervals to the time of production. "Exhibitions" are a digital adaptation of Goffman's (1959) notions of identity "performance" and "front and back stage," and imply that the world is not only a stage but also a "library and a gallery ... a participatory exhibit" (2010, p. 377).

Notably, the ideas of "exhibition" and "the lowest common denominator" imply some degree of curatorship. This occurs both at the level of the artist (read: CEO) and the exhibition space (read: the Twitter platform). In the case of Twitter, the curatorship role is performed by the user interface and the various algorithms that structure Twitter to display information in a certain manner. To that end, Twitter employs some 1,800 engineers to ensure its smooth operation (Twitter, 2015) and ultimately, to help produce the public performance of the CEOs and other users. Subsequently, this study considers Twitter and broadly speaking, technology, as an important actor – not just a neutral container – in shaping organizations and the practice of CEO (Güney & Cresswell, 2012; Latour, 1992; Taylor & Van Every, 2000).

With the exception of two notable works by Geho, Smith, and Lewis (2010) and Domo + CEO.com, there is a gap in the scholarly body of works exploring CEOs' personal tweeting. Briefly, Geho et al., examine the Twitter uses of entrepreneurs and small business owners (though not explicitly CEOs or exclusively personal Twitter accounts) and find that the most frequent purpose of Tweets, 79%, was broadly speaking information sharing, marketing and promotion (ibid.). Domo + CEO. com conduct annual surveys on CEO's social media practices but they focus entirely on Fortune 500 CEOs and primarily provide big-picture, quantitative analyses about use. Their reports show that in 2014 only 42 of all Fortune 500 CEOs were on Twitter; they also look at CEO engagement across four other platforms.

Since there are very limited studies of CEOs' personal Twitter uses we may turn to others in the public eye, such as celebrities, for further guidance. Indeed, high-profile CEOs certainly can have thousands, if not millions of followers, which puts them on par with celebrities. Marwick and boyd (2011) argue that "Twitter demonstrates the transformation of 'celebrity' from a personal quality linked to fame to a set of practices that circulate through modern social media" (p. 156). Therefore, celebrity, seen as a communicative practice, becomes something that may be captured and analyzed.

Further, Marwick and boyd (2011) contend that "celebrity" is practiced on Twitter "through the appearance and performance of backstage access" (p. 139). CEOs who share seemingly banal personal information, such as their lunch preferences, perform a backstage-revelatory act. Yet, "while celebrity practice is theoretically open to all, it is not an equalizer or democratizing discourse. Indeed, in order to successfully practice celebrity, fans must recognize the power differentials intrinsic to the relationship" (ibid.). This implicit need for inequality is also true in the case of CEOs as well, and as we shall see further on, the algorithms behind Twitter, something Hogan may refer to as the implicit curatorship role of the technology, certainly become an important accomplice in creating and maintaining this hierarchy.

Constituting an organization: the CCO approach

As we come to acknowledge that traditional markers such as physicality decreasingly determine the boundaries of organizations it is natural to wonder: what does? Jacobs (2008) suggests that business is now structured around actions such as sending e-mails late at night or on the weekends. Similarly, CEOs are now judged by additional criteria, such as their mediated selves and social media communication, during and outside of work. In other words, the communicative actions of and around organizations become key episodes for constructing and deconstructing their DNA. It then follows that if we accept communication as a constitutive force in our organizations then a change in communicative behaviors could lead to different organizational formations.

Here we may turn to some organizational research to help us better understand the link between communication and organization. One of the foundational developments in organizational thought can be traced to Karl Weick (1969, 1979), who described the term *organization* as a verb as opposed to a noun. Weick also drew attention to the social construction and human agency involved in organizations by arguing that communication is not just a container; it is the very substance through which organization occurs. This presented a radical departure from previous works, which saw the organization as a static entity (McPhee & Zaug, 2000, 2009). Since Weick's fundamental implication was that organizing happens through social interaction, the next step was for scholars to explore the nature of those interactions.

McPhee and Zaug's four flows model emerged as a response to this gap in research. The model was first presented at a conference in 2000, under the title "The Communicative Constitution of Organizations: A Framework for Explanation," and became one of the first recorded uses of the phrase "Communicative Constitution of Organizations," abbreviated as CCO. The four constituting flows are: membership negotiation, organizational self-structuring,[7] activity coordination, and institutional positioning. These flows are equally important and analytically distinct, yet they share some porous boundaries and are open to various combinations. Moving forward, they will help us analyze how various CEO Tweets contribute toward the constitution of an organization.

The four flows

Table 2.1 contains a description of each of the flows along with an example of corresponding CEO Tweets (Figure 2.1).

Study design

The CEOs for this study were identified via an online search and selected through a convenience sample (with the exception of David Barger, CEO of JetBlue, whose interview was obtained through an opportune, in-person encounter). The three main criteria for selecting CEOs were (1) that CEOs managed their own, personal Twitter accounts, (2) that they came from diverse business backgrounds, and (3) that they were responsive to the study.

More than 40 CEOs were initially contacted via e-mail or other electronic message, such as LinkedIn mail, and about a quarter replied positively to participating. Of the CEOs who were contacted, the highest success rate came via e-mail communication, where CEOs responded

Table 2.1 Four flows categorization

Flow	Example Tweets
Membership Negotiation is a form of direct or indirect communication with others, such as the recruitment or reinforcement of existing members/employees.	"@MatrixGroup seeks a project manager" "@FranklinNicole Thx for the mention. How are things? How's biz? Miss you at the @MatrixGroup holiday party"
Self Structuring refers to any mention of official internal procedures, policies, and feedback.	e.g. A shared link to evaluation or policy documents.
Institutional Positioning is a form of external communication, which negotiates relationships with other companies and institutions. This flow includes sharing promotional information and instances of networking.	"@salesforce! #2 on @BloombergNews @businessweek 50 — #2/50 best performing"
Activity Coordination refers primarily to internal work processes such as challenges, tasks, and protocols. It also includes information about the CEO's own workflow and whereabouts.	"@MatrixGroup PMs & Directors have been discussing task management apps. Anyone tried #TheSecretWeapon?"

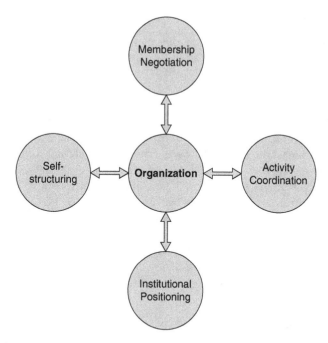

Figure 2.1 McPhee & Zaug's four flows framework

almost instantaneously. In fact, the majority responded within an hour of the e-mail request being sent. The rest of the CEOs typically responded within a day. Interestingly, soliciting CEOs for this study via Twitter did not yield any success.

The data collection took place in two stages: first, each CEO's Twitter feed was actively monitored for a period of three months (October 1–December 31, 2012) and a total 2,086 Tweets were captured using NVivo10 and coded by hand. Second, the Twitter data was triangulated through personal interviews and questionnaires from the CEOs. This dual data analysis offers a more contextualized set of findings along with the ability to observe the level of reflexivity and correlation between the CEOs' prescriptive and descriptive Twitter practices (Glaser & Strauss, 1967; Krippendorff, 2013) (Table 2.2).

Findings: Twitter uses

The Twitter content analyses and CEO interviews revealed a variety of practices. While no two CEOs were found to have the same tweeting

Table 2.2 Profile of CEOs and companies*

Company	CEO**	Business	Founder?***	Year****	# Employees	State
Zoom Active	Dallas Alexander @dallasalexander	Web Design Company	Yes	2008	10–20	AZ
JetBlue	David Barger @davebarger	Airline Company	No	1999	15,000+	NY
Brazen Careerist	Ed Barrientos @SnowCrash65	Self Branding	No	2008	10–15	DC
Quintain Marketing	Kathleen Booth @WorkMommyWork	Marketing/Branding	Yes (co-founder)	2006	4	MD
Shoulder2Shoulder	Ken Falke @ken2s	Veteran Media & Technology	Yes	2011	1–5	VA
Sumazi	Sumaya Kazi @sumaya	Social Networking Consulting	Yes	2010	1–5	CA
Veenome	Kevin Lenane @kevinlenane	Video Content Extraction	Yes	2011	5–10	DC
Zillow Inc.	Spencer Rascoff @spencerrascoff	Real Estate Information	Yes	2005	300+	WA
Furia Rubel Communications, Inc.	Gina Rubel @GinaRubel	Integrated Marketing Agency (law firm specialty)	Yes	2002	5–10	PA
Ziglar Inc.	Tom Ziglar @TomZiglar	Inspirational Talks/Self Improvement	No (family member of founder)	1970	3–10	TX

* All data reflects CEOs and their companies as of March 17, 2013..
** An important distinction is to be made between CEOs' personal Twitter accounts and practices (accounts held and maintained by the CEOs themselves), and corporate Twitter accounts and practices (accounts held and maintained by companies, which are often managed by communication staff). Although all of the CEOs in question had corporate accounts this study exclusively engages with their personal ones.
*** "Founder" refers to whether the CEO in question is also a founder/founding member of the company.
**** "Year" refers to year the company was founded.

behaviors, there were some emergent patterns. For instance, the most common CEO response to the question "why do you use Twitter?" was a desire to establish oneself as an industry expert, to connect with others, and to grow a personal brand. Then, unanimously, the CEOs stated that their personal Twitter accounts were mainly professional or hybrid (personal and professional) in nature. It is also worth highlighting that the majority of the CEOs in this study were the founders of their organizations, and seven out of the ten CEOs announced their role as a CEO on their personal Twitter profile.

Figure 2.2 shows that CEOs' tweeting practices seemed to fluctuate. Notably, some of the highest peaks of Tweets occurred in early and late October and were directly related to the 2012 Presidential debates (October 3–22) and Hurricane Sandy (October 22–29). This suggests that most CEOs were engaging not only with their organizations but also with the world around them.

Figure 2.3 shows that two thirds of all tweeting occurred within the loose boundaries of the working day, 7am–7pm. However, another third of the tweeting took place between 7pm and 7am, or what could be considered outside of normal working hours for most people. (Very few of these were pre-scheduled Tweets, and differences in time zone were accounted for.)

Upon a first reading, tweeting outside of work hours suggests the CEOs do tend to use Twitter not only as a work-related medium but also as a personal tool. Upon a closer reading, however, one may conclude that work in our technologically enabled society has no clear boundaries.

The interview with Suamaya Kazi, CEO of Sumazi, also supports the idea of an integrated relationship between CEOs' personal Twitter practices and their daily lives. Kazi stated that there was no timeframe she specifically set aside for her tweeting; instead, she noted that when she

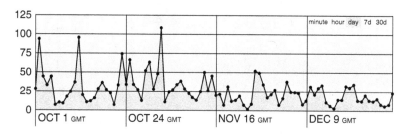

Figure 2.2 Twitter activity

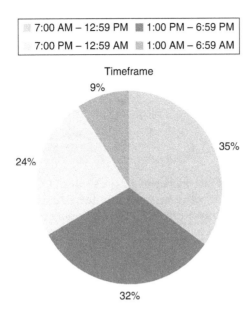

| ▨ 7:00 AM – 12:59 PM | ▦ 1:00 PM – 6:59 PM |
| 7:00 PM – 12:59 AM | ▩ 1:00 AM – 6:59 AM |

Timeframe

9%

35%

24%

32%

Figure 2.3   CEO Tweeting times

woke up, she would naturally turn to her phone and be met with a slew of notifications from e-mail, Facebook and Twitter. Then, as the day progressed, she would use her personal Twitter account whenever the occasion organically arose. The fact that all of these updates appeared on the same mobile platform, her phone, is already an indication of a blurred work/personal life space.

The four flows

The content analyses of the 2,086 CEO Tweets did provide evidence for the use of the four flows, suggesting that the CEOs' personal Twitter accounts are related to their organizations but perhaps, in less direct and traditional ways than one might expect. The most frequently encountered flow was activity coordination, but the largest percentage of the Tweets (63%) fell under a "non-flow" category. In essence, the majority of the Tweets could not be categorized into one of the framework's four flows.

This is indicative not so much of the banal or non-organizational nature of CEOs' personal Tweets but potentially of different organizational realities where constitution occurs through social interactions that are less structured around and physically bound to an organization.

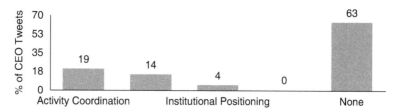

Figure 2.4   CEO Tweet flows

This is an important consideration for the study of CCO, and it suggests that we could benefit by expanding our understanding of what type of communication is constitutive of organizations. Perhaps, we need to adapt the four flows framework accordingly – an issue addressed further on (Figure 2.4).

Activity coordination

The most prevalent flow among the CEOs was activity coordination, accounting for 19% of the total CEO Tweets. Examples of activity coordination include travel and important or interesting work updates, which suggests that through the use of Twitter the physical organizations are extended to include whatever region of the world their CEOs are presently in. Further, the mobile nature of Twitter makes it easy, perhaps even desirable, for CEOs to give snapshots of their work and thoughts on the go:

> Stuck on a train, stopped in the snow somewhere in NJ. Wish i was watching #dcweek #dctech keynote. Will consume @skeevis morsels instead
> Kevin Lenane, CEO of Veenome

A particularly interesting application of activity coordination could be seen across the Tweets of David Barger, CEO of JetBlue. Barger was one of several CEOs who tweeted actively during and post Hurricane Sandy in October 2012, because his company's headquarters were based in an area that was directly impacted. Barger tweeted regular information to propagate the coordination efforts of his large company, to send out flight operation updates, and to boost staff morale.

> A huge thank you to our Crewmembers, for supporting our Customers and each other during #HurricaneSandy! How are you doing?
> David Barger, CEO of JetBlue

While most activity coordination was concerned with relatively light-hearted organizational information Barger's Tweets showed a powerful application of Twitter as a timely and important communication tool in moments of organizational crises. This type of organizational Twitter use certainly warrants further exploration and has the potential to become a valuable resource in many organizations' crisis communication response plans.

Membership negotiation

Membership negotiation was the second most frequently encountered flow, totaling up to 14% of the sampled Tweets. This flow presents a particularly nuanced concept because it raises the fundamental issue of what it means to be a "member." According to Rafaeli (1996), there are various shades of membership, whereby "membership is a matter of degree" (p. 6). Seen as a relational quality, membership becomes a loose variable, which expands beyond the traditional staff member to include other organizational actors such as customers and suppliers, too (Ansari & Phillips, 2011). As seen in CEO Tweets, this flow did indeed consist primarily of communication with non-organizational persons:

> To my new followers, allow me to introduce myself: https://t.co/u4Y54uCn
>
> Sumaya Kazi, CEO of Sumazi

In her interview, Kazi mentioned that she had many more followers on her personal Twitter account (26,256), than her corporate Twitter account (1,903). Furthermore, she felt like it was an achievement to "convert" somebody who was first her personal follower to then become a corporate follower, too. She also noted that the more platforms (meaning multiple Twitter accounts and other forms of social media) a person engaged in, the stronger their brand loyalty would typically be.

This was corroborated by Tom Ziglar, CEO of Ziglar Inc., who stated that true fans of the Ziglar organization followed it across Twitter, Facebook, and other platforms, and by Alexander Dallas, CEO of Zoom Active, who stated that his personal Twitter account lowered the cost of new customer acquisition. This is consistent with market research, which suggests that a personal or emotional connection with a brand, organization or CEO is key for establishing a loyal customer base (Chaudhuri & Holbrook, 2001).

Of course, membership negotiation also occurred through more explicit Tweets, which served to directly seek new organizational members or to reinforce the status of persons already affiliated with the organization:

> We're hiring! If you know a Software Engineer interested in working @ Sumazi, let us know! http://t.co/VDzYRkET #jobs #hiring #sanfrancisco
>
> Sumaya Kazi, CEO of Sumazi

> I'm looking at the account of an @zillow Premier Agent who has received 104 contacts from Zillow shoppers in the last 30 days. She's stoked.
>
> Spencer Rascoff, CEO of Zillow

Notably, seven of the ten CEOs had many more account followers than people they themselves followed. In some cases this discrepancy was as high as 136:1. This is quite a clear indication of uneven power distribution; although both followers and CEOs are seemingly able to communicate freely via Twitter the CEOs ultimately are the ones in higher demand and in a position to reaffirm others' membership. Marwick and boyd call this practice "micro-celebrity," whereby the power dynamic is a key differentiation between CEOs (the micro-celebrities) and their followers (2011).

Institutional positioning

Institutional positioning was the third most prevalent flow, at 4% of the total sampled Tweets. The low frequency was consistent with previous research, which found that celebrities, sports stars, and even companies tended to shy away from what could be considered overtly promotional content on Twitter (Case & King, 2011; Hambrick et al., 2010). Instead, the type of institutional positioning found involved positive acknowledgments of others in the industry, which allowed CEOs to position themselves as direct or indirect colleagues of theirs.

Furthermore, in the cases of smaller companies, or those in which the CEOs openly appropriated the brand, institutional positioning seemed analogous to Self Positioning:

> At the @HaasFounders mixer. Great group to learn from & share with. Thanks @berolz for running this great network! http://t.co/2sk9jbe6
>
> Sumaya Kazi, CEO of Sumazi

There were also numerous examples of institutional positioning in non-overtly business oriented contexts. This serves to further extend the boundary of an organization by including other mutually reaffirmative organizations or communities.

> Two carloads of clothes and supplies headed to NY/NJ with the Red Cross. http://t.co/t2VcTbQd
>
> Gina Rubel, CEO of Furia Rubel
> Communications Inc.

Self structuring

The finding that self structuring was not prevalent on Twitter suggests that the medium may have some characteristics that make it inherently better suited to certain communicative exchanges over others. Perhaps, the most obvious explanation for the lack of self structuring Tweets could be that this sort of communication is traditionally reserved for more "serious" and controlled environments. Since self structuring frequently includes working with official or confidential documents it would appear that a more fixed environment and known audience would be preferable.

Another reason why it was rare to see examples of the self structuring flow could be that Twitter as a medium tends to be forward facing, based on current information and trends, while self structuring as an activity tends to be reflective. Further still, it could be that self structuring occurs through other "unofficial" means, which could suggest we need to expand our definition of the concept and the guiding framework.

The "non flow"

The vast majority, 63% of the Tweets, from this sample did not readily fit into one of McPhee and Zaug's four organizational flows. However, it is probably naïve to assume that the explanation for the non-flow Tweets is simply that they are not related to organizational communication at all. Rather, it is more fruitful to seek alternative explanations.

One such explanation is that the non-flow Tweets (the majority of which pertained to relationship formation, self positioning, organizational culture, and open leadership) are important communicative acts for any organization but are not always easily quantifiable or explicitly business-related. For example, sharing links to articles of general interest was a prevalent activity on Twitter (86% of the total Tweets were coded as sharing some type of content). This activity positions the CEOs, and by extension, their companies, as thought and industry leaders.

CEOs like Gina Rubel of Furia Rubel Communications Inc. noted that her local business community looked up to her as a leader precisely for her information-sharing practices. That, in turn, implies a certain cutting-edge and savvyness, which can lead to positive institutional positioning, membership negotiation, and so on. In this manner we are able to see how, albeit tangentially, seemingly work-irrelevant CEO Tweets can filter in and be connected to the larger organizational picture. Thus, a plausible way of expanding McPhee and Zaug's framework could be by adding a fifth category called "content sharing."

Additional characteristics

The majority of Tweets, almost 50%, fell within some variation of a direct post. This means that the CEOs often communicated directly with someone or with specific constituencies (Figure 2.5).

Notably, it was quite rare for the CEOs to use Twitter to ask questions. This finding further reinforces the status distinction between the CEOs and their followers, and implies that the CEOs' role is mainly to supply information and to provide answers rather than to pose questions and to overtly seek information. This presents a power dynamic centered on knowledge; followers come to the CEOs for information, not vice versa. CEOs thus become "information brokers," publicly providing and facilitating the dissemination of knowledge.

Combinations of flows

It may be somewhat surprising that given the 140-character limit to the Tweets, certain ones could still be classified as belonging to more than one flow. Various combinations occurred in around 10% of the total sample, and the most prevalent grouping of flows was activity coordination and membership negotiation. The significance of these multiple flows draws attention to the idea that communication, by its very nature, is polysemic. Even with the 140-character limit Tweets could still evoke a multiplicity of meanings.

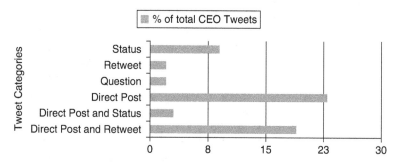

Figure 2.5   CEO Tweet typology

These combinatory Tweets also indicate a level of CEO awareness that messages could be read by a multitude of audiences, and therefore should be suitable and appealing for a variety of people. Furthermore, the existence of multiple messages, meanings and interpretations suggests that organizational structure and complexity are just as much a function of multiple flows of communication and combinations of audiences as they are of physical location and size.

Big birds, small birds

As hinted at by Shaywitz (2012), the size of the company did have a significant impact on the CEOs' Twitter output. In cases of larger organizations, such as Barger's JetBlue and Rascoff's Zillow (with over 15,000 and 300 employees, respectively), Twitter was used simultaneously as a megaphone to amplify the CEO's voice and as a glue to promote company culture and cohesion. In these larger organizations Twitter occupied a unique space as a communicative medium; while in the past most employees in large companies would not have had a daily reason to communicate with – or to hear directly from – their CEOs, Twitter opens up, at least theoretically, this possibility.

Worth noting too, was that the CEOs who had the lowest percent of non-flow Tweets in their feeds, Barger (23%) and Rascoff (46%) were the CEOs of the two biggest companies. In comparison, the average non-flow Tweets for the other CEOs was 69%. This supports the idea that CEOs of larger companies use Twitter as an organizational tool to foster cohesion and a sense of corporate culture among existing members. It also suggests that perhaps they experience greater rewards and pressures to do so.

In the case of the CEOs from the smaller-sized companies Twitter was primarily used to coordinate activities with outside constituencies. As Kazi, CEO of Sumazi (a small start-up company) said, Twitter for her was a community of likeminded strangers. Thus, based on the size of their organizations, we can potentially explain and predict certain CEO communicative behaviors.

Keywords

The content analyses pointed toward an overtly positive, humorous, and congratulatory tone in the CEOs' Tweets. According to a word frequency search, it appeared that one of the most used words that showed up in every CEOs' list regardless of their industry, size of company, or personal background, was "great." Perhaps, this was a function of the publicness of the Tweets. Since the CEOs seemed keenly aware of their online visibility they would also likely be cautious of attaching any negative attention to themselves or to their organizations.

Another less anticipated finding was the discovery of the frequent Tweets about women in the workplace (sometimes referred to by different words like "females"). These mentions could be seen equally across female and male CEOs' posts. (Incidentally, Warren Buffet has only tweeted five times, and his second Tweet was a link to his essay on why women are key to America's prosperity (Adams, 2013).)

In addition, female CEOs such as Booth and Rubel openly stated on their Twitter profiles that they were mothers as well as successful business owners. This trend aligns with the modern-day working reality in the United States, where women make up nearly half of the workforce (Bureau of Labor Statistics, Annual Averages, 2012). More importantly, it also implies that our organizations are indicative of our values and our societies.

The role of technology

Several findings from this study suggest that technology (in this case the Twitter interface) is not a neutral actor when it comes to the communicative constitution of organizations. For instance, Lenane mentioned that his Twitter feed was akin to an interests and hobbies section on a resumé. To borrow from Hogan's (2010) concept, Twitter is a space for public exhibitions whereby communication receives an air of durability and an option to be viewed at one's convenience. A CEO's remarks about their travels, favorite sports teams or political views all present pieces of curated information, which assemble over time and become reified into a Twitter feed or into an extension of the CEO persona and his or her organization for the world to see.

Another salient feature is the possibility of tracking and measuring Tweets. Most of the CEOs interviewed dedicated a significant effort to being active on their personal Twitter account, and they were certainly aware of the reach of their message. For example, Ziglar noted that he used trackable links to see how far and wide his content had spread, and Rascoff, in a separate interview, stated that he used three screens at work: one for work, one for e-mail, and a third dedicated to monitoring Twitter (Hagey, 2012).

The ability to track almost instantaneously the online diffusion of certain messages or the general sentiments toward a leader and their company is something unique to the digital CEO. This form of feedback, facilitated by technology, also allows for the relatively fast modification of an exhibition, if necessary. Yet, as evidenced by Rascoff's practice, it is something that requires a conscious effort and an integration into one's life.

Of course, not everything about a CEOs' personal Twitter output is traceable. Kazi emphasized this point in her interview, and stated that it was not just about numbers. Further, unless communicated, positive or negative affects arising from CEOs' Tweets are not necessarily readily apparent, which also potentially goes to explain the broader trend of hesitation from the CEO population toward using Twitter.

Conclusions and future directions

The interviews and content analyses in this chapter painted a picture of personal tweeting practices as curated exhibitions of the CEOs and their organizations. We saw a blurring and an extending of what would be considered traditional organizational communication topics, members, and temporal and spatial boundaries. In addition, the application of the four flows framework demonstrated a heavy slant toward activity coordination communication, which seems quite natural given the structure of the medium.

It is worth mentioning a couple of limitations of this study, too. First, a larger and even more diverse sample of CEOs would certainly yield a more colorful and corroborated set of results. However, due to practical constraints, the present study is better understood as an exploratory step into the practice of CCO in the new media context. It also fills a gap in research about CEOs' social media practices and suggest a way to amend the four flows framework to better reflect current organizational realities. Second, the four flows framework provided somewhat of a limitation since it did not account for the majority of CEOs' Tweets. Consequently, a way to improve the framework would be by adding a fifth flow, content sharing, which would provide a more accurate account of the communicative landscape of modern organizations and certainly for CEOs' Twitter uses.

Nonetheless, it is necessary to note that McPhee and Zaug first presented their four flows framework in 2000, about six years prior to the emergence of Twitter and many of the other social media we see as firmly embedded within our organizations today. Therefore, it is unreasonable to expect the four flows to be fully accommodating to current communicative evolutions. Despite this, the framework still serves as a useful heuristic for professionals and academics alike. Moreover, it helps to conceptualize an organization in textual terms and to think through how specific types of communication can contribute toward its structuring.

Ultimately, this study suggests that an organization is more than just a combination of work-related events. It is a dynamic space of interaction where multiple communicative flows converge to create organizational realities and findings such as the "non-flow" imply the need for additional research to elucidate this space and the process of CCO. As CEOs continue to adopt Twitter and other new media platforms, we are presented with the opportunity to unpack their communicative acts and to shed light on their practices as telling of 21st-century organizations, leaders, and societies.

Five key takeaways

1. Twitter use simultaneously extends and blurs the traditional organization.
2. CEOs on Twitter often engage in acts of "information broking"; this helps to position them and their companies as thought and industry leaders.
3. CEOs of smaller-sized businesses tend to use Twitter for external, outreach purposes.
4. CEOs of larger-sized businesses tend to use Twitter for internal, company culture-building goals.
5. Studying communication flows as the boundaries of organizations allows for a more dynamic understanding of an organization's structure.

Notes

1. See IBM CEO Survey, 2012.
2. See BRANDFog, 2012; Cruz & Mendelsohn, 2012.
3. See CEO.com and Domo Report, 2014.
4. See Love in *Business Insider*, 2011.
5. See Gow, 2013.
6. This study focuses exclusively on Twitter accounts that belong to and are managed personally by CEOs.
7. For brevity's sake, "organizational self structuring" is called "self structuring" from here on.

References

Adams, S. (August 7, 2013). Less than a third of top CEOs are on social media. *Forbes*. Retrieved from: http://www.forbes.com/sites/susanadams/2013/08/07/less-than-a-third-of-top-ceos-are-on-social-media/.

Ansari, S., & Phillips, N. (2011). Text me! New consumer practices and change in organizational fields. *Organization Science, 22* (6), 1579–1599.

boyd, d. (2008). Taken out of Context: American Teen Sociality in Networked Publics (PhD Dissertation), University of California, Berkeley, USA.

BRANDFog (2012). *CEO, Social Media and Leadership Survey*. Retrieved from: http://www.brandfog.com/CEOSocialMediaSurvey/BRANDfog_2012_CEO_Survey.pdf.

Bureau of Labor Statistics, Current Population Survey, Table 3: Employment Status of the Civilian Noninstitutional Population by Age, Sex, and Race. *Annual Averages 2012* (2013).

Case, C., & King, D. (2011). Twitter usage in the Fortune 50: A marketing opportunity? *Journal of Marketing Development and Competitiveness, 5* (3), 94–101.

CEO.com and Domo Report (2014). *2014 CEO.com Social CEO Report.* Retrieved from: http://www.ceo.com/social-ceo-report-2014-report/.

Chaudhuri, A., & Holbrook, M. (2001). The chain of effects from brand trust and brand affect to brand performance: The role of brand loyalty. *The Journal of Marketing, 65* (2), 81–93.

Cruz, B., & Mendelsohn, J. (2012). Why social media matters to your business. *Chadwick Martin Bailey Survey.* Retrieved from: http://www.cmbinfo.com/cmb-cms/wp-content/uploads/2010/04/Why_Social_Media_Matters_2010.pdf.

Geho, P., Smith, S., & Lewis, S. (2010). Is Twitter a viable commercial use platform for small businesses? An empirical study targeting two audiences in the small business community. *The Entrepreneurial Executive, 15*, 73–85.

Glaser, B. & Strauss, A. (1967). *The Discovery of Grounded Theory: Strategies for Qualitative Research.* Chicago: Aldine Publishing.

Goffman, E. (1959). *The Presentation of Self in Everyday Life.* New York: Anchor.

Gow, G. (April 24, 2013). Why CEOs should NOT be involved in social media. *Crimson Marketing Blog: Corporate Marketing.* Retrieved from: http://crimson marketing.com/why-ceos-should-not-be-involved-in-social-media/.

Güney, S., & Cresswell, A. (2012). Technology-as-text in the communicative constitution of organization. *Information and Organization, 22* (2), 154–167.

Hagey, P. (November 27, 2012). Zillow's "Social CEO" sounds off on Twitter, company's future. *Key Realty Inc.* Retrieved from: http://www.keyrealty.us/2012/11/27/zillows-social-ceo-sounds-off-on-twitter-companys-future/.

Hambrick, M., Simmons, J., Greenhalgh, G., & Greenwell, T. (2010). Understanding professional athletes' use of Twitter: A content analysis of athlete Tweets. *International Journal of Sport Communication, 3*, 454–471.

Hogan, B. (2010). The presentation of self in the age of social media: Distinguishing performances and exhibitions online. *Bulletin of Science Technology & Society, 30* (6), 377–386.

Ingram, M. (September 28, 2012). Interview with Dick Costollo. *Bloomberg Businessweek Technology.* Retrieved from: http://www.businessweek.com/articles/2012-11-28/dick-costolo-twitter-is-a-reinvention-of-the-town-square-but-with-tv#p1.

Jacobs, G. (2008). Saying something or having something to say: Attention seeking, the breakdown of privacy, and the promise of discourse in the blogosphere. *Fast Capitalism, 4* (1). Retrieved from: http://www.uta.edu/huma/agger/fastcapitalism/4_1/jacobs.html.

Krippendorff, K. (2013). *Content Analysis: An Introduction to Its Methodology* (3rd edition). Thousand Oaks, California: Sage.

Latour, B. (1992) Where Are the Missing Masses? The Sociology of a Few Mundane Artifacts. In W. E. Bijker & J. Law (Eds), *Shaping Technology/Building Society: Studies in Sociotechnical Change* (pp. 225–258). Cambridge, Mass: MIT Press.

Love, D. (May 16, 2011). 13 people who got fired for Tweeting. *Business Insider Blog: Strategy.* Retrieved from: http://www.businessinsider.com/twitter-fired-2011-5?op=1.

Marwick, A., & boyd, d. (2010). I Tweet honestly, I Tweet passionately: Twitter users, context collapse, and the imagined audience. *New Media and Society, 13* (1), 114–133.

Marwick, A., & boyd, d. (2011). To see and be seen: Celebrity practice on Twitter. *Convergence: The International Journal of Research into New Media Technologies, 17* (2), 139–158.

McPhee, R., & Zaug, P. (2000). The communicative constitution of organizations: A framework for explanation. Paper presented to the annual conference of the Western States Communication Association, Sacramento, CA.

McPhee, R., & Zaug, P. (2009). The communicative constitution of organizations: A framework for explanation. In L. Putnam & A. Nicotera (Eds), *Building Theories of Organization: The Constitutive Role of Communication* (pp. 21–48). New York: Routledge.

Melewar, T. (2003). Determinants of the corporate identity construct. *Journal of Marketing Communications, 9* (4), 195–220.

Norris, S., & Porter, T. (2011). The changing face of leadership: Making an impression in the technically mediated landscape. *Journal of Leadership Studies, 4* (4), 69–73.

Nyström, S. (2009). The dynamics of professional identity formation: Graduates' transitions from higher education to working life. *Vocations and Learning, 2* (1), 1–18.

Papacharissi, Z. (2012). Without you, I'm nothing: Performances of the self on Twitter. *International Journal of Communication, 6,* 1989–2006.

Rafaeli, A. (1996). What is an organization.? Who are its members? In. C. Cooper & S. Jackson (Eds), *Creating Tomorrow's Organizations: A Handbook for Future Research in Organizational Behaviour* (pp. 121–139). Chichester: John Wiley & Sons.

Schick, J. (March 20, 2013). Mastering the age of social business. Innovation insights blog. *Wired Magazine Online.* Retrieved from: http://www.wired.com/insights/2013/03/mastering-the-age-of-social-business/.

Shaywitz, D. (September 28, 2012). No, most CEOs shouldn't be on Twitter. *Forbes Magazine Online.* Retrieved from: http://www.forbes.com/sites/davidshaywitz/2012/09/28/no-most-ceos-shouldnt-be-on-twitter/.

Taylor, J., & Van Every, E. (2000). *The Emergent Organization: Communication as its Site and Surface.* Mahwah, NJ: LEA.

Twitter (2015). *About* (Web log). Retrieved from: https://twitter.com/about.

Weick, K. (1969). *The Social Psychology of Organizing.* Reading, MA: Addison-Wesley.

Weick, K. (1979). *The Social Psychology of Organizing* (2nd Ed.). Reading, MA: Addison-Wesley.

Wenger, E. (1998). *Communities of Practice: Learning, Meaning, and Identity.* Cambridge: Cambridge University Press.

3
Utterance Chunking in Instant Messaging: A Resource for Interaction Management

Kris M. Markman

Modern organizations have an array of communication tools available for interacting with both internal and external audiences. While email continues to dominate much workplace interaction, the use of instant messaging (IM) continues to grow (Garrett & Danziger, 2007), prompting scholars to look at how it is used in a variety of organizational contexts. In this chapter, I first give a background on the research into IM use in organizations. I will then look at IM as a form of conversation, and discuss why adopting a language-based approach to the study of IM is useful for communication professionals. I illustrate this discussion with an examination of one particular phenomenon, utterance chunking, in task-based IM interactions. Finally, I will conclude by discussing the implications of this research for business discourse and make some suggestions for future research in this area.

Instant messaging in organizations

While email remains the dominant computer-mediated communication (CMC) tool in most organizations (D'Urso & Pierce, 2009; Skovholt & Svennevig, 2013), IM is becoming more important in a number of business settings, particularly in multinational organizations (Hunt, 2009; Yuan et al., 2013). One survey of MBA students in the United States found that 53% worked in organizations that supported IM use (Glass & Li, 2010), while an industry survey found that 84% of responding organizations used corporate-sanctioned, or enterprise, IM (EIM) (Radicati & Hoang, 2011). A case study of one high-tech organization found both email and IM to be the dominant communication media, over both the phone and face-to-face (Turner et al., 2006). The differences in rates of IM usage noted across these studies can be explained, in part, by the different organizational contexts. In particular, having a critical mass of IM users in a workplace is one of the most important factors that influences people's decision to adopt the technology (Cameron & Webster, 2005). In other words, people will be more likely to use IM when they perceive that enough of their colleagues are using the technology. In cases where a critical mass of IM usage has not been achieved, however, other factors can influence IM adoption, such as the influence of peers (To et al., 2008). Similarly, organizational support was found to be a significant influence on Chinese professionals' use of IM at work (Ou & Davison, 2011).

Culture may also have an influence on what factors affect employees' decisions to use IM at work. For example, To et al. (2008) found that the perceived usefulness of IM was not an influence on IM adoption among the Taiwanese professionals they surveyed, whereas Luo et al. (2010) found perceived usefulness to be positively related to the use of IM in a U.S.-based survey.

Affordances and constraints of workplace IM

IM has a number of advantages as a workplace communication tool. In particular, it allows for near synchronous interaction, when all parties are logged in at the same time, but can also serve as an asynchronous medium (see Darics, 2014). Used synchronously, IM allows for easy coordination and collaboration, and the presence awareness systems built into most IM platforms make it easy to tell when others are available and afford quick responses (Pazos et al., 2013; Quan-Haase et al., 2005; Shaw et al., 2007; Stephens, 2008). In addition to coordination, IM is frequently used for asking and answering questions, information exchange, and other types of task discussion (Hung et al., 2008; Luor et al., 2010; Pazos et al., 2013; Quan-Haase et al., 2005). Thomas and Akdere (2013) also argue that IM can be a beneficial tool for learning and training in organizations. However, IM, despite its highly synchronous nature, may not be perceived as being as effective for more ambiguous conversations, such as reaching understanding (Hung et al., 2008). IM may also be perceived as affording more privacy when compared with the phone, since IM conversations cannot be overheard (Cameron & Webster, 2005).

Several studies have examined the use of IM as a multitasking tool, and in particular, how IM might serve as a source of interruptions in workflow or productivity. In their interviews with members of four different organizations, Cameron and Webster (2005) found that IM was used for multitasking conversations, either by allowing a second channel of communication with an existing conversational partner, or by allowing workers to carry on conversations with multiple partners. IM was also used to "queue jump" to get the attention of a colleague who was engaged in a conversation with a third party. Cameron and Webster's interviewees had mixed opinions on the interruptive nature of IM, with some respondents indicating that it could cause a break in task focus, while others felt IM was less interruptive than other technologies, such as the telephone. Interestingly, survey research from the United States has found that workplace IM users reported being interrupted less frequently than non-users, and that IM did not contribute to an increase in overall levels of work communication (Garrett & Danziger, 2007). Garrett and Danziger argued that IM can be used as an interaction management tool, "allowing users to create communication practices that minimize some types of interruption and negotiate the timing of others" (p. 36). Licoppe's (2010) qualitative analysis of IM use at work illustrated some of these interaction management strategies, and showed how they "constituted a situated, artful accomplishment" (p. 300). Ou and Davison (2011) found that IM use contributed to work interruptions, but it was not the only, nor the major, source of work interruptions for the Chinese professionals they surveyed. In addition, Ou and Davison found that IM use contributed to a perception of improved communication quality, and interactivity, and led to an increase in perceptions of mutual trust. IM interruptions do not necessarily lead to a reduction in work quality, either. In a case study of administrative workers at a technical college in the U.S., Mansi and Levy (2013) found that accuracy on both simple and complex tasks was not affected by IM interruptions. However, complex spatial tasks took longer to complete due to interruptions, while symbolic tasks were not affected.

In addition to being used by individuals working alone, IM is also a tool that allows for multitasking during group events, such as meetings, particularly when the norms of the organization support the use of IM and other tools for extra-meeting communication (Dennis et al., 2010; Stephens & Davis, 2009; Yuan et al., 2013). Observations by Dennis et al. of two U.S.-based companies found that many IMs sent and received during meetings were not related to the meeting at hand. Those that were, however, could have several functions, including allowing interaction by others not present at the meeting, aiding in directing the meeting, and serving as a clarification tool. In addition, Dennis et al. found that these IMs, which they termed "invisible whispers," could serve social support needs as well as task support needs. However, using IM to multitask during meetings can lead to information overload (Dennis et al., 2010).

Finally, researchers have also identified several personal benefits and drawbacks to workplace IM use. Members of a global virtual team frequently chose IM over richer media such as videoconferencing, as a way of maintaining work–life balance (Ruppel et al., 2013). The use of IM has been found to improve perceptions of working relationships both within and between departments (Cho et al., 2005). Quan-Haase et al. (2005) found that IM was sometimes used to communicate with superiors about sensitive topics, such as disagreements or difficult decisions. They argued that in the use of IM for these conversations increases the social distance, making it easier for employees to communicate with their supervisors. However, culture also plays a role in the relational benefits of IM, as Cho et al. found the opposite in their study of IM use in a Korean company. The presence awareness feature of IM, often seen as a benefit, can also cause strain in the workplace when people feel pressured to be available (Turner et al., 2006) even to the point of working while on vacation (Gibbs et al., 2013).

Instant messaging as conversation

Research on computer-mediated conversation has documented how the structure of these interactions varies from that of spoken conversation, due to the constraints and affordances of the medium (e.g., Baron, 2010, 2013; Beisswenger, 2008; Darics, 2014; Jacobs & Garcia, 2013; Lee, 2007; Markman, 2009, 2013; Ong, 2011; Panyametheekul & Herring, 2003; Schonfeldt & Golato, 2003). In particular, several researchers have noted that group chat conversations can have problems with coherence, in part due to the inability to precisely time when messages arrive in the chat room (Herring, 1999; Markman, 2013; Stromer-Galley & Martinson, 2009). Berglund (2009) argued that many of the coherence issues associated with multi-party chat may be mitigated in IM by the reduced number of participants, and thus this medium is worthy of additional study. But despite a growing body of research on the impact of IM in the workplace, very few studies examine discourse or linguistic elements in workplace IM conversations. A language-based approach to the study of IM can help shed light on findings from previous workplace research. For example, several studies have noted that IM is generally perceived to be an informal communication channel (Cho et al., 2005; Luo et al., 2010; Quan-Haase et al., 2005; Stephens, 2008; Yuan et al., 2013). Darics' (2010) study of IM use among virtual team members illustrates how that sense of informality can be achieved. Darics found that several orthographic strategies, such as repeated letters, emoticons, and the use of all-capitals, along with various politeness strategies adapted from spoken conversation fostered a sense of an informal workplace and enhanced cooperation. Her study shows that by developing an understanding of how specific linguistic strategies contribute to a sense of informality in IM, practitioners can begin to cultivate a more mindful awareness of their own workplace IM use.

Cooper and Johnson (2014) compared the use of IM to audio for price negotiation discussions. Although their research was conducted in a laboratory setting, the conditions were designed to mimic the negotiations typically found on e-commerce sites. Overall they discovered that critical comments had more impact in IM, making it less likely that the participants would reach an agreement. Similarly, comments that threatened self-esteem increased the likelihood that participants would fail to reach an agreement in their negotiations. Other discourse-based research on workplace IM has examined how virtual team members use IM for both synchronous and asynchronous interactions (Darics, 2014), and how professionals in highly connected organizations use "quick questions" in IM conversations as a resource for collaborating on knowledge-intensive tasks (Licoppe et al., 2014).

In the next section, I discuss a specific linguistic strategy frequently found in IM conversations – utterance chunking – and provide an analysis of how this phenomenon is deployed in persuasive, task-based IM conversations. Although the data examined here are not drawn from a workplace context, research has shown that IM is sometimes used in organizations for solving conflict, such as resolving a disagreement (Pazos et al., 2013). In addition, IM may be used for persuasive interactions during e-commerce negotiations (Cooper & Johnson, 2014). Thus, we can draw conclusions from the study of experimentally generated IM conversations that are analogous to situations that might occur in workplace IM use.

Case study: utterance chunking in task-based IM conversations

What is utterance chunking? One linguistic feature of IM conversations that has been found to be common in social IM is utterance chunking (Baron, 2010). Utterance chunking is defined as the breaking down of "single utterances into several components, which are then transmitted seriatim, rather than typing out the entire utterance and then transmitting it all of a piece" (Baron, online). Utterance chunking has also been identified in business IM conversations (Mackiewicz & Lam, 2009). Mackiewicz and Lam (2009) used a discourse analytic approach to examine coherence in IM interaction between a director and her employee. They found that by breaking up longer turns into shorter, rapidly sent transmissions, utterance chunking served as a resource for providing coherence in workplace IM conversations.

The data examined below are drawn from two laboratory studies. The first examined IM conversations between pairs that had no prior history (Strangers), while the second involved pairs that had a prior relationship (Prior History). In the Strangers study, participants were asked to persuade a research assistant to either adopt or reject a particular health-related policy. In the Prior History study, participants were assigned to opposing sides of a printer use policy and asked to persuade their partner of their side. In both studies, the persuasive tasks were similar to types of conversations that might occur in a sales or negotiation setting in the workplace. The IM transcripts were saved from all conversations and each participant's computer screen was video recorded, allowing the analysis of both the final record of each conversation along with a moment-by-moment recording of how participants composed their IM transmissions.

In most commercially available IM systems, participants type their messages into a composition box at the bottom of the IM window. Once the participant hits enter or clicks send, the message is displayed in the main IM window. Unlike some very early dyadic CMC systems (Anderson et al., 2010), in IM the text typed into the composition box is typically sent as a complete unit, rather than being displayed as it is being typed. Following Baron (2010), I refer to this chunk of text as a transmission unit (TU). Utterance chunking occurs when a complete grammatical unit, such as a sentence, is spread out over multiple TUs. Examples 1–4 illustrate common forms of utterance chunking.

Example 1: Prior History – Pair 11

```
    [15:56:29] <F11A>Well stop the unnecessary printing
    jobs in the computer labs
➔   [15:56:36] <F11A> you are saving paper
➔   [15:57:07] <F11A> and you learn to use alternatives
    to paper printing!
    [15:57:21] <F11A> other alternatives*
```

Example 2: Strangers 19

> (1:49:37 PM) C: so what do you think about gardasil?
➜ (1:50:07 PM) P19: I believe gardasil is a very useful vaccine
➜ (1:50:25 PM) P19: and that every girl should be vaccainated
> (1:51:02 PM) C: i think it's a good thing for the most part

Example 3: Strangers 11

> (2:54:43 PM) P11: its may seem crazy but even the children who are n the sixth grade needs it
➜ (2:55:12 PM) C: yea i know its sad how young kids are starting these days
➜ (2:55:42 PM) C: but i also feel like it would be a little scary for those young girls who arent sexually active
> (2:56:03 PM) C: and what if boys in they're grade teased them for it or something?

Example 4: Prior History – Pair 51

➜ [12:07:17] <M51A> ya, but part of people's complaints on campus have to do with finances
➜ [12:07:30] <M51A> because college students are poor
> [12:07:45] <M51B> see! that's exactly WHY they shouldn't be doing this

The marked TUs in Examples 1–3 illustrate how coordinating conjunctions can be used to link multiple TUs into a single utterance. In Examples 1 and 2, "and" is used to link the second TU grammatically to the preceding TU, whereas in Example 3 "but" is the cue that links the two TUs. It is also important to note that the presence of coordinating conjunctions does not de facto indicate utterance chunking, as can be seen in the last line in Example 3. Although here the confederate starts her TU with "and," it is clear that here it indicates an additional thought in her ongoing argument, rather than a grammatical connection to the preceding TUs, particularly given that the last TU is phrased as a question, where as the preceding TUs were part of a statement of opinion. In Example 4 the subordinating conjunction "because" acts similarly to the previous examples by grammatically linking the two TUs.

Example 5: Strangers 6

> (12:01:19 PM) P6: i think the state shoulndt be getting too far into forcing vaccines
> → (12:01:53 PM) P6: nobody should be forced to have medical procedures
> → (12:02:05 PM) P6: or treatments really
> → (12:02:17 PM) P6: if they dont want to
> (12:02:59 PM) P6: what about you?

Example 5 shows a slightly more complex use of conjunctions to mark utterance chunking. While all of the TUs in this extract are from the same person, Participant six, only the three marked TUs are linked as a single utterance. The first of the three marked TUs is plausibly complete, but the use of "or" in the second TU and "if" in the third grammatically link all three TUs into the same sentence.

Example 6: Prior History – Pair 38

> [13:50:06] <M38A> You don't know that. And it could be they use all 500 because they paid for all 500 up front
> → [13:50:20] <M38A> if they were charge on a per page basis
> → [13:50:26] <M38A> it would be a different story

Finally, Example 6 illustrates another way that utterances can be broken in separate TUs. In this extract, the TU at 13:50:20 is incomplete, as the "if" clause needs a "then" clause to finish the sentence. Although the "then" is only implied in the next TU, the clause provides grammatical closure to the sentence and links the two TUs into a single utterance.

The previous examples have shown that one simple way to chunk an utterance over multiple TUs is to end them at natural break points, such as conjunctions. This is seems to be the most common way that utterance chunking is manifested in IM, in both these data and in previous studies (Baron, 2010). Baron found that, after conjunctions, the next most common way to chunk an utterance into multiple TUs was to start the second TU with an independent clause. Less frequently found were breaks at adverbs and adverbial phrases, adjectives and adjectival phrases, noun phrases, and verb phrases. Examples 7 and 8 show some of these additional ways of chunking utterances.

Example 7: Strangers 31

> (12:20:22 PM) P31: well, being that HPV is spread through sexual contact even if you have no symptoms you can have the virus.

→ (12:20:34 PM) P31: and HPV can cause cervical cancer
→ (12:20:48 PM) P31: for women, and other types of cancer
   for men
→ (12:20:54 PM) P31: so it's not just the women at risk.
   (12:21:27 PM) P31: There are so many different types
   of genital HPV, some can even cause genital warts
   _____
→ (12:24:53 PM) P31: Another thing,
→ (12:25:15 PM) P31: Gardasil is still pretty new, so they
   don't know the long tem effects that the vaccine may have
→ (12:25:37 PM) P31: and it doesn't protect girls against all
   strains of HPV
   (12:26:20 PM) C: yea i know the vaccines new so that
   whole long term side effect thing is a big question
   mark, but i have to wonder if any "side effects" would
   be nearly as severe as cancer and/or genital warts?

Example 7 contains two instances of utterance chunking from different times in the same conversation. The first sequence, from 12:20:34 to 12:20:54 consists of three TUs that form a single utterance. Although the first TU in this sequence starts with "and," the period at the end of the prior TU marks it as complete, and therefore the TU at 12:20:34 is the start of a new thought, as in Example 3 above. However, rather than break at the conjunction, this participant instead breaks the TU at the prepositional phrase ("for women"), and then breaks at the conjunction "so" for the third TU. In the second sequence, from 12:24:53 to 12:25:37, the first TU is an adjectival phrase that, along with the comma, forecasts the continuation of this utterance, which is then broken down into two subsequent TUs, broken at the more common point of the conjunction.

Example 8: Strangers 15

   (2:21:01 PM) C: true- so then those girls that are sexually
   active can go get the shot and the girls who aren't can have
   the option to not get it until a little later when they feel
   like they're ready
→ (2:21:12 PM) C: i'm not saying i don
→ (2:21:15 PM) C: t
→ (2:21:20 PM) C: think the shots a good thing
→ (2:21:32 PM) C: im just saying 6th grade might be too early

➡   (2:21:44 PM) C: and that maybe people should be able
to decide for themselves
(2:24:03 PM) P15: well with some girls yes its to early but
if they are sexually active then they should otherwwise
it shold be vountary. yes they should have the decision to
deside for themselves but its to help the community. And
the people around them.

Example 8 contains a combination of techniques, including a more idio-
syncratic formulation of utterance chunking. Based on the analysis of the
screen recordings, the isolated "t" at 2:21:15 appears to be an error. While
composing the TU that is posted at 2:21:12, the confederate types "I'm
not saying I don;t t" and then backspaces to correct the typo. However,
it appears that she hit enter rather than the apostrophe (located next to
each other on the keyboard) and typed the t before noticing her mistake.
She pauses briefly, deletes and retypes the "t" and hits enter, and then
proceeds to type the TU that posts at 2:21:20. Thus it seems plausible
that her original intention was to break the utterance into three TUs (two
independent clauses and a dependent clause with coordinating conjunction), but having made a typing error instead breaks the first TU in the
middle of the verb phrase, a less natural place for a break to occur.

Thus far I have shown how utterance chunking in task-based conversations is typically accomplished through breaking up utterances
into multiple TUs that are linked grammatically. These findings are
consistent with the social IM conversations analyzed by Baron (2010).
Baron argues that utterance chunking in IM is a feature that makes it
more similar to speech versus formal writing. Indeed, Mackiewicz and
Lam (2009) found that utterance chunking can be used deliberately in
workplace IM in order to cultivate a more speech-like, conversational
style. For practitioners, then, an understanding of utterance chunking
in IM offers an additional perspective on why IM is often perceived as
an informal communication channel, and can also contribute to the
development of a mindful awareness of IM style.

Utterance chunking as strategy: Holding the floor. It's important to
note that while utterance chunking may often be a naturally occurring
feature of IM conversation, it can also be used purposefully. Mackiewicz
and Lam (2009) found that utterance chunking was frequently used
strategically in the IM conversations they studied. In particular, they
found that the director acknowledged that she often chunked her utterances as an attempt to hold the conversational floor. In CMC, a conversational floor is more than just who is taking a turn at talk, in part

because IM systems allow participants to type and send whenever they want. Instead, the floor is the sense of what the conversation is about, including the topic and the overall speech activity (such as explaining, chatting, arguing, etc.) (Simpson, 2005, 2013). Simpson noted that participants work together to produce the conversational floor in CMC, and that floors can be monologic, where one participant dominates (called the speaker-and-supporter floor), or collaborative. However, in persuasive or negotiation-type situations, such as the ones being examined here, participants may be particularly motivated to gain and hold the floor in order to garner support for their ideas. Examples 9–12 illustrate different ways that utterance chunking can be used towards this end.

Example 9: Prior History – Pair 38

> [13:49:14] <M38A> We as students, in order to save money,
> would resort to alternatives to paper printing
→ [13:49:22] <M38A> Don
→ [13:49:24] <M38A> t
→ [13:49:26] <M38A> ya
→ [13:49:28] <M38A> think?
> [13:49:32] <M38B> i agree.. but it seems most students
> use that many sheets of paper espiesally for the
> commuters.

In Example 9 the first two marked TUs appear to be a typo, similar to Example 8 above. The screen recordings reveal that this participant first types "Dont" then backspaces to delete the "t," but again hits enter instead of the apostrophe. However, the pacing of his typing in this excerpt suggests that the rest of this utterance was deliberately spread over the next two TUs. By making each TU a single word, he is adding visual force to his argument, by occupying more vertical space in the IM window. In addition, most modern IM systems have some type of conversational monitoring element built in to them, which alerts one partner when the other is composing a transmission. By sending shorter TUs in rapid succession, IM participants are potentially able to exploit this technical feature by announcing their intention to continue, thereby adding to the visual dimension and increasing their chances of holding the floor. In fact, it is possible that typing longer utterances in lieu of chunking them into shorter TUs may work against floor holding, despite the conversational monitoring features, as is illustrated in Example 10.

Example 10: Prior History – Pair 4

> [11:09:30] <M4> its still cumbersome...you have to put
> in all types of credit card information and stuff...
➜ [11:09:54] <F4> ... AND ?
➜ [11:09:56] <F4> POINT?
> [11:10:03] <M4> and how can it teach them to be more
> environmental if they can just go and print somewhere
> else such as thier home
> [11:10:08] <F4> when you order clothes offline ...
> you have to do that too

Analysis of the screen recordings reveals that immediately after M4's TU posts at 11:09:30, the conversational monitor (in this system located at the top of the IM window next to the IM partner's screen name) indicates that he is continuing to type. After waiting for 19 seconds, F4 begins typing in her composition box, even though the IM window indicates that her partner is still composing a message. Her two TUs at 11:09:54 and 11:09:56 are plausibly interpretable as a single utterance, broken up (and with the addition of all capital letters) as a way of getting the attention of her partner. In fact, she starts typing the post at 11:10:08, just four seconds after sending her previous TU, even though her partner is still typing. It is of course impossible to know if the outcome would have been different had M4 chunked his utterance into multiple TUs, but this example does show that typing longer TUs may be dis-preferred by some IM partners, and therefore it may be advantageous to be more deliberate about the use of utterance chunking.

The last two examples show how utterance chunking can add rhetorical force to the visual force achieved by sending multiple, short TUs in rapid succession.

Example 11: Prior History – Pair 13

> [12:12:27] <F13B> i dont use the printers here
➜ [12:12:40] <F13A> well i do
➜ [12:12:43] <F13A> a lot
➜ [12:12:45] <F13A> all day
➜ [12:12:47] <F13A> every day
> [12:13:03] <F13B>1. it will reduce the amount of
> printing on campus... becuase students will only print
> what they are willing to pay for.

Example 12: Prior History – Pair 3

```
[14:42:56] <F3A> so paper will be saved cuz they're
using alternatives, like email
[14:43:10] <F3B> students arent gonna wanna waste their
money
[14:43:13] <F3A> the printers wont be as jammed wiht print
jobs anymore
```
→ `[14:43:18] <F3B> and sometimes you have to print`
→ `[14:43:22] <F3B> like homework`
→ `[14:43:25] <F3B> readings`
→ `[14:43:31] <F3B> something to have in class`
```
[14:43:31] <F3A> not necessarily
[14:43:36] <F3B> it wont be saving money
```

In Example 11, F13A's first TU is a direct response to the prior turn by her partner. She then continues to type a series of modifying phrases that function to upgrade each prior TU with a stronger statement. In doing so, she not only gains the visual force of multiple TUs, but she adds rhetorical power to her argument by adding emphasis in each successive chunk. The screen recordings indicate that participant F13B started typing her next message before her partner's TU posted at 12:12:40, but that she pauses for several seconds after the TUs at 12:12:45 and 12:12:47 post, which may indicate that this use of utterance chunking was successful at least momentarily garnering attention.

In Example 12, participant F3B accomplishes something similar through the use of additional examples to extend her utterance. Based on an analysis of the screen recordings, the utterance chunked across TUs 14:43:18 to 14:43:31 was most likely a response to her partner's TU at 14:42:56, rather than to the immediately preceding TU. Participant F3B has already started typing her TU at 14:43:10 when the previous message posts. After she finishes typing, she pauses for seven seconds before hitting enter, and then immediately starts typing the TU that gets posted at 14:43:18. This suggests that she was reading the post that "interrupted" hers, and that her next TU is a rebuttal to her partner's argument. She is able to rhetorically extend her argument and hold the floor by quickly composing a series of short TUs to provide additional examples. Once again, the screen recordings show that she may have been at least partially successful, in that her partner did not start typing again until after the TU at 14:43:25 had posted (although the conversation monitor indicated that F3B was still composing).

Discussion: utterance chunking and interaction management in workplace IM

The growing body of research on workplace IM demonstrates the importance of this medium to 21st-century businesses. The numerous surveys of IM usage have helped to clarify how widespread IM usage is, the factors that influence IM adoption, and the various tasks that are accomplished through communication in this medium. In addition, research on IM interruptions has generally shown the medium to be a help, rather than a hindrance, to productivity. What is missing from this literature, however, is a critical mass of studies that examine in-depth the discursive features and functions of workplace IM conversations. The analysis presented in this chapter has been one attempt to fill that gap, but is limited in scope by being drawn from lab-based task discussions, rather than bona-fide workplace interactions. However, other research on IM shows that the particular linguistic phenomenon discussed here, utterance chunking, does occur in business settings (Mackiewicz & Lam, 2009). In addition, the persuasive nature of the conversations presented here are analogous to some types of workplace IM discourse (Cooper & Johnson, 2014; Pazos et al., 2013). It is therefore useful to discuss how insights from this analysis can be applied to business communication settings.

By using a qualitative, micro-analytic perspective, I have illustrated both how utterance chunking is typically formulated in IM conversations, and also how it might serve as a means of managing interaction. In particular, utterance chunking can be used strategically in business settings to cultivate a more informal style, which could be useful in a variety of settings. For example, researchers and industry watchers have noted a rise in the use of chat for providing online customer support ("Can I help the next customer ... online?," 2006; Klie, 2012; Sarrel, 2007). Communication professionals could incorporate a discussion of utterance chunking into training materials for online customer support staff. By understanding how to make their IM conversations seem more natural and friendly, online customer service workers could help increase customer trust. In organizations that value friendliness and informality as part of the culture, understanding utterance chunking could help employees make their IM conversations conform to that norm (see also Darics, 2010). In addition, utterance chunking can be used in IM conversations between coworkers as a way of lowering the social distance between interlocutors in order to broach disagreements or conflicts. However, in cultural contexts where maintaining formality is important, developing a more mindful awareness of IM construction, and particularly an awareness of utterance chunking, may help participants avoid the practice when informality is not desired. Utterance chunking may also increase the perception of interactivity in IM conversations, which can in turn lead to an increase in mutual trust in the workplace (Ou & Davison, 2011). Professionals who are multitasking and maintaining multiple simultaneous conversations may also want to strategically avoid utterance chunking, because it could cause miscommunications if people are not paying close attention to the IM conversation.

In this chapter I have also shown that utterance chunking serves as a way for IM participants to try to hold the floor, and potentially make their contributions to the conversation more noticeable. Floor-holding can be a way of signaling power or status in other types of CMC (Herring, 2010; Simpson, 2005), and one study of workplace IM use has demonstrated that supervisors may use utterance chunking strategically to hold the floor in conversations with their employees (Mackiewicz & Lam, 2009). However, supervisors who are trying to build more collaborative relationships with their employees may want to consider avoiding utterance chunking in IM conversations when it might be perceived as dominating the conversation.

Finally, while this research focused on persuasive task conversations, utterance chunking may also be useful in other types of task conversations that IM is typically used for in organizations. Using utterance chunking to break down complex information into bite-sized pieces, for example, may help make IM a more suitable medium for explaining processes, giving directions, or other ambiguous tasks. Overall, by being mindful of how IM conversations are constructed, practitioners can help employees maximize the usefulness of this important workplace communication technology.

Conclusion

In this chapter I have shown that IM continues to be an important communication tool in 21st-century organizations. However, despite the overall increase in research on workplace IM, relatively few of those studies take a discourse-based approach. I have shown that, through a close analysis of the discursive features of IM, scholars can contribute to both the literature and to the needs of practitioners by helping professionals become more mindful about the way they manage their IM interactions. Scholars of business discourse should look to the research on email discourse in the workplace (e.g., Hössjer, 2013; Skovholt & Svennevig,

2006, 2013; Turnage, 2013; Waldvogel, 2007) as a jumping-off point for future studies of IM. Such research would also allow a comparison to the research on social IM (e.g., Baron, 2010; Berglund, 2009; Ling & Baron, 2007; Tagliamonte & Denis, 2008), in order to further our understanding of which aspects of IM discourse may be more universal, and which are context-dependent.

References

Anderson, F. J., Beard, K. F., & Walther, B. J. (2010). Turn-taking and the local management of conversation in a highly simultaneous computer-mediated communication system. *Language@Internet, 7* (7). Retrieved from: http://www.languageatinternet.org/articles/2010/2804.

Baron, N. S. (2010). Discourse structures in instant messaging: The case of utterance breaks. *Language@Internet, 7* (2). Retrieved from: http://www.languageatinternet.de/articles/2010/2651/index_html/.

Baron, N. S. (2013). Instant messaging. In S. C. Herring, D. Stein, & T. Virtanen (Eds), *Pragmatics of Computer-Mediated Communication* (pp. 135–161). Berlin: De Gruyter Mouton.

Beisswenger, M. (2008). Situated chat analysis as a window to the user's perspective: Aspects of temporal and sequential organization. *Language@Internet, 5* (6). Retrieved from: http://www.languageatinternet.de/articles/2008/1532/index_html/.

Berglund, T. Ö. (2009). Disrupted turn adjacency and coherence maintenance in instant messaging conversations. *Language@Internet, 6* (2). Retrieved from: http://www.languageatinternet.de/articles/2009/2106.

Cameron, A. F., & Webster, J. (2005). Unintended consequences of emerging communication technologies: Instant Messaging in the workplace. *Computers in Human Behavior, 21* (1), 85–103. doi: 10.1016/j.chb.2003.12.001.

Can I help the next customer ... online? (June 2006). *CRM Magazine, 10,* 11.

Cho, H.-K., Trier, M., & Kim, E. (2005). The use of instant messaging in working relationship development: A case study. *Journal of Computer-Mediated Communication, 10* (4). doi: 10.1111/j.1083-6101.2005.tb00280.x.

Cooper, R. B., & Johnson, N. A. (2014). So close yet no agreement: The effects of threats to self-esteem when using instant messaging and audio during seller–buyer negotiations. *Decision Support Systems, 57,* 115–126. doi: 10.1016/j.dss.2013.08.005.

Darics, E. (2010). Politeness in computer-mediated discourse of a virtual team. *Journal of Politeness Research, 6,* 129–150. doi: 10.1515/JPLR.2010.007.

Darics, E. (2014). The blurring boundaries between synchronicity and asynchronicity: New communicative situations in work-related instant messaging. *International Journal of Business Communication.* doi: 10.1177/2329488414525440.

Dennis, A. R., Rennecker, J. A., & Hansen, S. (2010). Invisible whispering: Restructuring collaborative decision making with instant messaging. *Decision Sciences, 41* (4), 845–886. doi: 10.1111/j.1540-5915.2010.00290.x.

D'Urso, S. C., & Pierce, K. M. (2009). Connected to the organization: A survey of communication technologies in the modern organizational landscape. *Communication Research Reports, 26,* 75–81.

Garrett, R. K., & Danziger, J. N. (2007). IM = Interruption management? Instant messaging and disruption in the workplace. *Journal of Computer-Mediated Communication, 13* (1), 23–42. doi: 10.1111/j.1083-6101.2007.00384.x.

Gibbs, J. L., Rozaidi, N. A., & Eisenberg, J. (2013). Overcoming the "ideology of openness": Probing the affordances of social media for organizational knowledge sharing. *Journal of Computer-Mediated Communication, 19* (1), 102–120. doi: 10.1111/jcc4.12034.

Glass, R., & Li, S. (2010). Social influence and instant messaging adoption. *Journal of Computer Information Systems, 51* (2), 24–30.

Herring, S. C. (1999). Interactional coherence in CMC. *Journal of Computer-Mediated Communication, 4* (4). Retrieved from: http://www.ascusc.org/jcmc/vol4/issue4/herring.html.

Herring, S. C. (2010). Who's got the floor in computer-mediated conversation? Edelsky's gender patterns revisited. *Language@Internet, 7*. Retrieved from: http://www.languageatinternet.org/articles/2010/2857.

Hössjer, A. (2013). Small talk, politeness, and email communication in the workplace. In S. C. Herring, D. Stein, & T. Virtanen (Eds), *Pragmatics of Computer-Mediated Communication* (pp. 613–638). Berlin: De Gruyter Mouton.

Hung, Y. T. C., Duyen, N. T. T., Kong, W.-C., & Chua, A.-L. (2008). Reexamining media capacity theories using workplace instant messaging. *IEEE Transactions on Professional Communication, 51* (4), 352–368. doi: 10.1109/TPC.2008.2007861.

Hunt, S. (2009). Instant Messenger communication in a multinational corporation. *Academy of Information & Management Sciences Journal, 12* (1/2), 65–70.

Jacobs, J. B., & Garcia, A. C. (2013). Repair in chat room interaction. In S. C. Herring, D. Stein, & T. Virtanen (Eds), *Pragmatics of Computer-Mediated Communication* (pp. 565–587). Berlin: De Gruyter Mouton.

Klie, L. (June 2012). Web chat and speech analytics are set to surge. *CRM Magazine, 16*, 17.

Lee, C. K.-M. (2007). Affordances and text-making practices in online instant messaging. *Written Communication, 24* (3), 223–249. doi: 10.1177/0741088307303215.

Licoppe, C. (2010). The "crisis of the summons": A transformation in the pragmatics of "notifications," from phone rings to instant messaging. *Information Society, 26* (4), 288–302. doi: 10.1080/01972243.2010.489859.

Licoppe, C., Cudicio, R., & Proulx, S. (2014). Instant messaging requests in connected organizations: "Quick questions" and the moral economy of contribution. *Discourse Studies, 16* (4), 488–513. doi: 10.1177/1461445613519021.

Ling, R., & Baron, N. S. (2007). Text messaging and IM: Linguistic comparison of American college data. *Journal of Language and Social Psychology, 26*, 291–298.

Luo, X., Gurung, A., & Shim, J. P. (2010). Understanding the determinants of user acceptance of enterprise instant messaging: An empirical study. *Journal of Organizational Computing & Electronic Commerce, 20* (2), 155–181. doi: 10.1080/10919391003709179.

Luor, T., Wu, L.-L., Lu, H.-P., & Tao, Y.-H. (2010). The effect of emoticons in simplex and complex task-oriented communication: An empirical study of instant messaging. *Computers in Human Behavior, 26* (5), 889–895. doi: http://dx.doi.org/10.1016/j.chb.2010.02.003.

Mackiewicz, J., & Lam, C. (2009). Coherence in workplace instant messages. *Journal of Technical Writing and Communication, 39*, 417–431.

Mansi, G., & Levy, Y. (2013). Do instant messaging interruptions help or hinder knowledge workers' task performance? *International Journal of Information Management, 33* (3), 591–596. doi: 10.1016/j.ijinfomgt.2013.01.011.

Markman, K. M. (2009). "So what shall we talk about": Openings and closings in chat-based virtual meetings. *Journal of Business Communication, 46,* 150–170.

Markman, K. M. (2013). Conversational coherence in small group chat. In S. C. Herring, D. Stein, & T. Virtanen (Eds), *Pragmatics of Computer-Mediated Communication* (pp. 539–564). Berlin: De Gruyter Mouton.

Ong, K. K. W. (2011). Disagreement, confusion, disapproval, turn elicitation and floor holding: Actions as accomplished by ellipsis marks-only turns and blank turns in quasisynchronous chats. *Discourse Studies, 13,* 211–234.

Ou, C. X. J., & Davison, R. M. (2011). Interactive or interruptive? Instant messaging at work. *Decision Support Systems, 52* (1), 61–72. doi: 10.1016/j.dss.2011.05.004.

Panyametheekul, S., & Herring, S. C. (2003). Gender and turn allocation in a Thai chat room. *Journal of Computer-Mediated Communication, 9* (1). Retrieved from: http://www.ascusc.org/jcmc/vol9/issue1/panya_herring.html.

Pazos, P., Chung, J. M., & Micari, M. (2013). Instant messaging as a task-support tool in information technology organizations. *Journal of Business Communication, 50* (1), 68–86. doi: 10.1177/0021943612465181.

Quan-Haase, A., Cothrel, J., & Wellman, B. (2005). Instant messaging for collaboration: A case study of a high-tech firm. *Journal of Computer-Mediated Communication, 10* (4). doi: 10.1111/j.1083-6101.2005.tb00276.x.

Radicati, S., & Hoang, Q. (2011). *Survey: Instant Messaging, Social Networking, Unified Communications, 2011–2012.* Palo Alto, CA: The Radicati Group, Inc.

Ruppel, C. P., Gong, B., & Tworoger, L. C. (2013). Using communication choices as a boundary-management strategy: How choices of communication media affect the work–life balance of teleworkers in a global virtual team. *Journal of Business and Technical Communication, 27* (4), 436–471. doi: 10.1177/1050651913490941.

Sarrel, M. D. (December 2007). Give your web site a human touch. *PC Magazine, 26, 94.*

Schonfeldt, J., & Golato, A. (2003). Repair in chats: A conversation analytic approach. *Research on Language & Social Interaction, 36,* 241–284.

Shaw, B., Scheufele, D. A., & Catalano, S. (2007). The role of presence awareness in organizational communication: An exploratory field experiment. *Behaviour & Information Technology, 26* (5), 377–384. doi: 10.1080/01449290500484450.

Simpson, J. (2005). Conversational floors in synchronous text-based CMC discourse. *Discourse Studies, 7,* 337–361.

Simpson, J. (2013). Conversational floor in computer-mediated discourse. In S. C. Herring, D. Stein, & T. Virtanen (Eds), *Pragmatics of Computer-Mediated Communication* (pp. 516–538). Berlin: De Gruyter Mouton.

Skovholt, K., & Svennevig, J. (2006). Email copies in workplace interaction. *Journal of Computer-Mediated Communication, 12* (1), 42–65. doi: 10.1111/j.1083-6101.2006.00314.x.

Skovholt, K., & Svennevig, J. (2013). Responses and non-responses in workplace emails. In S. C. Herring, D. Stein, & T. Virtanen (Eds), *Pragmatics of Computer-Mediated Communication* (pp. 589–611). Berlin: De Gruyter Mouton.

Stephens, K. K. (2008). Optimizing costs in workplace instant messaging use. *IEEE Transactions on Professional Communication, 51* (4), 369–380.

Stephens, K. K., & Davis, J. (2009). The social influences on electronic multitasking in organizational meetings. *Management Communication Quarterly, 23*, 63–83.

Stromer-Galley, J., & Martinson, A. M. (2009). Coherence in political computer-mediated communication: Analyzing topic relevance and drift in chat. *Discourse & Communication, 3* (2), 195–216. doi: 10.1177/1750481309102452.

Tagliamonte, S. A., & Denis, D. (2008). Linguistic ruin? LOL! Instant messaging and teen language. *American Speech, 83* (1), 3–34.

Thomas, K. J., & Akdere, M. (2013). Social media as collaborative media in workplace learning. *Human Resource Development Review, 12* (3), 329–344. doi: 10.1177/1534484312472331.

To, P.-L., Liao, C., Chiang, J. C., Shih, M.-L., & Chang, C.-Y. (2008). An empirical investigation of the factors affecting the adoption of instant messaging in organizations. *Computer Standards & Interfaces, 30* (3), 148–156. doi: http://dx.doi.org/10.1016/j.csi.2007.08.019.

Turnage, A. (2013). Technological resistance: A metaphor analysis of Enron e-mail messages. *Communication Quarterly, 61* (5), 519–538. doi: 10.1080/01463373.2013.803995.

Turner, J. W., Grube, J. A., Tinsley, C. H., Lee, C., & O'Pell, C. (2006). Exploring the dominant media: How does media use reflect organizational norms and affect performance? *Journal of Business Communication, 43* (3), 220–250. doi: 10.1177/0021943606288772.

Waldvogel, J. (2007). Greetings and closings in workplace email. *Journal of Computer-Mediated Communication, 12* (2), 456–477. doi: 10.1111/j.1083-6101.2007.00333.x.

Yuan, Y. C., Zhao, X., Liao, Q., & Chi, C. (2013). The use of different information and communication technologies to support knowledge sharing in organizations: From e-mail to micro-blogging. *Journal of the American Society for Information Science and Technology, 64* (8), 1659–1670. doi: 10.1002/asi.22863.

4

Some Linguistic and Pragmatic Aspects of Italian Business Email

Nives Lenassi

Introduction

A few years ago a major research project was carried out at the Faculty of Economics in Ljubljana within which various Italian business correspondence texts were studied. Among other facts and tendencies, the analysis also revealed that authentic email messages written in the Italian corporate world encompass a vast variety of texts depending on a complex set of situational factors. For this reason it is possible to find messages characterized by different levels of formality (from highly formal to typically less formal) and by various traits that depend on the form or system of communication (from properties pertaining exclusively to written communication to features that have distinctive characteristics of ordinary spontaneous conversation). This situation results from the fact that email can take over the function of other transmission media (such as a letter, a fax or a message left on an answering machine) or simply serve as a device used to send attached documents. Furthermore, business email messages are institutional texts whose production depends on various linguistic and extralinguistic factors such as the age, gender, and education of the writer, as well as environment, intention, mood, time available, the writer's feelings about the adequacy of the medium and its reliability, the relationship between the communicators, computer literacy and experience, trust in email communication, organizational culture, and mastery of various genres (see Nidorfer Šiškovič, 2010, p. 60, and the cited work of Mallon & Oppenheim, 2002).

The education level of persons who write email messages is above average: these are usually people who can also write traditional letters. The case is, however, different as far as the age of email authors is concerned: many are probably so young that they are not used to writing traditional letters and are not acquainted with traditional paper-based communication (see Baron, 2002, p. 31; Lorenzetti & Schirru, 2006, p. 91). For this reason the traditional letter model cannot serve as a reference point for an email analysis. Another reason why traditional letters cannot be considered as a valid basis from which to observe electronic messages is that email often tends to imitate spoken language, representing the dialogical nature of communication (Antonelli, 2007; Baron, 1998, 2000; Peticca, 2005).

The characteristics of Italian email messages are presented in various works and refer to a corpus of texts written for social purposes (Fiorentino, 2002, 2004, 2008), for didactic purposes (Absalom & Pais Marden, 2004), and for academic purposes in student–teacher interaction (Fiorentino, 2011; Sciubba, 2010). The studies reveal typical characteristics at various linguistic levels, which are also presented in the analyses carried out by Antonelli (2007), D'Achille (2006), Lorenzetti and Schirru (2006), and Vergaro (2005). For other typical traits found in non-Italian messages, but equally important given global communication trends, see also Darics (2013), Dresner and Herring (2010), Kalman and Gergle (2014), Kankaanranta (2006), and Vandergriff (2013).

The Italian email messages presented in the contributions mentioned here were written for non-business purposes, and so not all the findings can be relevant to the present study. What is significant for the present research is the manner in which the electronic messages are analyzed, together with the ascertainment of parameters that influence email production and of certain linguistic choices. For this reason the collected authentic business email messages were analyzed taking into account particular aspects of text production relevant for non-native speakers who have business contacts with Italian firms: register, passive voice, and verb tenses. Although the categories selected for a more detailed description shed only partial light on the vast range of variables considered in the process of email composition revealed during the research project, their presentation here contributes to the understanding of some linguistic and pragmatic aspects of the texts studied. Thus, it might be of interest for people involved in bilingual interactions other than ELF, and people exposed to intercultural communication and computer-mediated discourse research focusing on languages other than English.

Materials and methods

As stated above, the results of this study, which combines qualitative and quantitative research methods, are part of a larger research project whose aim was to examine Italian business correspondence texts in order to improve language teaching effectiveness for Slovene university-level economics students. The study was conducted at various linguistic levels on a large number of prototypical and authentic texts; these included a corpus of 275 authentic email messages written by Italian native speakers. In these texts only the central part, the body of the message, was studied. This means that the documentary parts such as the time of sending, the sender, the receiver, the subject, and the signature block (the sender's name, the company name, etc.) were not considered because some companies offered only texts in which these data were previously deleted, whereas others sent the messages in their original forms. At this point it is necessary to acknowledge that such data deletion poses some problems: time represents a major contextualization cue affecting message construction and production; the information about the sender(s) and receiver(s) contributes to the relations layers of the messages; the name of the company provides data from which to start analyzing tendencies/guidelines within a single corporate culture; and so on.

The texts, collected (in some cases with considerable difficulties) between 2005 and 2013, represent external or international communication in different stages of business transactions: some include correspondence referring to a business transaction from the first contact to the next or even final contact, whereas others are merely single texts representing parts of transactions whose beginning and final texts were not offered for the study. There are, therefore, "chain initiators," embedded messages (a series of internal messages) and "chain terminators" (see also Gimenez, 2005, pp. 235–6). The collected materials offered by businesspersons working in the secondary (manufacturing, construction), tertiary (transportation, distribution, tourism, insurance) and quarternary (culture, education) sectors display significant diversity at the linguistic and pragmatic levels, as already pointed out above: they differ in length (the shortest text contains six words and the longest 306), topic (new product introduction letter, offer, request, complaint, information about the attached document, etc.), number of recipients (one vs. many; i.e., flyers), register (formal, semiformal, informal), and relationship between sender and recipient (social closeness vs. social distance).

Register

There are numerous definitions of the term *register* and problems arising from it (see, for example, Berruto, 2011; Lee, 2001), as well as possible denominations for single types of registers (Berruto, 1993, p. 73; D'Achille, 2006, p. 35; Dardano & Trifone, 1995, p. 62). For the purpose of this study the texts were divided into three categories by register: formal (texts conforming to accepted and established rules), semiformal (formal texts with occasional conversational features), and informal (texts imitating spoken discourse). Coveri et al. (1998, pp. 146–7) specify that the level of in/formality depends on the situational context of the communicative process and on the function or objectives of the interaction: the register is therefore predictable considering the text typology and medium. In Italian, the formal or consultative register corresponds to the written language and the standard and neostandard language variant, whereas the informal register refers predominantly to spoken language. Useful criteria for the distinction between formal and informal are major or minor explicitness/implicitness, lexical and morphological coding/non-coding, and resort to extralinguistic communication factors (proxemic, kinesic, etc.).

One of the parameters that creates part of the situational context and is relevant for this study is the social distance or closeness between the communicators. In the case of social distance, displayed by the use of the pronoun *Lei* for singular or *Voi* for plural (for problems emerging from the capitalized or lower case *voi*, see Lenassi, 2013a), the text usually calls for a formal communicative process that conforms to accepted and established rules. This is the case in Example 1, in which one can find recurrent business correspondence verbalizations such as *in riferimento a* (with reference to), *sono ad inviarVi in allegato* (please find attached), *debitamente firmato e timbrato* (duly signed and stamped), and *RingraziandoVi per la collaborazione Vi porgo distinti saluti* (Thank you for your cooperation. Yours faithfully):

Example 1
Buongiorno,
in riferimento al codice sulla privacy Dlgs. N. 196 del 30 giugno 2003 sono ad inviarVi in allegato l'informativa resa all'interessato per il trattamento dei dati personali comuni e il consenso al trattamento dei dati personali.
Vi chiedo di restituirci, debitamente firmato e timbrato il mudulo di consenso al trattamento dei dati personali al n. fax _____.
RingraziandoVi per la collaborazione Vi porgo distinti saluti.
C* R** (MZ 1)

(Good day,
With reference to the regulations on privacy Legislative Decree N. 196 of June 30, 2003 please find attached the information sent to

the applicant for processing personal data and permission to process the personal data.
I would like to ask you to send back permission to process personal data form duly signed and stamped to the fax no. _____
Thank you for your cooperation.
Yours faithfully)

The only less formal element is the opening salutation *Buon giorno* (good morning or good afternoon), recurrent in face-to-face conversations, but also frequently used in email instead of the formal *Egregi Signori* or *Gentili Signori* (Dear Sirs) to diminish the formality level. The presence of the spoken discourse feature, used here for pragmatic factors, is an interesting element of code switching, frequently present in less formal messages. This type of register alternation may provide a means to suggest how the text is to be interpreted (see also Nilep, 2006, p. 9).

Features of conversational interaction imply that, at some point in the past, social closeness between communicators was established and such a relationship often requires no salutation, as in Example 2. The absence of the prefatory greeting also indicates that the text is part of a previously started communicative chain, exchanged in a short period of time, in which the salutation is neither written by the sender nor expected by the receiver. The message itself is semantically insufficient; that is, without the previous message(s), it is hardly comprehensible.

Example 2
Si, scusa. È l'abitudine.
In allegato il DDT corretto.
Buon lavoro a te,
S* (AT 2)

(Yes, I'm sorry. It's [because of] habit.
In the attachment the correct DN.
Good work to you.)

The next indication of the lower degree of formality in Example 2, which seems to be a message left on an answering machine, is the presence of various spoken discourse features, such as the brief discourse markers *si* (instead of the orthographically correct *sì* [yes]) and *scusa* (I'm sorry) with its phatic function; that is, to establish contact with the receiver, stimulating his/her approval or involvement (see D'Achille, 2006, p. 186). A further trait of the oral language is the concise explanation for the mistake made in one of the preceding messages È l'abitudine (It's [because of] the habit) and the closing paragraph expressing the wish *Buon lavoro a te* (Good work to you). The *emoticon* (the only one found in the texts studied), another typically informal element, is used to achieve an approving receiver's interpretation of the apology and the reason given. An additional interesting feature is the verb omission of *In allegato il DDT corretto* (In the attachment the correct DN [delivery note]), recalling the telegraphic language of one time (see also Baron, 2002, p. 34). In contrast to the past, when telegram senders' tendency to elide parts of speech that did not impair the meaning of the telegram was associated with cost savings, today's senders primarily omit various terms to comply with the global tendency to be efficient, probably trying to respond to initiatives from the business world in the shortest possible period of time. (See, however, Darics, 2013; this claims that professional communicators do spend time composing and proofreading their messages and that the majority of cues are conscious signs with meaning.) The inclusion of the telegram variety, which could be interpreted either as an element of code switching or an element of the *economy principle*, in the texts studied, however, is characteristic only of four senders who wrote a total of eight messages (i.e., 2.9% of the texts).

Examples 1 and 2 display the characteristics usually expected in business written interpersonal interaction: formal register for social distance and less formal for social closeness (see Table 4.1). However, there are intermediate stages closely related to various factors that influence email composition; one of the most salient is the topic (offer, request, complaint, payment reminder, etc.). In Example 3 the receiver, although on first-name terms with the sender, is invited to pay the invoice in a formal message, to match the formality of the situation: *con la presente sono a sollecitaTi* (This is to remind you), *se hai provveduto al pagamento, non tener conto di quanto sopra* (If the payment has been made, disregard the above). The formal verbalization is, however, mitigated with the opening

Table 4.1 Register in email messages functioning as business letters

FM, SD	39.0%
FM, SC	3.3%
SF, SD	44.4%
SF, SC	13.3%

FM – formal message	SC – social closeness
SF – semiformal message	SD – social distance

Cara B* (Dear B*) and closing *Tanti saluti* (Best), usually featuring in informal messages, to match the relationship between the correspondents. The opening and the close therefore represent another example of code switching, which – like every element of code switching presented up to this point – is to be interpreted with regard to the communicators' opinions on this phenomenon, with special reference to business and social effects.

Example 3
Cara B*,
Con la presente sono a sollecitarTi il pagamento della nostra fattura: Fatt. N. 16990 del 7.7. di euro ___ scaduta il 5.10.
Se hai gia' provveduto al pagamento, non tener conto di quanto sopra e Ti chiedo cortesemente di inviarmi via fax la copia del bonifico bancario.
Tanti saluti
B* (Bo 8)

(Dear B*,
This is to remind you about paying the invoice:
Invoice N. 16990 of 7.7. of _____EUR, due Oct 5.
If the payment has already been made, disregard the above. I would like to ask you to send me a copy of the bank transfer by fax, please.
Best)

Spoken discourse features may signal evidence of hastily planned and unedited texts, resulting in semiformal messages, which are also largely present in the case of social closeness, expressed by the use of the familiar second-person pronoun *tu*. Table 4.1 indicates that 13.3% of such messages are in the corpus. The texts taken into consideration in this table, however, refer only to the 90 messages that functioned as traditional letters. An email as a message left on an answering machine and as a device for transmitting attachments was not considered because such a message is often very short, containing only recurrent formulaic expressions and therefore less interesting for the purpose of this study. In the case of social closeness some of these messages tend to be rather informal (see Lenassi, 2012b, p. 202).

It interesting to note in Table 4.1 that the prevailing relationship in the corpus studied is social distance: in such a relationship the senders are slightly more prone to create semiformal messages (44.4%). These texts tend to be formal, but have some elements that indicate a lower degree of formality, occasionally displaying the informality of dialogue and informal written language with some evidence of scarce editing. Following closely are formal messages (39.0%) for socially distant relationships, indicating that in international trade messages analyzed almost half of correspondents who are not on first-name terms with their foreign business partners see it as more appropriate to create or maintain certain distance. What draws particular attention is the low number of messages for socially close relationships (3.3% and 13.3%). This is explained by the fact that correspondents who are on first-name terms usually choose (1) to construct telephone-conversation-like messages to require or offer some brief information (as mentioned before, such texts are not considered in the table) or (2) to send letter-like documents in the attachments (these were not considered in the study because they were simply referred to in the message but not actually sent to the author of the research).

As already observed, a typical feature of email composition is the use of spoken discourse elements (see Lenassi, 2012b), often present in salutations and closings. These have a relevant demarcation function of denoting the beginning and the end of texts (see D'Achille, 2006, p. 186). Salutations may be seen as the first indications of the message register, although this is not always the case, as seen in Examples 1 and 3, in which informal salutations open formal messages. This could indicate a lower degree of formality and a general attenuation of the formal/informal bipolarity: in communicative situations for which formality was in force in the past, today semi-informality has set in despite the asymmetrical interaction, as pointed out by Coveri et al. (1998, p. 148). Leaving aside the fact that both formal and less formal messages can open with no salutation, Table 4.2 clearly indicates that the prevailing elements of salutations in the analyzed corpus refer to the spoken language and informal written messages, whereas characteristic formal openings such as *Gentile, Alla cortese attenzione di, Egregio* and *Spettabile* are evidently less frequent.

The closings (Table 4.3) present a slightly different tendency: the typical business correspondence conclusion *Cordiali saluti* is still the preferred way of concluding a message, followed by the still more formal variant *Distinti saluti,* or no salutation at all and various verbalizations, usually

Table 4.2 Salutations in the analyzed corpus

no salutation (22.9%), *Buongiorno* (21.5%), receiver's name (15.7%), *Ciao* (15.7%), *Gentile/Gentili* (14.9%), *Cara* + receiver's name (11.4%), *Cari (colleghi/amici)* (5.2%), *Alla cortese attenzione di* (2.2%), *Salve* (2.2%), *Egregio/Egregi* (1.7%), *Spettabile* (1.3%), *Dear all* (0.4%)

Table 4.3 Closings in the analyzed corpus

Cordiali saluti (28.8%), *Distinti saluti* (13.3%), no salutation (11.4%), *Ciao* (10.2%), *Saluti* (9.7%), expressions of good wishes (9.3%), *Cari saluti* (6.4%), *Grazie* (5.9%), *A presto* (2.1%), *Un abbraccio* (0.8%), *Best wishes* (0.8%), *Tanti saluti* (0.4%), *Migliori saluti* (0.4%), *A più tardi* (0.4%)

---

featuring in spoken language or informal messages. Given some qualitative differences in the openings and conclusions resulting from Tables 4.2 and 4.3, further study and analysis would be necessary to discover parameters governing the choice of single elements. However, considering this chapter's space limitations, these will be dealt with separately. (For the presence of English language elements such as *Dear all* in Table 4.2 and *Best wishes* in Table 4.3, see also Lenassi, 2012a; Lenassi, 2013b.)

The 275 messages collected and studied from various aspects, whose complexity cannot be presented here in detail, show that communicators chose different stages of formality/semiformality/informality in business emails to find the most functional verbalization in a given situation. Sometimes the level chosen in the opening of the message is respected throughout the text: for example, the formality of the opening *Egregi Signori* is continued in the body of the text until the equally formal closing *Distinti saluti* or the informal *Ciao* opens and closes the body of the text, which throughout clearly displays conversational traits. Sometimes, however, email users resort to single elements of code switching (by including spoken conversation traits or informal written language features), as seen in some of the examples presented here. On the one hand, such a tendency can be ascribed to the desire to adhere to the formality of writing for professional purposes; on the other, to the desire to create the involvement expected in close relationships.

There are many aspects to be considered when selecting the register level, which is of particular importance for non-native speakers. The failure to choose the appropriate register will probably not compromise relations between communicators, but it may result in a less favorable evaluation of the non-native speakers' social skills and, more importantly, might have a serious effect on the business at hand – influencing, for example, compliance, efficiency, and willingness to cooperate.

Passive voice

Passive voice is a structure frequently used in business correspondence and often associated with formal register (see Raso & Da Pieve, 2002, p. 252). Selection of the passive sentence structure makes it possible to avoid mentioning the agent (if he/she is unknown or the text producer does not want to mention him/her) and also allows selection of the topic–comment structure considered appropriate to the context, which is determined by various pragmatic factors. This thus makes it possible to communicate in an impersonal way but also to abbreviate the text by using participial structures, eliding the auxiliary verbs *essere* and *venire* in:

(a) Relative clauses, for example: *la merce <u>ordinata</u> ieri verrà spedita entro questa settimana* (the merchandise <u>ordered</u> yesterday will be sent within this week) instead of *la merce <u>che è stata ordinataa</u> ieri verrà spedita entro questa settimana* (the merchandise <u>which was ordered</u> yesterday will be sent within this week); and in
(b) Adverbial clauses, for example: *appena <u>caricato</u>, il camion è partito* (once <u>loaded</u>, the truck left) instead of *appena <u>era stato caricato</u>, il camion è partito* (once the truck <u>had been loaded</u>, it left).

In business correspondence the passive voice is seen as an indication of a formal and impersonal relationship with the text receiver: by using it, the senders communicate that, in a way, they are distancing themselves from the text content (Van Mulken & Van der Meer, 2005, p. 105). For example, when the receiver receives a request that he/she does not want or cannot grant, it is possible to use the passive voice in order to indicate that he/she does not take responsibility. Such linguistic behavior allows the text producer to maintain face (Brown & Levinson, 1987, p. 13), as, in Example 4, say, in which the author uses nine verb forms, five of which are passive. The text refers to the control visit to shops that are being built in Slovenia under the surveillance of the Italy-based mother company. In order not to communicate directly that all the visits have already been arranged by the Italian supervisor, the text writer uses finite *(le visite /.../ verranno effettuate,* i.e., the visits /.../ will be made, *si prega di,* i.e., (you) are asked to) and non-finite passive constructions *(quelle indicate,* i.e., those indicated, *visite concordate,* i.e., visits agreed upon, *settimane indicate,* i.e., weeks indicated) with no agent specification.

Example 4
Egregi signori,
Vi invio il prospetto delle visite ai cantieri E***. Oltre a quelle <u>indicate</u>, <u>verranno effettuate</u> altre visite <u>concordate</u> di volta in volta in base alle rispettive esigenze, con sufficiente preavviso. Avendo già programmato le visite per tutte le piattaforme, <u>si prega</u> di attendersi alle

date del prospetto. Le visite avverranno di norma nelle giornate di mercoledì e giovedì delle settimane indicate.
Cordiali saluti.
E*** SPA
Ufficio tecnico
F. C** (EE 14)

(Dear Sirs,
I am sending you the schedule of the visits to the E*** construction sites. Besides those indicated, other visits will be made, agreed upon each time on the basis of requirements, with suitable notice. Having already planned the visits for all the platforms, you are asked to note the dates of the schedule. The visits will normally take place on Wednesdays and Thursdays of the weeks indicated.
Best regards)

However, agent specification can be present; its presence is the means with which the intended information structure of the text can be reached when arranging single language items into the planned topic–comment structure (see Example 5):

Example 5
T* le mando le normative, le questioni sono due: /.../
La Direttiva di riferimento è la 2002/95/CE ed il campo di applicazione nel quale occorre valutare se rientrano i nostri prodotti è definito dall'allegato I /.../ (K 18)

(T* I am sending you the regulations, the issues are the following: /.../ The Directive is 2002/95/CE and the area in which it is necessary to evaluate whether our products meet the requirements is defined by the attachment I /.../)

The planning of the designed information structure can be recognized in numerous other texts in which – contrary to what has been seen up to now – no passive is used. This is not surprising given the use of nominalizations, which adequately meet the requirements of clear information structuring (Example 6):

Example 6
D*,
la settimana prossima produrremo il c***. Come sai, se ne hai bisogno, ci serve un ordine programma in base alle tue necessità. Se per ora non hai richieste, prevediamo la prossima produzione a gennaio.

Saluti e grazie

S* S** (O 2)

(D*,

next week we will produce the c***. As you know, if you need it, we need an <u>order</u> of the program based on your <u>requirements</u>. If for the time being you have no <u>requests</u>, we are planning the next <u>production</u> in January. Best and thank you)

In Example 6, characterized by a less formal register and socially close relationship between the communicators, there are nominalizations such as *ordine* (order), *necessità* (requirements), *richieste* (requests), and *produzione* (production). However, this does not mean that in less formal texts nominalization prevails over the passive voice. This can be confirmed by Example 7, containing numerous spoken discourse features (the receiver's name in the opening, a direct question, a double question mark, suspension points, the closing) and also the passive constructions *era stato fatto* (had been produced) and *veniamo scartati* (we are dismissed):

Example 7

D*

Ma la richiesta è la stessa dello scorso anno?

Perché mi dicono che il materiale già <u>era stato fatto</u> ma il problema era la traspirabilità (ti allego i test e documentazione....), quindi, se anche mettiamo in produzione un'altra volta lo stesso art. Poi <u>veniamo</u> ancora <u>scartati</u> per i problemi tecnici....

Cosa facciamo?? Fammi sapere...

Grazie, ciao

P*** SpA (O 5)

(D*

But the request is the same as last year?

Because they are telling me that the material <u>had</u> already <u>been produced</u> but the problem was the breathability (I am attaching the tests and the documentation....) so, if we start producing the same art. again. Then we <u>are dismissed</u> because of technical problems....

What shall we do?? Let me know...

Thank you, best)

The choice of the active/passive voice is determined by numerous parameters, which are often genre-based and situation-specific. For this reason the passive is typically avoided by non-native speakers: to develop various grammatical, lexical, and textual elements necessary to appropriately describe a situation/state and to offer the most adequate perspective in order to guide the receiver's attention and consequently to achieve the purpose of communication (see also Nuzzo, 2012, p. 82), the passive needs to be studied from different perspectives and introduced into either formal or less formal email texts destined to be used as teaching materials.

Verb forms

Less competent non-native speakers of Italian are often convinced that in order to communicate effectively with Italian partners it is essential to use the same basic verb tenses, and that the subjunctive is not a commonly utilized structure and it will never be necessary for them to use it. They tend to believe that native speakers do not use the entire series of verb tenses available in the language. It is to be stressed, however, that on this point they are not completely wrong: in the spoken language the subjunctive is relatively less frequent (see Antonelli, 2007, p. 43), but in business email production, native speakers generally adhere to the norm. To find out the extent to which this tendency is respected, all the collected messages were analyzed according to the presence of single verb tenses. The parameters taken into account were the number of different verb tenses in single messages, the topic, and the number of words.

Focusing first on the presence of single verb forms in the texts analyzed, it is necessary to observe the absence of *trapassato remoto, passato remoto,* and *futuro composto*. Given their particular use and relevance in the text construction process, their absence in the genre studied is expected (see, for example, Miklič, 2012). All other verb forms are extensively present, predominantly in emails referring to negotiations, descriptions of the working process, the first contacts with firms and various conflicts in which the sender justifies the various reasons that caused the conflict in detail and politely. In such cases it is important that verbalization is well planned and that the sender is seen as a competent person, able to compose polite and situationally appropriate messages. This is made possible by the use of various coordinate and subordinate syntax patterns in which the architecture of Italian verbal tenses is very complex.

In complete contrast to the texts briefly discussed above, messages with only one verb form largely used *presente dell'indicativo*. This characteristic is displayed in 34 messages, containing a small number of words: from six (to refer to the attached documents) up to 50 words (to order or offer goods/services). In some instances it is also possible to find texts with no verbal tenses: the eight messages of this nature refer to attached documents and contain a low number of words.

Text length is a relevant factor for the use of verbal forms. Moreover, sentence length and number of sentences can be viewed as an indication of wordiness and thus the formality of the message: there is a tendency to use more words and sentences to write a formal text as opposed to an informal text such as a note or a memorandum (see Van Mulken & Van der Meer, 2005, p. 105). Email, however, has its own distinguishing features: in our corpus, less formal messages are usually shorter than formal ones, but there are also short formal ones, especially when email is used merely as a means for transmitting an attachment. Taking into consideration the features indicated, it can be inferred that email length depends on the complexity of the situation (presence vs. absence of controversies), the text position in the communication chain (beginning vs. intermediate and final; see also Gimenez, 2005, pp. 235–6), the register (formal, semiformal, informal), and the role of the medium (letter/fax, answering machine, transmission device for attachments).

The study confirms the expected connection between the number of words and the variety of verb tenses: a large number of words results in the use of many different verb forms (see Table 4.4). In the corpus there are some messages with more than 200 words per text, containing from 6 to 12 different verb forms. The topics of the texts mentioned can be summed up as follows: attempts to solve a complex situation (A 2, A 9), letters of promotion (SA 4, Z 4), and detailed information about the cooperation (EE 30, IN 1, OV 3):

The data collected show that the use of verb forms in authentic texts is not as straightforward as foreign language users would prefer or expect them to be. As far as the use of verb forms is concerned, the analyses show that the most complex texts are those in which the sender relays information about conflict situations and expresses the desire to solve them as well as texts in which the senders promote their activities or offer detailed information about the joint work undertaken or planned. To be able to compose messages dealing with such topics it is necessary to know well the expected macrostructural elements and to plan and carry out verbalization successfully, always bearing in mind future reciprocal business cooperation. If all the aspects mentioned are considered, it cannot be supposed that composing professional emails is a simple process. Non-native speakers who exchange email messages with Italian firms should be aware of numerous factors affecting single communicative processes, together with the complexity of Italian

94 *Nives Lenassi*

Table 4.4 Verb forms in lengthy messages

Topic	Text code	Number of single verb forms	Number of different verb forms	Number of words
Request to re-examine the decision taken	A 2	Pr 6, PP 4, TP 3, F 3, Pr' 1, IM'1, TP' 1, Im 1, C 1, CC 3, Inf 4, Ppa 7	12	306
Negotiating	A 9	Pr 16, PP 6, F 2, Pr' 1, IM' 1, Inf 6, Ppa 2, G 1	8	214
Information about data access	EE 30	Pr 12, PP 3, IM 1, C 2, Inf 3, Ppa 1, G 2	7	213
Instructions for employees	IN 1	Pr 10, PP 6, F 1, PP' 2, IM' 1, Im 5, Inf 10, Ppa 3, GG 1	9	293
Information about the planned cooperation	OV 3	Pr 11, PP 2, F 2, C 1, Pr' 2, Ppa 1, Inf 7	7	254
Letter of promotion	SA 4	Pr 10, PP 3, Inf 8, Ppa 3, Ppr 2, G 2	6	307
Letter of promotion	Z 4	Pr 10, F 7, PP 3, G 2, Im 7, Inf 6, Ppa 3	7	237

Pr presente dell'indicativo, PP passato prossimo, F futuro semplice, C condizionale semplice, CC condizionale composto, Im imperativo, IM imperfetto dell'indicativo, Pr' presente del congiuntivo, PP' passato del congiuntivo, IM' imperfetto del congiuntivo, G gerundio semplice, GG gerundio composto, Inf infinito semplice, Ppr participio presente, Ppa participio passato

verb tenses, which serve to express significant temporal, aspectual, and modal meanings as well as relevant logical and semantic aspects, and their peculiarities for foreign language users (see Miklič, 1997; Miklič, 2008; Miklič & Ožbot, 2007).

Conclusion

Within its variety of functions, email is still often used as a traditional letter in which one can notice various degrees of analogy to face-to-face conversation, especially in socially distant relationships. In such a relationship participants in communicative events frequently formulate messages that can be defined as semiformal, displaying characteristic traits of spoken discourse. The study also shows the notable presence of formal messages written in socially distant relationships, with all the typical features of traditional letters: distinctive business correspondence phrases and patterns, and frequent use of the passive voice. The analyses reveal that the passive can be found in all the topics because it makes it possible to avoid mentioning certain information and to structure the text in such a manner that the theme–rheme structure is adequately realized. As a result of these characteristics, the passive can be found in either finite or in infinite verb forms with special reference to the participial construction, which has gained considerable importance given the widespread tendency to follow the economy principle. However, clear information structuring, enabled by the passive voice, can also be achieved with nominalizations: if adequately distributed in the text the nominalized lexical units meet the requirements of clear information structuring.

As for the use of verb tenses interwoven into a complex verb system, the analyses show that numerous different tense forms are found in composite, lengthy, and rather formal texts, with an elaborated message organization. In these messages the senders (respecting their social distance/closeness with the receivers) give information about conflict situations and express the desire to solve them, justify their points of view or stimulate the addressees to act by offering them various types of information regarding the work completed or planned and by presenting new goods or services.

Although all business texts are institutionalized, they are, nevertheless, written by individuals in particular business settings, and as such subject to specific encoding depending on extralinguistic parameters that are sometimes not easy to determine and usually intertwined with each other. Despite such an intricate combination of different parameters it is necessary to sensitize not only foreign language speakers but also persons dealing with communication teaching and training in companies to some relevant elements occurring in this text production. The findings of this analysis confirm that in specific situations within the corporate world specific linguistic knowledge is indispensable. For this reason it is important that in foreign business language teaching or in communication teaching and training, students or employees are faced with circumstances and texts that differ from everyday routine, usually calling for short and simple messages. In complex situations, good language competence is expected at all levels: with linguistically correct and pragmatically adequate language, senders demonstrate their good acquaintance levels with international corporate culture and respect for the receiver.

References

Absalom, M., & Pais Marden, M. (2004) Email communication and language learning at university – an Australian case study. *Computer Assisted Language Learning, 17* (3–4), 403–440.

Antonelli, G. (2007). *L'italiano nella società della comunicazione*. Bologna: il Mulino.

Baron, N. (1998). Letters by phone or speech by other means: The linguistics of email. *Language and Communication, 18*, 133–170.

Baron, N. (2000). *Alphabet to Email: How Written Language Evolved and Where It's Heading*. London: Routledge.

Baron, N. (2002). Who sets email style: Prescriptivism, coping strategies, and democratizing communication access. Retrieved from College of Arts and Sciences, American University, Washington, DC website: http://www.american.edu/cas/lfs/faculty-docs/upload/2003-Paper-Who-Sets-Email-Style.pdf.

Berruto, G. (1993). Varietà diamesiche, diastratiche, diafasiche. In A. A. Sobrero (Ed.), *Introduzione all'italiano contemporaneo* (pp. 37–92). Bari: Laterza.

Berruto, G. (2011). Registri, generi, stili: alcune considerazioni su categorie mal definite. In M. Cerruti, E. Corino, & C. Onesti (Eds), *Formale e informale. La variazione di registro nella comunicazione elettronica* (pp. 15–35). Rome: Carocci.

Brown, P., & Levinson, P. (1987). *Politeness: Some Universals in Language Usage*. Cambridge: Cambridge University Press.

Coveri, L., Benucci, A., & Diadori, P. (1998). *Le varietà dell'italiano. Manuale di sociolinguistica* (5th edition). Rome: Bonacci.

D'Achille, P. (2006). *L'italiano contemporaneo* (2nd edition). Bologna: il Mulino.

Dardano, M., & Trifone, P. (1995). *Grammatica italiana con nozioni di linguistica* (3rd edition). Bologna: Zanichelli.

Darics, E. (2013). Non-verbal signalling in digital discourse: The case of letter repetition. *Discourse, Context & Media, 2*, 141–148. Retrieved from: http://dx.doi.org/10.1016/j.dcm.2013.07.002.

Dresner, E., & Herring, S. C. (2010). Functions of the nonverbal in CMC: Emoticons and illocutionary force. *Communication Theory, 20* (3), 249–268.

Fiorentino, G. (2002). Computer-mediated communication: lingua e testualità nei messaggi di posta elettronica in italiano. In R. Bauer & H. Goebel (Eds), *Parallela IX. Testo, variazione, informatica* (pp. 187–208). Wilhelmsfeld: Egert.

Fiorentino, G. (2004). Scrivere come si parla. Variabilità diamesica e CMC: il caso dell'e-mail. *Horizonte, 8*, 83–110.

Fiorentino, G. (2008). Scrittura elettronica: il caso della posta elettronica. In F. Orletti (Ed.), *Scrittura e nuovi media* (2nd edition) (pp. 69–112). Rome: Carocci.

Fiorentino, G. (2011). Scrittura liquida e grammatica essenziale. In U. Cardinale (Ed.), *A scuola d'italiano a 150 anni dall'Unità* (pp. 219–241). Bologna: il Mulino.

Gimenez, J. C. (2005). Unpacking business emails: Message embeddedness in international business email communication. In M. Gotti & P. Gillaerts (Eds), *Genre Variation in Business Letters. Linguistic Insights* (pp. 235–255). Bern: Peter Lang.

Kalman, Y. M., & Gergle, D. (2014). Letter repetitions in computer mediated communication: A unique link between spoken and online language. *Computers in Human Behaviour, 34*, 187–193.

Kankaanranta, A. (2006). "Hej seppo. could you pls comment on this!" – internal email communication in lingua franca English in a multinational company. *Business Communication Quarterly, 69* (2), 216–225.

Lee, D. (2001). Genres, registers, text types, domains, and styles: Clarifying the concepts and navigating a path through the BNC jungle. *Language Learning & Technology, 5* (3), 37–72.

Lenassi, N. (2012a). The use of anglicisms in authentic Italian and Slovene commercial correspondence. In A. Akbarov & V. Cook (Eds), *Contemporary Foreign Language Education: Linking Theory into Practice* (pp. 473–480). Sarajevo: International Burch University.

Lenassi, N. (2012b).Tratti del parlato nelle e-mail d'affari in lingua italiana scambiate tra partner italiani e sloveni. *Linguistica, 52,* 201–211.

Lenassi, N. (2013a). Graphemic characteristics of Italian business texts produced by Italian and Slovene speakers. In P. Vičič, V. Ipavec, & A. Plos (Eds), *Proceedings of the Sixth International Language Conference on the Importance of Learning Professional Foreign Languages for Communication between Cultures, 19 and 20 September 2013, University of Maribor, Faculty of Logistics, Slovenia* (pp. 164–174). Celje: Faculty of Logistics.

Lenassi, N. (2013b). Elementi di lingue straniere nella corrispondenza commerciale italiana. *Linguistica, 53,* 221–237.

Lorenzetti, L., & Schirru, G. (2006). La lingua italiana nei nuovi mezzi di comunicazione: SMS, posta elettronica e Internet. In S. Gensini (Ed.), *Fare comunicazione. Teoria ed esercizi* (pp. 71–98). Rome: Carocci.

Mallon, R., & Oppenheim, C. (2002). Style used in electronic mail. *ASLIB Proceeedings, 54* (1), 8–22.

Miklič, T. (1997). Segnalazione della temporalità nel testo: che cosa aiuta il ricevente a collocare le azioni sull'asse temporale. In L. Agostiniani, P. Bonucci, G. Giannecchini, F. Lorenzi, & L. Reali (Eds), *Atti del Terzo convegno della Società internazionale di linguistica e filologia italiana* (pp. 477–505). Napoli: Edizioni Scientifiche Italiane.

Miklič, T. (2008). Alcuni aspetti di tipo pragmatico e di quello retorico-narratologico nell'uso del sistema verbale italiano: con possibili implicazioni per l'insegnamento L2. *Linguistica, 48,* 103–120.

Miklič, T. (2012). Alcuni moduli narrativi e l'uso dei paradigmi verbali in chiave contrastiva: riflessioni sulla necessità di includere la presentazione delle funzioni retoriche testuali nell'educazione linguistica materna e nell'insegnamento delle lingue straniere. In M. Ljubičić, I. Peša, & V. Kovačić (Eds), *Zbornik Međunarodnoga znanstvenog skupa u spomen na prof. dr. Josipa Jerneja (1909–2005), Filozofski fakultet, Zagreb, 13–14 studenoga 2009* (pp. 101–117). Zagreb: Filozofski Fakultet, FF Press.

Miklič, T., & Ožbot, M. (2007). Teaching the uses of Italian verb forms to Slovene speakers. *Linguistica, 47,* 65–76.

Nidorfer Šiškovič, M. (2010). pragmatičnojezikoslovna analiza elektronskih poslovnih pisem v slovenščini. Doctoral dissertation. Ljubljana: Faculty of Arts.

Nilep, C. (2006). "Code switching" in sociocultural linguistics. *Colorado Research in Linguistics, 19.* Boulder: University of Colorado. Retrieved from University of Colorado website: http://www.colorado.edu/linguistics/CRIL/Volume19_Issue1/paper_NILEP.pdf.

Nuzzo, E. (2012). Imparare la costruzione passiva in italiano L 2. *Studi Italiani di Linguistica Teorica e Applicata, 41* (1), 67–84.

Peticca, S. (2005). Il linguaggio delle e-mail. In M. Baldini & D. Marucci (Eds), *La parola nella galassia elettronica* (pp. 93–101). Rome: Armando.

Raso, T., & Da Pieve, A. (2002). Il linguaggio burocratico. In F. Bruni & T. Raso (Eds), *Manuale dell'italiano professionale* (pp. 248–276). Bologna: Zanichelli.

Sciubba, M. E. (2010). Salutations, openings and closings in today academic emails. *Studi Italiani di Linguistica Teorica e Applicata, 39* (2), 243–264.

Vandergriff, I. (2013). Emotive communication online: A contextual analysis of computer- mediated communication (CMC) cues. *Journal of Pragmatics, 51,* 1–12. doi: http://dx.doi.org/10.1016/j.pragma.2013.02.008.

Van Mulken, M., & Van Der Meer, W. (2005). Are you being served? A genre analysis of American and Dutch company replies to customer inquiries. *English for Specific Purposes, 24,* 93–109.

Vergaro, C. (2005).»*Dear sirs... con la presente ci pregiamo di...«. Il genere business letter in italiano e in inglese.* Rome: Aracne.

Part II
New Modes of Communication: New Conventions

5
Doing Leadership in a Virtual Team: Analyzing Addressing Devices, Requests, and Emoticons in a Leader's E-mail Messages

Karianne Skovholt

Introduction

Leadership is primarily accomplished through communication. It involves managing many types of oral and written communication genres and thus requires good communication skills. To be a leader in the Internet Age additionally involves managing groups of people in virtual teams by use of email. For many years, information technology experts have regarded email as an "old-fashioned" way of communication that will very soon disappear (Dürscheid & Frehner, 2011, p. 48). However, smart phones with Internet connection and email applications have given email a renewed importance for employees in all kinds of professions. In today's work life, achievements of professional and institutional goals are to a great extent accomplished through email communication. Official figures show that 92% of Norwegian enterprises are connected to Internet (Statistics Norway, 2013), and for many leaders, as well as for other employees, email is the primary communication tool for providing information, inviting others to meetings and coordinating tasks. Over 30 years after email entered work life, it has become one of the most important communication tools for office workers in governmental, municipal, and business-related communication.

In spite of the dominant role of email in organizational activities, research on the use of email and the discursive practices involved with professional email communication is currently lacking. Studying a leader's linguistic and discursive strategies, which is the main objective in this chapter, is important in order to reveal and account for discursive practices and patterns that in a professional context can be viewed as functional or dysfunctional, depending on the aim of the ongoing activity (cf. Heritage, 2011, p. 339).

A virtual team is a group of people who collaborate across space, time, and organizational boundaries, and who use electronic media, such as email, as the primary communication tool (Bell & Kozlowski, 2002, p. 13; Skovholt, 2009; Yoo & Alavi, 2004). The Canadian/American sociologist and Internet researcher Barry Wellman has claimed that working in virtual teams and computer-mediated networks has changed the social organization of the workplace. Today, work life can be characterized as "networked individualism," in which "boundaries are permeable, interactions are with diverse others, connections switch between multiple networks, and hierarchies can be flatter and recursive [...]" (Wellman, 2001, p.10). The community exists more in the informal networks than predefined work-groups. Rather than fitting into the same group as those around them, each person has his/her own "personal community." A risk with the networked individualism, according to Wellman, is that social life at the workplace may be fragmented, and that no one fully knows their colleagues:

> Where person-to-person community is individualizing, role-to-role community deconstructs a holistic individual identity. A person becomes only the sum of her roles, and there is the danger of alienation. The compartmentalization of personal life – within the household and within the community – may create an insecure milieu where no one fully knows anyone. (Wellman, 2001, p. 17)

Many scholars have claimed that the outcome of virtual teamwork is dependent of the leader's ability to resolve miscommunication and conflict, and to facilitate a collegial working environment among team members (Berry, 2011; Darics, 2014) based on trust (Jarvenpaa & Leidner, 1999; Yoo & Alavi, 2004). In spite of its many advantages, the absence of physical presence is considered to be a drawback of email communication (Berry, 2011, p. 189). Scholars from organizational studies have identified lists of skills that leaders of virtual teams *should* have, but very few studies address how virtual leadership *is actually accomplished* through email interaction (Bell & Kozlowski, 2002; Darics, 2010; Darics, 2012; Fairhurst, 2007; Skovholt, 2009), or identify which discursive devices leaders may use in order to create motivation and coherence in a virtual team. These questions are addressed in this chapter.

More specifically, the chapter examines how a leader of a distributed work group (Agenda) in a Norwegian telecommunication company (TCM) performs leadership using email as the primary communication tool. The study has a discursive approach to leadership, that is, examining leadership as it practically unfolds through written discourse (Boden, 1994; Fairhurst, 2007; Heritage, 1984; Holmes & Marra, 2004). Within the frame of interactional sociolinguistics the study analyzes how leadership is linguistically accomplished in the leader's day-to-day email interaction with her subordinates. The main goal is to identify the discursive devices the leader uses to engage, coordinate, and maintain group performance in the virtual team. In terms of politeness theory, the study also examines how the leader, by performing requests, positions herself in relation to the group.

In the current study, leadership is defined as a *discursive phenomenon*, involving a person's *communicative skills*. Rather than analyzing leadership as a predefined phenomenon, the current study analyzes "leadership as it happens" (Fairhurst, 2007, p. 25) and views leadership as a phenomenon that is practically and repeatedly achieved in particular discourses by and through language use. This view corresponds with a project within interactional sociolinguistics known as "Language in the Workplace." Scholars within this project define leadership as a "communicative performance":

> [Leadership is] a consistent communicative performance which, by influencing others, facilitates acceptable outcomes for the organization (transactional/task-oriented goal), and which maintains harmony within the team or community of practice (relational/people-oriented goal). (Holmes, 2005, p. 1780)

Leadership is seen as a process, or an activity. The focus is on the "interpersonal interaction processes and the communication which takes place between people, rather than simply on what a leader achieves" (Holmes, 2005, p. 1780). As a practical consequence of the definition above, analyses of leadership include close reading of leaders' actual spoken and written exchanges. In the present study, this primarily involves the Agenda-leader's day-to-day email interaction with her group members, in addition to some of her external partners.

Previous research on leadership discourse

Relatively little is known about how leadership is actually carried out in computer-mediated conversation (Bell & Kozlowski, 2002). However, a few studies have looked more closely at leadership in *face-to-face conversations*. While several studies in Conversation Analysis (CA) have focused on expert–lay communication (cf. Arminen, 2005; Drew & Heritage, 1992), only a few linguistically oriented studies have explored leader–subordinate interaction (Asmuβ, 2008; Clifton, 2006). Within Interactional Sociolinguistics, researchers in the project called "Language in the Workplace" have conducted several studies on leadership conversations (cf. Holmes, 2005; Holmes & Marra, 2004; Stubbe et al., 2003; Vine, 2004). These previous studies on leadership conversations establish useful background knowledge for the current study on virtual leadership.

How leadership is carried out in *virtual teams* has primarily been studied in organizational studies. These either address emergent leadership (Yoo & Alavi, 2004), or explore leadership as a pre-formulated position, presenting assumptions on how virtual leadership ideally should be accomplished (Bell & Kozlowski, 2002). In what follows, the most relevant research from both conversational studies and organizational studies is reviewed.

Leadership discourse

Scholars from the "Language in the Workplace" – project analyze leadership conversations predominantly with predominant reference to gender differences and, moreover, to how power is enacted in leadership discourse (Holmes, 2005; Holmes & Marra, 2004; Mullany, 2004; Stubbe et al., 2003). They use examples from interactions recorded in a number of New Zealand workplaces. In general, their analyses seem to agree that a "consensus view" (Vine, 2004, p. 167) of power in the workplaces exists. There seems to be a tendency toward minimizing power differences in the interactions between individuals of different status, between leaders and their subordinates. This is done by using different types of positive politeness strategies in order to mitigate the repressive content of an utterance. One such strategy is the use of humour. Inspired by the Language in the Workplace project, sociolinguist Mullany (2004) shows how leaders use humour as a linguistic strategy to hide the use of power when attempting to gain compliance from subordinates in business meetings. By using humour, the meeting chair disguises the oppressive authoritarian nature of their messages and minimizes the appearance of status difference.

Power may also be overtly expressed in a leader's speech, as explored in Vine (2004). She focused on the overt expression of power in management style. By combining a quantitative and qualitative method, Vine showed how leaders "do power" in the workplace. Drawing on speech act theory, Vine (2004) identified and counted what she called the "control acts" in the data (mainly directives, requests, and advisories). According to the author, previous studies on people's perception of control acts and appropriate forms (imperatives, declaratives, interrogatives) showed that "more powerful people are seen as having the right to use direct forms such as imperatives" (Vine, 2004, p. 153). She thus expected to find a preponderance of forceful forms (imperatives) in the data. The use of an imperative is considered to be a very forceful way of giving a directive, while the use of an interrogative is considered to be the least forceful. Vine's results showed that managers made requests to a far greater extent than subordinates did. The directive acts were expressed as imperatives, interrogatives, and declaratives. However, imperatives accounted for only 28% of the leaders' speech acts. The largest proportion were expressed as declaratives.

Vine's results indicate that leaders favour request forms that are less powerful. Drawing on politeness theory, she shows the ways that leaders in this workplace mark or minimize power differences when performing requests. These leaders generally mitigate their control acts, and Vine (2004) finds that communicating and maintaining good relations with other employees play key roles in this workplace (Vine, 2004, p. 165). Of great interest for the current study, Vine (2004) concludes that the leaders "use a range of forms to express control acts and always use mitigation. The power relations between managers and their staff is evident in the number of control acts uttered to them, *but is not necessarily apparent in the way these are realised*" (Vine, 2004, p. 165 [my emphasis]).

The studies from the "Language in the Workplace" project show that leaders tend to minimize power differences. While power is enacted explicitly through frequent requests, these requests are given a linguistic form that mitigates the power dynamic of the request.

Leadership in virtual teams

While the New Zealand project examines leadership conversation, the current study investigates leadership performed through email. Within the research on virtual teams[1] and virtual leadership, many studies discuss theoretically how leaders may effectively perform leadership (Berry, 2011) or lists the kinds of social skills that leaders of successful teams need (Malhotra et al., 2007). Only a handful of studies examine what leaders actually do through email discourse. However, only one of these examines leadership discourse within a linguistic framework (cf. Ho, 2011).

Many scholars have focused on the role that *trust* plays in the success of virtual teams (Iacono & Weisband, 1997; Jarvenpaa & Leidner, 1999; Yoo & Alavi, 2004; Berry, 2011). According to Berry, "effective social relationships are a required constant for effective collaborative work, virtual or face to face" (2011, p. 189). In a study on trust in global collaborative student groups, Jarvenpaa & Leidner (1999) combine statistical/quantitative methods (surveys with questions of trust) with qualitative methods (naturally occurring emails) in order to find out the degree of trust created within the groups. They found that *initiative* strengthened and unified the team, but that providing *response* was even more important. The authors attest that response is a trusted behaviour because it signals involvement. In addition, communication concerning tasks and projects also appears to be necessary to maintain trust. Social communication that complements, not substitutes, task communication may strengthen trust, but this depends on how explicitly members verbalize their commitment, excitement and optimism (Jarvenpaa & Leidner, 1999, p. 811). Similar results were found in Iacono & Weisband's (1997) investigation on trust. In a study on emergent leadership in a virtual team, Yoo & Alavi (2004) found that emergent leaders produce more emails, take more initiatives, and provide more socio-emotional support and feedback than other members. Hence, the studies on virtual teams seem in general to agree that trust may be created by both task-related messages in combination with explicitly verbalizing socio-emotional relations. However, these studies as a whole do not give enough consideration to what kinds of linguistic strategies leaders use.

Even though the scholars above base their findings on actual email discourse, they do not examine *doing virtual leadership* as an issue in itself. Scholars who do consider virtual leadership include Bell and Kozlowski (2002), who have developed a typology of virtual teams in order to draw implications for virtual leadership. However, their typology is not based on actual instances of email interaction, but on traditional models of leadership functions, that is normative models that identify general leadership functions that need to be accomplished in all teams. Bell and Kozlowski (2002) identify two major functions of leadership: *team development* (the development and shaping of team processes) and *performance management* (the monitoring and management of ongoing team performance and progress toward task accomplishment). The challenge for virtual leaders is to duplicate these functional roles in the virtual/distributed environment (Bell & Kozlowski, 2002, pp. 5–8). When teams cross institutional and cultural boundaries, often having different values and different sets of work procedures, it is more difficult for the leader to create coherence, or link employees together "so that they are 'insiders' in the team." This can be accomplished by building a unique "third" culture (Bell & Kozlowski, 2002, p. 37). In addition, it is more difficult for leaders to establish norms in virtual teams, with a more discrete lifecycle, than in teams that have been together longer

(Bell & Kozlowski, 2002, p. 40). Whereas Bell and Kozlowski outline normative expectations of leadership, the current study aims to examine leadership as it practically unfolds through email discourse. Bell and Kozlowski's emphasis on creating coherence and a "third culture" seems relevant for the current study.

Interesting for the current study is also Ho (2011), who identified the pragmatic functions of incorporating "intertextual and interdiscursive elements" in leaders' requests. He found that referring to a third person in requests served four functions: (1) distancing the leaders from the discourse and thus diverting possible forthcoming resentment to others; (2) convincing others to comply with the requests they made; (3) emphasizing selectively and strategically the various roles they were playing; and (4) managing rapport with the email recipients (Ho, 2011, p. 2534).

Due to the lack of empirical studies on how language contributes to the accomplishment of virtual leadership, there seems to be a need for descriptive and qualitative work on virtual teams with an explicit focus on the discursive processes involved (Asmuβ & Svennevig, 2009; Bell & Kozlowski, 2002, p. 47; Darics, 2010, p. 130; Fairhurst, 2007, p. 1). Hence, the current study seeks to answer:

- How is leadership carried out discursively through email interaction?

In order to answer this question, this study focuses on email interaction in one particular group, Agenda, addressing the following research questions:

- How does the leader of Agenda promote trust and build in-group solidarity?
- How does the leader of Agenda position herself *vis-à-vis* her subordinates when making requests?

Data and methodology

The data

The data for this study are emails collected from a distributed project group called "Agenda" in a Norwegian telecompany, "Telecom" (TCM). The leader of this group is named Line Myhre (LM),[2] and she is the person whose discourse is being analyzed. The email exchanges were gathered from August 2004 to December 2004, and amount to approximately 700 emails. Agenda's main task is to edit all confirmation letters that are distributed to customers in the private market. The group members formulate, revise, and standardize letters and templates, with the purpose of giving all letters a uniform style that communicates in a clear and polite way to customers. The group members are frequently contacted by various divisions within the company with requests to reformulate their letters. In order to give the letters a unified tone, they follow a set of guidelines concerning orthography, sentence structure, and style. The project group consists of 11 members, each representing a team from the different divisions of the company. All the team members speak Norwegian as their mother tongue. The emails were originally written in Norwegian, but are translated into English here.

Methodology

The research questions arise from a theoretical assumption that views language usage as a basic component of social relations. Within the frame of politeness theory (Brown & Levinson, 1987), analyzing language usage coincides with discovering how social relations are constructed. Since one of the aims of this chapter is to examine how the leader of a virtual team discursively establishes trust and creates social relations, an application of politeness theory is particularly relevant.

Politeness theory is rooted in the theories of Goffman (1967), and identifies five strategies that participants in interaction may use to protect and maintain one another's "face". Acts which threaten face, such as performing a request, are called 'face-threatening-acts' (FTA). Speakers may perform the FTA directly, *without* redressive action (Strategy 1 – going baldly on record, e.g. "Reformulate the letter"); they may perform the FTA *with* compensation, by using either positive (Strategy 2, e.g. "You are doing excellent work, but would you please reformulate the letter") or negative (Strategy 3, e.g. "I know you are busy, but could you pls reformulate the letter") politeness strategies. The speakers may choose to perform the FTA indirectly (Strategy 4 – off record, e.g. "The letter needs some justifications"), or simply avoid doing the FTA (Strategy 5) (Brown & Levinson 1987: 69).[3]

In workplace interaction where the participant's institutional roles and the organization's needs are in the foreground, complying with requests is more or less part of employees' job description. According to Kankaanranta (2005):

> The ranking of impositions within a company is affected by the job descriptions of the participants; for an outsider an imposition may

seem heavy but if it is part of a staff members' job description to do it or if the staff member has a legitimate right to presuppose it done, then requests involving the imposition will be handled as routine. (Kankaanranta, 2005, p. 111)

Depending on the employee's positions, they have a legitimate right to make requests or comply with requests. Hence, making requests is a part of routine, and will be treated as routine. However, the linguistic realization of the request provides interesting information about the social distance between the participants. Correspondingly, the linguistic realizations of the Agenda-leader's requests in the current study may signal how she positions herself *vis-à-vis* her subordinates.

In order to answer the first subquestion, how the leader promotes in-group solidarity, a close reading of all her messages was performed in order to identify linguistic markers (contextualization cues) of informal and personal style. These cues included addressing devices, metaphors, emoticons, and other personal expressions of engagement. In order to examine the second subquestion, how the leader positions herself in relation to the group, the leader's politeness strategies when making requests were identified.

Analysis

Building trust and promoting in-group solidarity

The Agenda-leader uses an informal, personal, and emotional style in most of her messages to the team. By using in-group identity markers she employs positive politeness strategies (cf. Brown & Levinson, 1987, p. 102). This is evident in how she addresses the group as a whole, how she creates metaphors and narrative schemas for the group to identify with, in how she provides feedback to the group, and finally how she uses emoticons to mitigate directives and to intensify expressives.

When posting messages to the whole Agenda group, the leader addresses her group by giving them characterizing *nicknames* ("Hi all letter-enthusiasts," "Hi Agendaese"). The nicknames function as attributive categorization devices. By selecting these words the sender creates a category that serves to characterize, include, and even compliment the receivers. Alternatively, the leader could have selected more neutral greetings, such as for instance "Hi," "To all members of Agenda," "Dear Agenda-members" etc., in order to signal more distance. Assigning her group positive characteristics in the salutations signals liking and solidarity, and contributes to creating a picture of a unified and well-functioning group. The addressing devices function as a politeness strategy that claims common ground, promotes group belonging, and makes a positive identification with a community.

The Agenda-leader uses additional rhetorical resources to create an attractive image of the group. In communication with the text-designer, the information director and the group as a whole, the leader uses a certain *metaphor*. From the start of its existence, Agenda has pursued a central role in the different divisions of Telecom, so that more employees may benefit from their letter services and linguistic/stylistic expertise. To promote her work group, the leader introduces Agenda to different divisions in the company, a project that she calls the "blessing-round" and the "blessing-journey" in her messages to the group. These metaphors draw an intertextual reference to the Norwegian royal couple and the blessing journey that traditionally follows a coronation of Norwegian monarchy in order to receive the people's blessing. By drawing a parallel between Agenda's presentation project and the royal blessing journey, the leader places her group members in a narrative scheme in which the group's position in the organization appears as important as that of the royal's. By playing with a narrative schema that (in a Norwegian context) is well known, she may contribute to building a success story in which the participants may see themselves. The Agenda leader even presents this project as an effort to "sell" Agenda to different divisions ("I'm leaving for a meeting now, but will be back after 3pm. I am going to sell AgendaPrivate to the Marketing Division today :-)"). By using metaphors from the world of finance and market economy, she presents Agenda as a valuable product that may be sold.

The Agenda-leader informs the group of their results and how their work is being evaluated by the top managers. She also congratulates them explicitly when they have achieved good results ("Congratulations on the good work and keep it up; we're getting attention from the top"). The leader tells her group that they are drawing attention from the upper management, and simultaneously encourages the group to work hard. TCM is a large, multinational corporation with approximately 1,100 employees in Norway. The distance between the upper management and employees is great, and in this context there might be strong competition in gaining attention from the leaders, and to be noticed and appreciated as an employee. When the Agenda-leader repeatedly stresses that the Agenda group receiving attention from the top, and even congratulates them, she is creating a picture of Agenda as a unique group, with great importance and value for the company. This might in itself serve as a rhetorical device to motivate the group and create stronger internal relations.

In 26 of her 88 messages the Agenda-leader uses *emoticons* (smileys). The emoticons accompany speech acts such as requests, thanks, greetings, wishes, appraisals, and admissions.

On the one hand, emoticons soften directive speech acts that are threatening to the recipient's negative face (or face-threatening acts). The Agenda-leader uses emoticons to soften requests, corrections, rejections, and complaints (Skovholt et al., 2014):

Example 1
Hi Maria,
(...) We are supposed to have a CONSISTENT AND CLEAR communication style.
Nice with a little clarification here ... :-)
rgds Line

In Example 1, the leader of the Agenda work group (Line) asks the text designer (Maria) to give her some information ("Nice with a little clarification here"). The request, which is formulated in the indicative mood, is articulated as a personal wish, rather than an institutional request. Within this context it must be interpreted as an indirect speech act (Brown & Levinson, 1987, p. 70), which functions as a request for information. The request is accompanied by a smiley, which serves to soften the illocutionary force of the request. In other words, the emoticon serves to modify the propositional content of the utterance and functions as a softening hedge. The request is presented with less authority, and the emoticon serves to downgrade the authoritative position of the leader.

On the other hand, the Agenda-leader's emoticons intensify expressive speech acts such as thanks ("great and thanks :-)"), greetings ("Hi Anna, long time no see:-)"), wishes ("I hope the home guard training was fine :-)"), appraisals ("They think that Agenda does an important and good job!:-)") and admissions ("I have probably read the signature incorrectly, so there you're probably right :-)"). These are speech acts that in the data are directed to the recipient's positive face (Skovholt et al., 2014). The use of emoticons in the leader's emails contributes to creating an informal style and may reduce social distance in the asymmetrical relations. In the next section, we will see that the leader's informal style is additionally reflected through her way of making requests.

The leader positioning herself vis-à-vis subordinates – the use of requests

The Agenda-leader performs requests by using positive politeness strategies (Strategy 2) in most of her requests to her team members. She compensates for the FTA by presenting the request as declaratives, and as wishes and hopes, rather than interrogatively designed commands. The constructions that are most frequent are "I need help from you to" ("I need help from you concerning the budgets of letters, internet and mobile"), "Hope you have/can" ("Hope it is possible for you to contact") and "nice if" ("but nice if you send me your comments on email – progression is important"). She expresses herself in psychological terms (wishes and hopes), rather than in normative ones (obligation). By presenting the requests as a *need* for help, a *wish* or a *hope*, the leader presents the request as a *personal wish*, rather than an *institutional obligation*. All in all, this contributes to downplay her institutional role, in favour of a more personal role. Alternatively the Agenda-leader could have presented her requests in a normative way, for instance, by using interrogatives and imperatives. These are more explicit ways of enacting institutional power. However, by using less forceful strategies and presenting the requests as needs and hopes, the leader is presenting the requests as speech acts that need little compensation. She is optimistic, assuming reciprocity and that the recipients will comply with the request, something that simultaneously implies common ground and familiarity with the recipients (cf. Brown & Levinson, 1987, p. 102). Instead of explicitly enacting power, the Agenda-leader downplays her institutional role in in order to building socio-emotional ties with her subordinates.

Furthermore, the Agenda-leader also goes off record (Strategy 4) in making her requests. Rather than make the request directly, she leaves it to the recipient to interpret the request based on the context or workplace routine:

Example 2
Are, concerning our talk. Here comes the document which sums up the signatures. **At the bottom on the page you have an A-point for Business and Networks.**

In Example 2 LM presents a declarative. In light of the institutional context, the declarative must be interpreted as a request. An "A-point" (Action point) in Agenda is a task description. When the employee responsible receives one, he knows that it is a request. By using the declarative form, the leader LM avoids presenting the request directly, and thereby she manifests less power.

So far, we have seen that the Agenda-leader uses positive politeness (Strategy 2) and *indirect strategies* (Strategy 4) when performing requests to the members of Agenda. However, when the Agenda-leader performs requests to, or negotiates with, partners outside of Agenda, she uses more *direct strategies*. These are often followed by an appeal to authority, or are anchored in her professional role as a leader:

Example 3
Hi Lise Marit,
Long time no see : -) I hope everything is okay in Steinkjer!! We in Agenda need your help to find concrete examples of sms's which we send our customers from Steinkjer. **Our leader in TCMP, Bente Knudsen, requested** an overview of the sms-texts. Will you [...] Thanks in advance.
Rgds Line

Example 4
Hi Katrine!
In Agenda we have for a long while worked with signatures **from Bente's wish** – and created a document for signatures in letters from TCMP. See attached document. [...] Can we [...]?
Thanks in advance!!!
Rgds Line

Example 5
Hi Stein! Thanks for info about a very good service! As leader of AgendaPrivate I have some comments/questions:
[...]
– Concerning Per Harald's title **it was decided in Bente Knudsens meeting** that the title is [...] and nice if the title could be changed to this in your letter.
Rgds Line

In Examples 3, 4, and 5 the speech acts are directed to partners outside of the Agenda group. The leader's requests are more direct, or baldly on record, than the request to her subordinates. The requests are for-mulated as interrogatives (Will you [...], Can we [...]). According to Brown and Levinson (1987) utterances such as: "Can you pass the salt" are indirect, but have become fully conventionalized and the FTA is no longer off record. In addition, in Example 5 LM refers to her own role as a leader, before she presents the request. This is a way of providing a contextual frame for the request as well as legitimizing her right to perform requests. In the examples above she refers to her superordinate, Bente Knudsen, also to legitimize and ground her request.

According to Ho (2011), referring to a third party is an interdiscursive or intertextual device, which functions as "distanc[e] the leader from the discourse and thus divert [...] the possible forthcoming resentment to others." By referring to a third party, the email author (LM) could reduce the resistance to comply with the request. The recipients, who might be unwilling to comply with the request, might feel less negatively toward the sender as the request originally was made by a third party, the authoritative Bente Knudsen (Ho, 2011, p. 2540).

In both examples, LM explicitly addresses and makes relevant her own authority or hierarchical position, in order to account for the request. This may be an efficient strategy to necessitate a quick response. As we shall see in the next example, the Agenda-leader also makes hierarchical positions and third parties relevant in order to reject a request or solve a conflict:

Example 6
Hi Eva! thanks for your response, but in my opinion too comprehensive. Abuse is one letter that needs a better tone of voice. As you saw in the previous mail, this is a letter that is sent from Internet, NOT a confirmation letter. Arvid wishes to prioritize this on behalf of TCM because we have increased bad will in this case. (cf. VG-article last week.)
[...]
Thanks in advance for your help on behalf of the abuse-group in Internet.
rgds Line

In a previous email, Line was criticized by a colleague in another department, Eva Engseth. Eva Engseth complained to Line that she has assigned new tasks to text designer Maria Monsen without consulting her (as MM's leader) to share information about the activity. Moreover, Engseth performs a whole range of requests to Line Myhre. In Example 6 Line Myhre *rejects* Eva Engseth's requests indirectly: first, by producing a dispreffered response ("thanks for your response, but [...]"); second, by giving an account ("Abuse is *one letter* that needs a better tone of voice"); and finally, by quoting a third party, the information director, Arvid Lervik's point of view (Arvid wishes to prioritize this) and Telecom's interests (on behalf of Telecom). Rejecting complaints and denying compliance with requests are FTAs. In this example Line Myhre performs her rejection of Eva Engseth on record, directly, and with very little effort at politeness. By underscoring words ("ett brev"/"one letter") and even using capital letters ("NOT"), she emphasizes the propositional content and signals strong emotional involvement and authority. By continuing to ground her rejection in Arvid Lervik's role as superordinate, and even copying him in, she shows that she has Lervik on her side. This strengthens her authority and makes it difficult for Engseth to reject the decision (cf. Skovholt & Svennevig, 2006).

Discussion

Summary

The Agenda-leader predominantly uses linguistic resources which are oriented towards an interpersonal level of communication. Her communication style is informal and displays a concern for the conversational partner's face.[4] The analysis identified four devices which promote in-group solidarity. First, by using addressing devices and positively charged she compliments (and categorizes) the members and invites them to identify with the picture/category she presents. Second, the leader makes use of metaphors as narrative devices. Metaphors such as "blessing journey" and "blessing round" contribute to creating a picture of the team as main characters in a success story. In addition, by using metaphors from economics ("to sell Agenda") the leader compares Agenda with a valuable product. Third, the Agenda-leader provides feedback to the group by informing them they have attention from top leaders. To have upper management's attention may signal that the group's work is making a real difference in the huge company. Providing this information may be a performance management device (Bell & Kozlowski, 2002), which might serve to strengthen relations within the team. Finally, she uses emoticons as a positive politeness strategy to soften requests and to intensify expressive utterances (Table 5.1).

A large part of the leader's messages to the group are requests. When she performs requests, she does not make her role as the leader explicitly relevant by being direct. Rather, she performs her directives in a with conventional indirectness and compensates for her requests by using positive politeness strategies that function to minimize the imposition. By presenting the requests as needs and hopes, she appears optimistic and assumes reciprocity. The Agenda-leader presupposes common ground and familiarity, something that makes her appear as an egalitarian leader who trusts her team members and encourages them

Table 5.1   Discursive devices used with group members

Discourse strategy	Example	Function
Addressing device	*Hi all letter enthusiasts* *Hi "Agendaese"*	Inclusion Complimentary
Metaphors	*blessing round* *blessing journey* *to sell Agenda*	Building success story Presenting the group as a valuable product
Feedback	*Congratulations on the good* *work and keep it up; we're* *getting attention from the top.*	Complimentary, appraising, encouraging, motivating and creating internal relations
Emoticons	*Nice with a little clarification* *here ... :-)* *Hi, Anna, long time no see:-)*	Softening directive speech acts Intensifying expressive speech acts
Requests performed as declaratives and as needs and hopes	*I need help from you* *Hope it is possible for you to* *contact ...* *Nice if you send me your* *comments on email ...*	Conventionally indirect Being optimistic Claiming common ground Imposing less power to the request

to act independently. The use of indirectness and positive politeness corresponds with findings in Mullany (2004) and the "Language in the Workplace project" (Holmes & Marra, 2004; Mullany, 2004; Vine, 2004).

Despite the fact that the Agenda appears in her verbal form as egalitarian and located within in-group communication, she constitutes herself more as an authority in relation to external co-workers. When writing messages to out-group partners, she tends to use a more formal style, as shown in Table 5.2.

When performing requests, she uses more direct strategies and grounds the act of requesting her position as a leader, or refers to third parties as superordinates. By referring to hierarchical roles, she is making power categories overtly relevant. This may be an effective device to pursue quick compliance to a request. Second, the Agenda-leader makes hierarchical categories explicitly relevant when managing conflicts.

This study has primarily shown that the Agenda-leader does not make hierarchical categories relevant when writing messages to the team members. Her authority is downplayed in favour of an emotional, personal relationship with her employees. These findings illustrate Fairhurst's point that hierarchical categorizations often remain unspoken

Table 5.2 Discursive devices used with external co-workers

Discourse strategy	Example	Function
Requests performed as interrogatives	*Will you [...]* *Can we [...]*	Direct strategies Imposing more power
Referring to a third person	<u>*Our leader in TCMP, Bente Knudsen,*</u> *requested an overview of the sms-text.* *In Agenda we have for a long while worked with signatures* <u>*from Bente's wish*</u> *– and [...]*	Placing the responsibility of the request to a superordinate Convincing the addressee to comply with the request Avoiding performing the request on behalf of oneself and maintaining harmonious relationship
Referring to own position as a leader	*As a leader of AgendaPrivate I have some comments/ questions: [...]*	Imposing more power to the request
Rejecting a request without politeness strategies and copying in superordinate	*Hi, Eva! Thanks for your response, but in my opinion too comprehensive [...]*	Strengthening own authority Imposing more power Makes it difficult to reject the leader's decision

(Fairhurst, 2007). Agenda-leader Line Myhre does not need to explicitly qualify herself as a each time she makes a request. Her appointed role as the leader of Agenda gives her an exclusive right to make requests to which members are obliged to respond. However, by using politeness strategies, the leader balances the need to accomplish certain tasks with caring for her addressees' face (cf. Darics, 2010). In addition, the institutional role is enacted implicitly by the rhetorical devices identified in this study. Her leadership role is constituted by and through the actions that she performs. Evaluating, motivating, and requesting are leadership actions (Vine, 2004). When Line Myhre posts messages to out-group co-workers, she does not have the same exclusive right, or cannot take for granted that the recipients will comply with her requests, since she is not their leader. Therefore, these requests need to be seen as grounded in her institutional role, or anchored in a superordinate's wish, decision or demand. Highlighting the role of the author may effect a higher chance of request compliance and simultaneously contribute to maintaining a harmonious relationship with her colleagues (cf. Ho, 2011, p. 2546).

Doing leadership is building trust

The leadership carried out in Agenda seems to a great extent to be grounded on trust. In the present chapter, this has been exemplified by the addressing devices, the nicknames, and the leader's use of positive politeness when performing requests. As mentioned, one of the challenges for leaders of virtual teams is to duplicate the two key functional leader roles to the virtual team (team development and performance management). According to Bell and Kozlowski (2002), this includes the leader's need to "closely monitor any changes in environmental conditions." Additionally, it includes motivating team members to "commit strongly to the overall team effort and need to facilitate team coherence, especially under high intensity conditions." In virtual teams, as in Agenda, where people rarely meet face-to-face, these functions are challenged. However, the leader seems to attempt to create a positive climate in the group, both with rhetorical devices, such as giving the group a nickname, and by providing receipts and acknowledgments in minimal responses. These characteristics belong to the team-development function (Bell & Kozlowski, 2002). In addition, arranging regular face-to-face meetings belongs to the performance management function. To conclude, it appears that the leader under study employs both of these important leader functions.

Computer-mediated communication provides great opportunities for leaders to distribute important information, make requests of and monitor their members. Even though the team members are physically distant, the technology facilitates constraint-free communication and "hyperconnectivity," that is, "the availability for people to communicate anywhere and anytime" (Quan-Haase & Wellman, 2006, p. 285). Email may foster social presence to a greater extent than face-to-face, in the sense that email messages are persistent and thus have more pervasive force. This makes it possible for leaders to appear powerful, even at a distance. Interestingly, with respect to the number of messages, the reminders and extent of feedback (Skovholt & Svennevig, 2013), the Agenda-leader appears as a powerful leader, displaying her authoritative position within the group's hierarchy. Simultaneously, her methods of creating in-group solidarity and performing requests show that her institutional role is understated as she enacts egalitarian leadership, building socio-emotional ties within the team.

Notes

1. For a definition of virtual team, see Skovholt, 2009, p. 66. This chapter is developed from the author's PhD thesis.

2. All the names of persons, groups, and departments in the data are replaced by pseudonyms. The emails were originally written in Norwegian, but are translated into English here.
3. For a brief discussion on the limitation of the politeness theory, see Skovholt, 2009, pp. 57f.
4. The emails from the leader to the group did not display the opposite style, such as, for instance, by using imperatives, going baldly on record, or using devices that foreground her power and the asymmetric discursive roles.

References

Arminen, I. (2005) *Institutional Interaction: Studies of Talk at Work*. Aldershot: Ashgate.

Asmuß, B. (2008). Performance appraisals: Preference organization in assessment sequences. *Journal of Business Communication, 45* (4), 408–429.

Asmuβ, B., & Svennevig, J. (2009). Meeting talk: An introduction [Special Issue]. *Journal of Business Communication, 46* (1), 3–22.

Bell, B. S., & Kozlowski, S. W. J. (2002). A typology of virtual teams implications for effective leadership. *Group and Organization Management, 27* (1), 14–49.

Berry, G. R. (2011). Enhancing effectiveness on virtual teams. Understanding why traditional team skills are insufficient. *Journal of Business Communication, 48* (2), 186–206.

Boden, D. (1994). *The Business of Talk. Organizations in Action*. Cambridge: Polity Press.

Brown, P., & Levinson, S. C. (1987). *Politeness: Some Universals in Language Usage*. Cambridge: Cambridge University Press.

Clifton, J. (2006). A conversation analytical approach to business communication: The case of leadership. *Journal of Business Communication, 43* (3), 202–219.

Darics, E. (2010). Politeness in computer-mediated discourse of a virtual team. *Journal of Politeness Research-Language Behaviour Culture, 6* (1), 129–150. doi: 10.1515/jplr.2010.007.

Darics, E. (2012). Instant Messaging in work-based virtual teams: The analysis of non-verbal communication used for the contextualisation of transactional and relational communicative goals. PhD thesis, Loughborough University, Loughborough.

Darics, E. (2014). Digital media in workplace interactions. In A. Georgakopoulou & T. Spilioti (Eds), *The Routledge Handbook of Language and Digital Communication*. London: Routledge.

Drew, P., & Heritage, J. (Eds) (1992). *Talk at Work. Interaction in Institutional Settings*. Cambridge: Cambridge University Press.

Dürscheid, C., & Frehner, C. (2011). Email communication. In Herring, S., Stein, D., & T. Virtanen (Eds), *Pragmatics of Computer-Mediated Communication* (pp. 35–54). Berlin/Boston: De Gruyter Mouton.

Fairhurst, G. (2007). *Discursive Leadership. In Conversation with Leadership Psychology*. Los Angeles, CA: Sage.

Goffman, E. (1967). *Interaction Ritual: Essays on Face to Face Behavior*. Garden City, NY: Doubleday.

Heritage, J. (1984). *Garfinkel and Ethnomethodology.* Cambridge and New York: Polity Press.

Heritage, J. (2011). The interaction order and clinical practice: Some observations on dysfunctions and action steps. *Patient Education and Counselling, 84* (3), 338–343.

Ho, V. (2011). What functions do intertextuality and interdiscursivity serve in request e-mail discourse? *Journal of Pragmatics, 43* (10), 2534–2547. doi: 10.1016/j.pragma.2011.04.002.

Holmes, J. (2005). Leadership talk: How do leaders 'do mentoring' and is gender relevant? *Journal of Pragmatics, 37*, 1779–1800.

Holmes, J., & Marra, M. (2004). Leadership and managing conflict in meetings. *Pragmatics, 14*, 439–462.

Iacono, C. S., & Weisband, S. P. (1997). Developing trust in virtual teams. *Proceedings of the Thirtieth Hawaii International Conference on System Sciences, 2* (7–10) January, 412–420. Los Alamitos, CA: IEEE Computer Society Press.

Jarvenpaa, S. L., & Leidner, D. E. (1999). Communication and trust in global virtual teams. *Organization Science, 10* (6), 791–815.

Kankaanranta, A. (2005). "Hej Seppo, Could you pls comment on this!" – internal email communication in Lingua Franca English in a multinational company, PhD thesis, University of Jyväskylä, Centre for Applied Language Studies.

Malhotra, A., Majchrzak, A., & Rosen, B. (2007). Leading virtual teams. *Academy of Management Perspectives, 21* (1), 60–70. doi: 10.5465/amp.2007.24286164.

Mullany, L. (2004). Gender, politeness and institutional power roles: Humour as tactic to gain compliance in workplace business meetings. *Multilingua, 23*, 13–37.

Quan-Haase, A., & Wellman, B. (2006). Hyperconnected networks: Computer-mediated community in a high-tech organization. In C. Heckscher & P. S. Adler (Eds), *The Firm as a Collaborative Community. Reconstructing Trust in the Knowledge Economy* (pp. 281–333). Oxford: Oxford University Press.

Skovholt, K., & Svennevig, J. (2006). Email copies in work-place interaction. *Journal of Computer-Mediated Communication, 12* (1), article 3. Retrieved from: http://jcmc.indiana.edu/vol12/issue1/skovholt.html.

Skovholt, Karianne (2009). Email Literacy in the Workplace. *A study of Interaction Norms, Leadership Communication, and Social Networks in a Norwegian Distributed Work Group.* PhD-dissertation. University of Oslo: Faculty of Education. Unpublished PhD-dissertation.

Skovholt, K., & Svennevig, J. (2013). Responses and non-responses in workplace emails. In S. Herring, S. Dieter, & T. Virtanen (Eds), *Pragmatics of Computer-Mediated Communication* (pp. 589–612). Berlin: De Gruyter Mouton.

Skovholt, K., Grønning, A., & Kankaanranta, A. (2014). The Communicative Functions of Emoticons in Workplace E-Mails: :-). *Journal of Computer-Mediated Communication, 19*, 780–797.

Statistics Norway (2013). Bruk av IKT i næringslivet [The use of ICT in business life]. Retrieved September 9, 2014 from: http://www.ssb.no/teknologi-og-innovasjon/statistikker/iktbrukn.

Stubbe, M., Lane, C., Hilder, J., Vine, E., Vine, B., Marra, M., Holmes, J., & Weatherall, A. (2003). Multiple discourse analyses of a workplace interaction. *Discourse Studies, 5* (3), 351–389.

Vine, B. (2004). *Getting Things Done at Work: The Discourse of Power in Workplace Interaction.* Philadelphia, PA: John Benjamins.

Wellman, B. (2001). Physical place and cyberplace: The rise of personalized networks. *International Urban and Regional Research, 25* (2), 227–252.

Yoo, Y., & Alavi, M. (2004). Emergent leadership in virtual teams: What do emergent leaders do? *Information and Organization, 14,* 27–58.

6

Swearing Is E-Business: Expletives in Instant Messaging in Hong Kong Workplaces

Bernie Chun Nam Mak and Carmen Lee

Introduction

This chapter explores an area that has received little attention in the field of discourse analysis, namely the use of expletives in computer-mediated workplace discourse. Generally, expletives have been associated with negative attributes such as being uneducated, anti-social, over-emotive, and provocative (Jay & Janschewitz, 2008). Nevertheless, scholars have contended that swearing can generate normal communicative effects (Christie, 2013). Early studies (e.g., Chaika, 1980; Hutton & Bolton, 2005) noted that swearing as covert prestige can bond adolescents in the street; some recent works (e.g., Daly et al., 2004) have discovered that the use of expletives in backstage workplace talk is strategic, rational, and business-oriented. But still, as Jay (2000) acknowledged, because of the taboo nature of swearing and the difficulty in collecting data, it has received very limited attention in academic research. With the increasing reliance on digital communication at work, swearing takes place not only in face-to-face interaction, but also in computer-mediated communication (CMC), such as in instant messaging, in the workplace. Despite a handful of scholarly works (e.g., Darics, 2013; Quan-Haase et al., 2005; Stephens, 2008) that have articulated the linguistic features of workplace instant messaging, there has been generally little research on swearing in workplace instant messaging, especially in Asian contexts. Studies on swearing by second language speakers of English have been equally scant (Nelson, 2014). Drawing on sets of English instant messages[1] produced by Hong Kong Chinese workers in two Hong Kong trading firms, this chapter investigates the impact of swearing in instant messaging in the backoffice as well as the involved acting out of identity and power.

The workplace, expletives, and instant messaging

In the body of research that explores different speech events (e.g., humor, small talk) in workplace discourse, the majority have drawn on Wenger's (1998) Communities of Practice (CofP) to theorize why these communicative behaviors can be considered to be both strategic and social in nature (see Holmes & Meyerhoff, 1999). According to Wenger (1998), a workplace can be understood as an ongoing process sustained by a CofP. He proposed that a workplace CofP contains three indispensable elements, namely joint enterprises, mutual engagements, and shared repertoires. Joint enterprises are the short- and long-term goals that make colleagues united and accountable to the workplace; mutual engagements are the regular and irregular ties through which colleagues achieve joint enterprises; and shared repertoires are the symbolic and behavioral norms gradually cultivated and repetitively practiced by colleagues in the process of mutual engagement. As joint enterprises keep emerging from the workplace, mutual engagements are continually needed, and shared repertoires are enacted in everyday workplace interaction. Following this conceptualization, recurring speech events as shared repertoires are ultimately aimed at getting things done (Holmes & Stubbe, 2003). Wenger (1998) additionally argued that social practices in a CofP enable a participating member not only to adhere to collective and existing norms for overall goals, but also in reification according to individual, immediate needs. This accounts for colleagues behaving differently in the same speech event when accomplishing the same goal. More importantly, as Darics (2010b) observed, the existence of a CofP is largely defined by its members' practice, whether offline or online (also see Wenger & Snyder, 2000). This elucidates the suitability for using communities of practice as the theoretical framework in the present study, which focuses on swearing as a speech event.

Use of expletives and swearing at work

Expletives are commonly referred to in lay terms as cursing, dirty words, and bad or obscene language (Hutton & Bolton, 2005; Stone et al., 2010). Here we use the terms expletives and swearwords interchangeably. Theoretically, the use of a swearword conveys two kinds of meaning: the literal, denotative meaning based on semantic knowledge, and the figurative, connotative meaning in a particular context. According to Stapleton (2010), denotative meanings of English swearwords fall into three taboo areas: excretory (e.g., shit, asshole), sexual (e.g., cunt, prick), and profanity (e.g., goddamn). Sociolinguists (e.g., Adams, 1999; Hughes, 2006) have reached a consensus that the connotative meanings of a swearword, which are stereotypically violent and offensive in public contexts, usually dominate over its denotative meanings as codified in dictionaries. Nevertheless, Jay (1981) and Christie (2013) suggest that the interpretation of the connotative meanings sometimes requires the understanding of the denotative meanings at first, especially those denoting sexual aggression (e.g., Moore, 2012), bodily behavior (e.g., Hobbs, 2013; Huang & Tian, 1990), and criminal concepts (e.g., Bolton & Hutton, 1995). Davis (1989) even argued that an expletive can be used literally in some intimate settings. In view of these observations, there are at least three approaches to understanding swearing in discourse:

- Using an expletive in which the denotative meanings are largely omitted (e.g., you are fucking lucky!);
- Using an expletive in which the denotative meanings are partly required to interpret the connotative meanings (e.g., what a cocksucker!); and
- Using an expletive in which the denotative meanings are largely retained (e.g., I need a piss after the long movie).

As Jay and Janschewitz (2008) observed, however, non-linguists are seldom aware of the multiple functions of expletives and thus they tend to disapprove of swearing behaviors. In 2013, a Hong Kong schoolteacher, Alpais Lam, was filmed shouting profanity at police officers to express her dissatisfaction with how the police handled a confrontation between protestors. The video immediately went viral, with netizens criticizing Lam for setting a bad example for her students (Kao, 2013). In reality, expletives have never ceased to exist for expressing feelings and attitudes in the street. Sometimes their historical taboo status even disappears with the shifting of social values (Hobbs, 2013). Some researchers (e.g., Andersson & Trudgill, 1990; Chen, 2004; Jay, 1981) have found different innovative uses of swearwords. In the workplace, some of their adaptive or maladaptive functions may imply affinity (Daly et al., 2004; Huang & Tian, 1990) and socialize into the subordinates' CofP (Mak, 2009). One interesting study is by Cook (2013) who explores the historical use of swearwords at war, and speculates that they were conducive to distancing soldiers from their previous civilian lives, relieving their internalized emotions, and singing for entertainment in such a dead-or-alive workplace. If swearing has such potential for interpersonal effect in the battlefield, it is likely to be productive, at least to some extent, in other workplaces as well. Unfortunately, research with respect to swearing at work is still in its infancy.

While the functions of expletives in the workplace remain under-explored, researchers have noted the construction of identity and power during the swearing process. For instance, Bailey and Timm (1976) and Hopper et al. (1980) noted that the use of expletives pertains to the situated identity that the speaker wants to create at the swearing moment. Jay (1981) explored how people swear to exercise power to redefine a situated context, while Chaika (1982) examined how swearing is used to express resistance to authority. Hughes (1992) added that those who swear actually marginalize those who are expected not to swear, and that expletives are often used as a tool to break official rules or formal norms. In these cases, identity and power start to fluctuate when one swears at another. These observations about swearing and power may also be applicable to the setting of instant messaging, because instant messaging generally imitates spontaneous speech in a community.

Instant messengers and instant messaging in the workplace

Instant messaging is a form of CMC that takes place via Instant Messengers (e.g., Windows Live Messenger[2] (WLM) and Tencent QQ), which allow a user to exchange synchronous instant messages with people or groups who have been added as contacts and have logged in through Internet-linked computers (e.g., Baron, 2010). Recently developed instant messengers have been integrated into social-network websites, surrounded by other CMC genres such as emailing and micro-blogging (e.g., Ellison et al., 2011). Users can always predesign their nicknames, head icons, recent sharing, and sometimes away messages before they interact through an instant messenger.

Much research into instant messaging has focused on interpersonal exchanges in non-professional settings. Among the limited studies of instant messaging in the workplace, Quan-Haase et al. (2005) examined how colleagues shift between media such as the telephone and instant messaging. From a linguistic point of view, Isaacs et al. (2002) pointed out that colleagues usually tolerate unimportant grammatical mistakes and rejection of instant response, and that they tend to omits opening and ending turns. Darics (2010a) concentrated on the use of ellipsis dots, emoticons, capitalization, laughter, and backchannels for politeness reasons in a virtual workplace; in another study, Darics (2013) explored how letter repetition in instant messaging goes beyond phonetic purposes to indicate intimacy and collegiality among colleagues. Other research also touched on the social or pedagogical functions of instant messaging at work, namely joking (Handel & Herbsleb, 2002), performing phatic exchanges (Chung & Nam, 2007), maintaining a minimal sense of group work (Quan-Haase et al., 2005), sharing work-related memory (Jacobs, 2006), arranging multitasks, and recording workplace knowledge for newcomers (Mak, Chui et al., 2012). There have been quantitative studies (e.g., Avrahami & Hudson, 2006; Iqbal & Horvitz, 2007) that articulated the communication features (e.g., response time, message length) of Instant Messaging at work as well.

The above literature survey suggests that the taboo nature of swearwords infuses them with the potency to exchange different meanings in a face-to-face or computer-mediated setting. Understanding its operation in professional communication is not only useful for linguists to conceptualize the register of swearing, but also inspiring for teachers and trainers to nurture their students with an appropriate attitude and practice towards the phenomenon. In view of this, the present study primarily investigates how expletives in workplace instant messaging have become functional to business, and explores how identity and power are constructed through strategic uses of expletives in online workplace discourse.

Data and methodology

The examples in this chapter come from a larger database of 60,000 English words of instant messaging that were collected from three white-collar Hong Kong workplaces in the period of March 2012–September 2013. For the purpose of this chapter, we focus on two workplaces. The first, Superstar Electronics Holdings (SEH-HK) (pseudonym), was a trading company engaged in the export business of computer hardware. The main participants were 15 full-time employees in the merchandising unit, who were Hong Kong Chinese ranging from 25 to 50 years old. The second research site was Sunshine Toys Limited (STL-HK) (pseudonym), in which nine full-time employees in the wholesale team were involved in the study. Seven of them were Hong Kong Chinese, while the other two were Shantouese who were based at the company's Shantou office in mainland China. The majority of these participants communicated regularly via instant messaging in addition to face-to-face talk. Their first language was Cantonese, and their English proficiency was largely non-native, but they preferred using English on instant messengers to save typing time. SEH-HK usually used WLM (or Skype later due to the discontinuation of WLM); STL-HK mainly used WLM (or Skype) and QQ.

In view of our research focus, we were interested in colleagues' internal instant messaging that was conducted mainly in English. After consideration of the criteria, six employees of SEH-HK and seven of STL-HK were invited to provide logs of their instant messages through computer-mediated files converted by the print-screen and file-export methods. In addition to words, we also requested the participants to supply necessary visual and online-behavioral information based on our interpretation of data in the open coding stage. After selective coding, we conducted face-to-face follow-up interviews with these 13 participants in order to gather contextual information on the representative examples. We particularly asked what had motivated them to swear in the way shown in the log, and other opinions they might have about the contents and development of the talk in general. Thirty instant messaging conversations (4,000 English words in total) with swearwords from SEH-HK and 50 from STL-HK (9,000 English words in total) were selected for in-depth analysis in the study reported in this chapter.

Gee's (2011) model of discourse analysis

We employ Gee's (2011) model of discourse analysis to explore swearing in our data. In particular, we draw on the notions of *practice, identities,* and *politics* in his model. Practice refers to the conversational goals being achieved; identities are concerned with what similarities are stressed or unstressed; and politics refers to what asymmetries of social goods result. The major tools we have adopted to analyze the examples are situated meanings (small "d") and discourses (capital "D").[3] The former addresses the contextual meanings in a single instant messaging interaction, while the latter addresses the broader process of language use developed by social–cultural practices in a CofP.

Swearing in workplace instant messaging

In our study, the most commonly found expletives in the two workplaces are *bloody, shit, damn,* and *fuck.* Colleagues usually swear when they have received instructions from their superiors. They also use more expletives when there are problems in shipping or express mail, when negotiation processes become difficult, and when they perform small talk. Since the participants are not native speakers of English, their use of English swearwords may draw on their Cantonese swearing conventions (see Dewaele, 2004).

Swearing in instant messaging for business and transaction purposes

The SEH-HK colleagues appear to swear more than the STL-HK members in task-oriented talk, but most circumstances in this regard originate from the similar goal of doing more business with fewer hurdles. In Example 1, a subordinate in SEH-HK is "fucked" through a top-down directive from his supervisor. Ricky, an assistant trade officer, was assigned to a deal with a Turkish buyer. The buyer, Kazi, had requested an older model of hard-disk enclosure with an adaptor; but Tommy, Ricky's immediate superior, told him to suggest a newer model.

Example 1

	Sender	Receiver	Message
1	Tommy	Ricky	ricky!!!!
→ 2	Tommy	Ricky	fuck you that kazi email us again
3	Tommy	Ricky	did you tell him we cant make that style with adaptor?
4	Ricky	Tommy	i reply him
5	Ricky	Tommy	tell him we have nwer models without use of adaptor
6	Tommy	Ricky	:@
→ 7	Tommy	Ricky	damn you should write clearly
8	Tommy	Ricky	dont just say newer model~~~
9	Tommy	Ricky	say our factory no longer produces this model
10	Tommy	Ricky	old model
11	Tommy	Ricky	it failed to pass the test you know
12	Ricky	Tommy	i see
13	Tommy	Ricky	leave this uncle to you
14	Tommy	Ricky	enjoy him :D

This example provides evidence for the use of expletives as an intensifier of directives in workplace instant messaging. However, the use needs to be interpreted with the unconventional use of emoticons and punctuation for communicating paralinguistic cues (e.g., Darics, 2010b). When Tommy calls Ricky, he imitates his shouting volume and aggressive tone by four exclamation marks (line 1). Subsequently, he initiates an imperative with the swearword "fuck" in the place of main verb (line 2). When asked why he "fucked" Ricky before scolding and questioning him (lines 2–3), Tommy in the interview explained:

> Like Cantonese, you swear fuck you before you complain the person in front of you. [This] was to show that I was angry at that point.

Hobbs (2013) divided the use of an expletive into literal use and figurative use. Here Tommy is using the expletive figuratively. The "fuck" carries anger directed at Ricky, but such anger needs to be understood on the basis of the denotative meaning that fucking is a penetrating behavior as a form of punishment. Additionally, the use is based on Tommy's knowledge of Cantonese swearing, as he implied in the interview. The grammatical construction of "fuck you" (line 2) and "damn you" (line 7) is ascribed to the formulaic saying of "屌你" in Cantonese swearing. Nevertheless, the swearing does not stop here. After Ricky retrieves how he communicated with Kazi (lines 4–5), Tommy shows an angry emoticon (line 6). Dresner and Herring (2010) state that such naked emoticons primarily communicate pragmatic meanings that map the speaker's facial expression (also see Provine et al., 2007). The pragmatic meanings are concretized in the next few lines, which include a series of directives proceeded by another swearword "damn" (lines 7–10), which is losing its offensive status nowadays (cf. Oliver & Rubin, 1975). While it intensifies the force of such directives, the degree is quickly decreased by the wave dashes (line 8), the informal term of address "uncle" to Kazi (line 13), and the humor "enjoy him" with the laughing face (line 14). They display a stylistic change from being bossy to being funny. When asked to explain these lines, Ricky in the interview reported:

> He sometimes laughs and uses foul language to ask people to do important and urgent things. [This] is easier to accept. And we sometimes name trouble[some] buyers like uncles, aunties, idiots [...] this is common for men and we get used to it.

Suggestively, the previous offensiveness, which is intensified by the swearwords, is mitigated by the computer-mediated paralinguistic cues afterwards. Throughout the conversation, Tommy's calling, swearing, questioning, and commanding Ricky emphasize his superior status in the hierarchy on the one hand, while on the other his later mitigating devices inch toward two less hierarchical selves. The supervisor not only shows his intellectuality of doing business, but also exercises his symbolic power by the strategic use of expletives in online communication. Ricky's passive and clear response also indicates his acceptance into the identity and power construction.

In another conversation in SEH-HK, a merchandiser trainee, Jenny, suggested processing a deal with an unimportant buyer from Taiwan by EXW (i.e., asking that buyer to come to the factory to collect the product) just now. Her official mentors, Charles and Ricky, believed that they should negotiate with different stakeholders before implementing EXW.

Example 2

	Sender	Receiver	Message
1	Charles	SEH-GRP	why not ask them to meet the moq?
2	Charles	SEH-GRP	we change the prepay
3	Jenny	SEH-GRP	–5%?
4	Charles	SEH-GRP	好難講, 睇餸食飯
			/hou2 naan4 gong2, tai2 sung3 sik6 faan6/
			[difficult to say, it depends]
→ 5	Ricky	SEH-GRP	shit
6	Ricky	SEH-GRP	just for this small buyer
7	Ricky	SEH-GRP	labour division jenny...
8	Ricky	SEH-GRP	I call the taiwan po
9	Ricky	SEH-GRP	you call john

As the Taiwan buyer wanted a small amount of products that did not meet the minimum order quantity (MOQ), Jenny suggested that SEH-HK ask the buyer to come to collect the products to save their delivery expenditure. Jenny's mentors, however, believed that they should persuade the buyer to purchase more and give her a better deal (lines 1–4). Now they go ahead in this direction. Ricky swears (line 5) before deciding the labor division (lines 6–9). It seems that the figurative use of "shit" is only directed at the "small buyer" (line 6). Yet, Ricky in the interview gave a surprising answer when asked to explain his swearing:

> Of course the deal requires some extra work, but we guys actually [felt] annoying [annoyed] when we need[ed] to include [Jenny]. I don't mean [that] she is troublesome. Every time when we [did] labor division, we had to think about her part because we had to let her learn but we could not give her difficult jobs. This is also workload.

Instead of intensifying the directives about calling John, the swearword is used as an implication of complaint about the careful consideration of the mentee when Ricky makes the decision on the labor division. His use of "shit" still projects his rank identity as someone's mentor, and implicates his authority over Jenny.

Example 3 exemplifies the use of *fuck*. The day before the conversation in the example, Patrick asked David to contact Peter in the mainland team to negotiate a price. David was asked to tell Peter to return a call to Patrick as well. Whereas David said that he had done so, Patrick did not hear from Peter, so just now he took the initiative to call him.

Example 3

	Sender	Receiver	Message
1	Patrick	David	i called him
2	Patrick	David	he said he forget and he will call the factory now
3	David	Patrick	i told him in qq
→ 4	Patrick	David	fuck your qq
5	Patrick	David	how many qq messages we make everyday?
6	Patrick	David	he will miss easily
7	David	Patrick	i see...sor

Hobbs (2013) proposed that when *fuck* is used as a transitive verb with a living direct object, it should be first interpreted as penetrating that living thing before moving to other possible connotations. Here, however, the direct object is the instant messenger QQ (line 4). What Patrick attacks, of course, is not the instant messenger, but the user of it. As the conversation unfolds, Patrick criticizes David for contacting Peter via QQ (lines 5–6), which might have led to messages being overlooked. The "fuck" is not only used to strengthen his criticism, but also carries the metalinguistic message about what counts as inappropriate use of QQ that makes the user worth offending. It consolidates Patrick's identity as the superior, and empowers him by imposing his view of using QQ on David. It is possible that, from Patrick's viewpoint, he is more competent in using instant messengers. This interpretation is supported by the acknowledgment and informal apology from David (line 7).

The above three examples demonstrate how swearwords are used in the process of giving directives to subordinates in a mitigated, non-ritualistic way. On the one hand, swearing primarily enforces the transmission of important transactional or business meanings; on the other hand, the usage generates subtle intrapersonal and interpersonal effects.

Swearing in instant messaging for affiliation and leisure purposes

Compared to the use of expletives in task-directed instant messaging, swearing in relational talk appears more loose, diversified, and humorous. Such usage takes place in STL-HK more than in SEH-HK. A typical instance is to swear at an outsider of the CofP, especially their business partners. Example 4 illustrates this through humorous use of innovative typography. In the morning before the conversation took place, Ricky had been to meet the business executive of a buying office. In the conversation, knowing that Ricky is back to the office, Charles asks him if there has been any development.

Example 4

	Sender	Receiver	Message
1	Charles	Ricky	how did he say?
2	Ricky	Charles	how did he say?
3	Ricky	Charles	he said
4	Ricky	Charles	"cif is a must or we can't make this business"
5	Ricky	Charles	he ask "do you know cif?"
6	Charles	Ricky	you should answer
→ 7	Charles	Ricky	"f????ck uuuu!!!"
8	Ricky	Charles	and I said
9	Ricky	Charles	"it is impossible for us to sign cif with this quantity"
10	Charles	Ricky	let's talk to Samuel first
→ 11	Ricky	Charles	really fuck him off
12	Charles	Ricky	relax
13	Charles	Ricky	you are not alone

In this episode, Charles suggests that Ricky should have sworn at the buyer, which is aimed at displaying emotional involvement and helping him release his anger (lines 6–7). After Ricky delimits the topic into the partner's impolite attitude and mimics how arrogant he sounded (lines 2–5), Charles appears to see Ricky's negative feelings at once and hence gives him such a recommendation. Nonetheless, the suggestion is not the common swearing expression "fuck you," but the wordplay "f????ck uuuu" plus three exclamation marks. When asked to explain why he had typed that way, Charles in the interview said:

> I learnt [it] from the Internet. The question mark means "what" like fill in the blanks and hides [the letter] "u," and the "u" after[wards] means "you" and the answer to that question mark. Funny right? I heard his experience and also felt angry but I thought he would find it funny.

The creative expletive is not invented by Charles. It is infused with unconventional punctuation marks (i.e. ????) and non-standard orthography (i.e., "u" as "you") (Herring, 2012). While the wordplay is intended to show understanding and attenuate Ricky's anger by making him laugh, Ricky continually whinges on his unpleasant meetings (lines 8–9), and he eventually cannot help swearing as well (line 11). Yet, Ricky's "fuck off" is different from Charles' "f????ck uuuu" in that the former mainly implicates his groan and moan about the buyer, while the latter is mainly aimed at cheering up Ricky. To that end, Ricky said in the interview:

> That guy [i.e., the business executive] was very impolite [so] I want[ed] to close [the] file. It was already bothering enough to go to their office and wait for a long time.

The meaning of "fuck off" used by Ricky is two-fold. While it connotatively signals his anger, it also implies the dictionary meaning of telling a troublemaker to go away. Although it is unclear how the business ends, the expletives result in much emphasis on their workgroup identity. That Charles plays out the expletive implies his intention to stress that he shares Ricky's feeling. After all, they are at the same rank and working closely with each other. On the other hand, when Ricky said "really fuck him off" (line 11), he echoes the cursing atmosphere formed by Charles. Likewise, they power up themselves through swearing at the stakeholder without his knowing. It is WLM backstage that allows them to do so.

Example 5 elucidates a humorous instance of swearing in STL-HK. Patrick is busy working with Ronald, a trade manager in the Shantou office, for an Indian distributor. The distributor had requested Patrick to post a sample by express mail, but did not mention who would be responsible for the charge. Patrick then made a long-distance call to the Indians.

Example 5

	Sender	Receiver	Message
1	Patrick	Ronald	Ronald
2	—	—	[Auto-reply] 您好，我现在有事不在，一会再和您联系。[nin2 hao3, wo3 xian4 zai4 you3 shi4 bu2 zai4, yi2 hui4 zai4 he2 nin2 lian2 xi4] /Hello, I am out, and I will reply to your message shortly./
→ 3	Patrick	Ronald	where are you fuckign when i need you?
4	—	—	[Auto-reply] 您好，我现在有事不在，一会再和您联系。
→ 5	Patrick	Ronald	fucking should do at night
6	—	—	[Auto-reply] 您好，我现在有事不在，一会再和您联系。
7	Ronald	Patrick	Back
→ 8	Ronald	Patrick	fucking at night?
→ 9	Patrick	Ronald	i talked with that fucking donnie

```
   10 Patrick Ronald   he refused to ask ups to come
   11 Patrick Ronald   he mean he refuse to pay for the sample
   12 Patrick Ronald   How
→  13 Ronald Patrick   if we ask factory again, they will fuck us...already
                       3 times
   14 Ronald Patrick   let me call factory
```

A remarkable point that arises in this snapshot is Patrick's creative use
of an expletive in QQ. While Ronald appears to be away according to
the system's auto-reply (lines 2, 4, 6), Patrick acts as if he was swearing
at him by swearing at the same system-generated message. When asked
why he did so, Patrick in the interview claimed:

> [I] was annoyed. It said he [was] not in front of [the] computer.
> I [had] some bad news [...] I [knew] he [was] out but when he came
> back he saw so many auto-replies [and] he [would] know I was chas-
> ing him.

His intended use of expletive seems both emotional and functional. He
plays with the auto-reply twice. The "fucking" is firstly used to display
his annoyance (line 3); its denotative meaning is largely omitted as
there is no evidence to justify any punishment or negative feeling from
Patrick to Ronald. In the second play of "fuck," in contrast, its literal
meaning of "having sex" is largely retained – so "fucking should do
at night" (line 5). The use overall can be interpreted to be humorous
swearing with an emphasis on atmosphere and intimacy (cf. Stapleton,
2010). The meaning is noted by Ronald when he comes back (line 8),
but Patrick quickly moves on to deliver the bad news (lines 9–11), in
which he uses "fucking" as a modifier again. Having learned about the
extra expenditure, Ronald joins in swearing by imagining how the factory will complain as well (line 13). Regarding why he swore as well,
Ronald in the interview explained:

> Every time we talk about him [i.e., Donnie] we want to fuck. We
> [have] talk[ed] for two months.

For Ronald, his swearing is to release work stress resulting from dealing
with this buyer, behind which is the implication of a workgroup identity shared with his legitimate partner in this deal, Patrick. As Nelson
(2014) observed, swearwords can be used as a marker of social identity
to express out-group distance in the workplace. But still, it is Patrick

who crafts such an identity through swearing at the auto-reply at first. So to speak, the expletive is a symbol to stress their shared negative feelings and attitude toward this buyer. Despite this, Patrick has increased the power of agenda-setting (cf. Holmes et al., 1999; Wodak et al., 2012) through his initial swearing, which frames the informality of the whole interaction. He also displays his technological skills through the innovative use of expletive targeting at the answering machine. It is the designed affordances of QQ that enables him to do so, because not all instant messengers support the function of auto-reply.

In the last example, the swearwords are used literally, to some extent, in social talk. Patrick saw his subordinate, Jeff, keep going to the washroom in the morning.

Example 6

	Sender	Receiver	Message
1	Patrick	Jeff	morning
2	Jeff	Patrick	morning
3	Patrick	Jeff	what happen? you go out and come back
4	Jeff	Patrick	stomache for 3 days
→ 5	Patrick	Jeff	why? no shit?
→ 6	Patrick	Jeff	or shit too much?
7	Patrick	Jeff	(lol)
8	Jeff	Patrick	@@
9	Patrick	Jeff	normal for adult men, we always sit
10	Patrick	Jeff	drink some cool tea
11	Jeff	Patrick	yes~~
→ 12	Patrick	Jeff	if you don't shit you will becoe busiess shit
13	Jeff	Patrick	(rotfl)

Although Jeff uses the politic English word "stomache" (typo of stomach ache) (line 4), Patrick uses "shit" twice when trying to find out what happened to Jeff (lines 5–6). The laughing-out-loud face suggests his informal and inoffensive tone (line 7). "Shit" here should be largely interpreted denotatively, which is rare in everyday settings. When asked about this, Patrick in the interview said:

> I don't know other [sayings] except poo, but "shit" [is] more common to me. We are men [who] don't mind.

Here Patrick additionally implicates how his limited knowledge of English slang may have motivated him to use the expletive. However, this does not deter him from further playing around the swearword. After Jeff agrees with Patrick's opinion about the "man problem" (lines 9–11), Patrick jokes that not shitting (i.e., suffering from constipation) will make a "business shit" (i.e., an unpleasant businessman) (line 12). The former shit literally refers to the bodily function; whereas the latter is with the connotative meanings of some negative attributes for a businessman. It is notable that the wordplay underlies the importance of business performance to Patrick. As he said in the interview:

> Business nowadays is tough enough and we cut off many staff [members], so we don't want sick guys. We want all people [i.e., STL-HK members] to [be] healthy to make money.

The talk surrounding "shit" not only highlights their gender identity (particularly when Patrick refers to the prototypical problem of constipation shared by adult men), but also links this gender identity to their profession through the final humorous remarks. However, such humor hides his authority and status in that it reminds Jeff of the importance of business in a top-down direction.

Discussion and conclusion

Unlike swearing in face-to-face contexts that sometimes appears to be spontaneous and accidental due to anger, surprise, and frustration (Hughes, 2006; Moore, 2012), the use of expletives in instant messaging requires conscious input through the keyboard. As Thurlow (2001) contended, the use of swearwords with creative typography is characterized by subverted traditional rules of writing. This is why swearing in WLM and QQ was more strategic and intentional in achieving transactional and relational goals in our corpus. Since our participants were second language speakers of English, they might not have acquired a wide range of English expletives, which might explain why only *fuck*, *shit*, and *damn* were widely used in our examples. Nevertheless, they were non-trivial in that they could be used transactionally in stressing directives (Example 1), whingeing over extra work (Example 2), and lecturing subordinates (Example 3); relationally, they could show shared negative feelings (Example 4), preface bad news (Example 5), and send regards to colleagues (Example 6). We argue that swearwords are versatile and functional in workplace instant messaging.

In this chapter, we also portrayed through our representative examples that colleagues' use of expletives interacted with both the denotative and connotative meanings. To our participants, the former was grounded on dictionaries, but the latter was based on their shared perception of the offensiveness of swearing in the white-collar workplace (cf. Nelson, 2014) and mutual experience of swearing as non-native English speakers in Hong Kong (cf. Danet, 2013; Dewaele, 2004; Jay & Janschewitz, 2008). These meanings not only constitute the members' participation in circulating the swearing norms in a CofP, but also fulfill their reification to satisfy their goals of instant messaging in a particular moment. Considering the discourse processes, we propose that the application and interpretation of swearwords in workplace talk depend on the shared repertoires of a CofP; and expletives generate an indirect effect on its joint enterprises, and that appropriate practices of swearing strengthen colleagues' mutual engagements. For example, computer-mediated paralinguistic cues, namely the non-standard use of numbers, punctuation, emoticons, and capitalization, definitely played an essential role in our dataset (see Herring, 2012). The swearing discourse become complicated with any associated offline workplace events and when it appears within other speech events, such as humor and code-switching.

Our analysis also illustrated how the use of expletives interplayed with the construction of identities and power. Identities and power were always fluid in the swearing moments in our examples. For instance, swearing could imply an emphasis on the identity of a superior (Examples 1, 2, 3) and the identity of peers in a workgroup (Examples 4, 5), and it could move the stressed gender identity to professional identity as well (Example 6). Likewise, the use of expletives was usually attached to the consolidation of authority (Examples 1, 2), increase of status (Example 3), control of topics and conversational atmosphere (Examples 4, 6), and display of technological ability (Example 5). In line with Baruch and Jenkins (2007), we found that swearwords could be an indirect indicator of identity and power in a workplace. Consequently, we propose that expletives, if normatively used in colleagues' instant messaging, provide an implicit channel to enact official authority or refigure institutional roles, resulting in their desired power distance and situated identities respectively. We believe that the perceived online autonomy further produces a superficially free cyberspace at work for ongoing acts of identity and power.

To conclude, we suggest that expletives in instant messaging can be a powerful tool, which needs an optimistic lens to observe or investigate. Swearing can be part of e-business. While the social stereotypes and popular myths permeating in a national culture can legitimize a CofP's use or avoidance of swearwords (Stapleton, 2010), any prescriptive ideas about swearing should not overwhelm the local conventions in an organizational culture. It typically happens backstage, but its influence and meaningfulness exist across and center stage. Since public-facing colleagues are often constrained by the requirement of presenting themselves as a nice person (Coates, 2000), they tend to suppress and hide their negative feelings to outsiders. In that case, swearing backstage *can* be a channel to release such pressure. Swearing in internal instant messaging, which outsiders cannot address, can be conducive to a relaxing time for releasing work-oriented pressure. Therefore, we extend the view of Hobbs (2013) that practitioners, rather than viewing all swearwords as inherently bad, should pay more attention to other possible connotations of and the reasons for using an expletive in a workplace interaction from an in-group perspective. As Jay and Janschewitz (2008) ventured, the use of expletives is not always a result of highly confrontational or aggressive acting, but often part of regular and normal conversation in a community. Still, swearing within two or more set of communities and cultural systems may cause miscommunication and undermining of relationships (Christie, 2013), so appropriate understanding of the background of conversational participant is exceedingly important. Finally, as Jacobs (2006) concluded, Instant Messaging is a productive response to the fast capitalist workplace, which is characterized by flexibility, adaptability, collaboration, and self-efficacy. With the prevalence of smartphones, colleagues can send instant messages not only on the desktop but also on their smartphones (e.g., Whatsapp has become a popular mobile instant messenger). Organizations should not neglect the role of instant messengers that allow their colleagues to perform any speech events, probably anytime and anywhere.

Notes

1. Since instant messengers are continually being upgraded, the description of instant messaging offered in this chapter may be different from what is actually in use at the time this chapter is read.
2. Windows Live Messenger was discontinued in 2013 (except in Mainland China); all existing users were requested to migrate to Skype from April 8, 2013 onwards.
3. The concepts of the lowercase "d" and capital "D" are used in the first and second editions of Gee's model. The former is conceptualized to be "situated meanings" and the latter to be "discourses" in the third edition, i.e., Gee (2011).

References

Adams, M. (1999). Another effing euphemism. *American Speech, 74* (1), 110–112.
Andersson, L., & Trudgill, P. (1990). *Bad Language*. Oxford, MA: Blackwell.

Avrahami, D., & Hudson, S. E. (2006). Communication characteristics of instant messaging: Effects and predictions of interpersonal relationships. *CSCW'06 Proceedings of the 2006 ACM Conference on Computer-Supported Cooperative Work* (pp. 505–514). New York, NY: ACM Press.

Bailey, L. A., & Timm, L. A. (1976). More on women's – and men's – expletives. *Anthropological Linguistics, 18*, 438–449.

Baron, N. S. (2010). Discourse structures in instant messaging: The case of utterance breaks. *Language@Internet, 4*. Retrieved from: http://www.languageatinternet.org/articles/2010/2651.

Baruch, Y., & Jenkins, S. (2007). Swearing at work and permissive leadership culture. *Leadership and Organization Development Journal, 28* (6), 492–507.

Bolton, K., & Hutton, C. (1995). Ban and banned language: Triad secret societies, the censorship of the Cantonese vernacular, and colonial language policy in Hong Kong. *Language in Society, 24*, 159–186.

Chaika, E. (1980). Jargons and language change. *Anthropological Linguistics, 22* (2), 77–96.

Chaika, E. (1982). *Language: The Social Mirror.* Rowley, MA: Newbury House.

Chen, Chap-man (2004). On the Hong Kong Chinese subtitling of English swearwords. *Meta: Translators' Journal, 49* (1), 135–147.

Christie, C. (2013). The relevance of taboo language: An analysis of the indexical values of swearwords. *Journal of Pragmatics, 58*, 152–169.

Chung, D., & Nam, C. S. (2007). An analysis of the variables predicting instant messenger use. *New Media and Society, 9* (2), 212–234.

Coates, J. (2000). Small talk and subversion: Female speakers backstage. In J. Coupland (Ed.), *Small Talk* (pp. 241–263). London: Longman.

Cook, T. (2013). Fighting words: Canadian soldiers' slang and swearing in the Great War. *War in History, 20* (3), 323–344.

Daly, N., Holmes, J., Newton, J., & Stubbe, M. (2004). Expletives as solidarity signals in FTAs on the factory floor. *Journal of Pragmatics, 36*, 945–964.

Danet, B. (2013). Flaming and linguistic impoliteness on a listserv. In S. C. Herring, D. Stein, & T. Virtanen (Eds), *Pragmatics of Computer-Mediated Communication* (pp. 639–664). Berlin: De Gruyter Mouton.

Darics, E. (2010a). Relational work in synchronous text-based CMC of virtual teams. In R. Taiwo (Ed.), *Handbook of Research on Discourse Behavior and Digital Communication: Language Structures and Social Interaction* (pp. 830–851). Hershey, PA: IGI Global.

Darics, E. (2010b). Politeness in computer-mediated discourse of a virtual team. *Journal of Politeness Research, 6*, 129–150.

Darics, E. (2013). Non-verbal signalling in digital discourse: The case of letter repetition. *Discourse, Context & Media, 2* (3), 141–148.

Davis, H. (1989). What makes bad language bad? *Language & Communication, 9* (1), 1–9.

Dewaele, S. M. (2004). The emotional force of swearwords and taboo words in the speech of multilinguals. *Journal of Multilingual and Multicultural Development, 25* (2–3), 204–222.

Dresner, E., & Herring, S. C. (2010). Functions of the non-verbal in CMC: Emoticons and illocutionary force. *Communication Theory, 20* (3), 249–268.

Ellison, N. B., Steinfield, C., & Lampe, C. (2011). Connection strategies: Social capital implications of Facebook-enabled communication practices. *New Media and Society, 13* (6), 873–892.

Gee, J. P. (2011). *An Introduction to Discourse Analysis: Theory and Method* (3rd edition). London: Routledge.

Handel, M., & Herbsleb, J. D. (2002). What is chat doing in the workplace? *CSCW'02 Proceedings of the 2002 ACM Conference on Computer Supported Cooperative Work* (pp. 1–10). New York, NY: ACM Press.

Herring, S. C. (2012). Grammar and electronic communication. In C. Chapelle (Ed.), *The Encyclopedia of Applied Linguistics* (pp. 2338–2346). Hoboken, NJ: Wiley-Blackwell. Retrieved from: http://ella.slis.indiana.edu/~herring/e-grammar.pdf.

Hobbs, P. (2013). Fuck as a metaphor for male sexual aggression. *Gender and Language, 7*(2), 149–176.

Holmes, J., & Meyerhoff, M. (1999). The community of practice: Theories and methodologies in language and gender research. *Language in Society, 28,* 173–183.

Holmes, J., & Stubbe, M. (2003). *Power and Politeness in the Workplace: A Sociolinguistic Analysis of Talk at Work*. London: Longman.

Holmes, J., Stubbe, M., & Vine, B. (1999). Constructing professional identity: "Doing power" in policy units. In S. Sarangi & C. Roberts (Eds), *Talk, Work and Institutional Order: Discourse in Medical, Mediation and Management Settings* (pp. 351–388). New York: De Mouton Gruyter.

Hopper, R., Coleman, L. G., & Daly, J. A. (1980). Expletives and androgyny. *Anthropological Linguistics, 22* (3), 131–137.

Huang, Hong-xu, & Tian, Gui-sen (1990). A sociolinguistic review of linguistic taboo in Chinese. *International Journal of the Sociology of Language, 81,* 63–85.

Hughes, G. (2006). *An Encyclopedia of Swearing: The Social History of Oaths, Profanity, Foul Language, and Ethnic Slurs in the English-speaking World*. Armonk, NY: Sharpe.

Hughes, S. E. (1992). Expletives of lower working-class women. *Language in Society, 21,* 291–303.

Hutton, C., & Bolton, K. (2005). *A Dictionary of Cantonese Slang: The Language of Hong Kong Movies, Street Gangs and City Life*. London: C. Hurst.

Iqbal, S. T., & Horvitz, E. (2007). Disruption and recovery of computing tasks: Field study, analysis, and directions. *Proceedings of the 2007 ACM SIGCHI Conference on Human Factors in Computing Systems* (pp. 677–686). New York, NY: ACM Press.

Isaacs, E., Walendowski, A., Whittaker, S., Schiano, D. J., & Kamm, C. (2002). The character, functions, and styles of instant messaging in the workplace. *CSCW'02 Proceedings of the 2002 ACM Conference on Computer Supported Cooperative Work* (pp. 11–20). New York: ACM Press.

Jacobs, G. E. (2006). Fast times and digital literacy: Participation roles and portfolio construction within instant messaging. *Journal of Literacy Research, 38* (2), 171–196.

Jay, T. B. (1981). Comprehending dirty-word descriptions. *Language and Speech, 24* (1), 29–38.

Jay, T. (2000). *Why we curse: A neuro-psycho-social theory of speech*. Philadelphia, PA: John Benjamins.

Jay, T. B., & Janschewitz, K. (2008). The pragmatics of swearing. *Journal of Politeness Research, 4,* 267–288.

Kao, E. (2013, September 2). Protesters call for suspension of teacher Alpais Lam. *South China Morning Post*. Retrieved from http://www.scmp.com/news/hong-kong/article/1301830/protesters-call-suspension-teacher-alpais-lam?page=all

Mak, B. C. N., Chui, H. L., & Liu, Y. Q. (2012). Instant messaging and microblogging: Situated-learning platforms for educationists and workplace mentors. *Social and Behavioral Sciences, 51*, 392–399.

Mak, C. N. (2009). Language and communication: A sociolinguistic study in newcomers' socialization into the workplace. Unpublished master's thesis, School of English, The University of Hong Kong, Hong Kong.

Moore, R. L. (2012). On swearwords and slang. *American Speech, 87* (2), 170–189.

Nelson, M. (2014). "You need help as usual, do you?": Joking and swearing for collegiality in a Swedish workplace. *Multilingua, 33* (1–2), 173–200.

Oliver, M. M., & Rubin, J. (1975). The use of expletives by some American women. *Anthropological Linguistics, 17* (5), 191–197.

Provine, R. R., Spencer, R., & Mandell, D. (2007). Emotional expression online: Emoticons punctuate website text messages. *Journal of Language and Social Psychology, 26* (3), 299–307.

Quan-Haase, A., Cothrel, J., & Wellman, B. (2005). Instant messaging for collaboration: A case study of a high-tech firm. *Journal of Computer-Mediated Communication, 10* (4). doi: 10.1111/j.1083-6101.2005.tb00276.x. Retrieved from: http://jcmc.indiana.edu/vol10/issue4/quan-haase.html.

Stapleton, K. (2010). Swearing. In M. A. Locher & S. L. Graham (Eds), *Interpersonal Pragmatics* (pp. 289–305). New York: Walter de Gruyter.

Stephens, K. K. (2008). Optimizing costs in workplace instant messaging use. *IEEE Transactions on Professional Communication, 51*, 369–380.

Stone, T. E., McMillan, M., & Hazelton, M. (2010). Swearing: Its prevalence in healthcare settings and impact on nursing practice. *Journal of Psychiatric and Mental Health Nursing, 17*, 528–534.

Thurlow, C. (2001). The Internet and language. In R. Mesthrie & R. Asher (Eds), *The Concise Encyclopedia of Sociolinguistics* (pp. 287–289). London: Pergamon.

Wenger, E. (1998). *Communities of Practice: Learning, Meaning, and Identity.* New York: Cambridge University Press.

Wenger, E. C., & Snyder, W. M. (2000). Communities of practice: The organizational frontier. *Harvard Business Review, 78* (1), 139–145.

Wodak, R., Krzyzanowski, M., & Forchtner, B. (2012). The interplay of language ideologies and contextual cues in multilingual interactions: Language choice and code-switching in European Union institutions. *Language in Society, 41*, 157–186.

7
Snuff Said! Conflicting Employee and Corporate Interests in the Pursuit of a Tobacco Client

Kristy Beers Fägersten

Introduction

This chapter presents an analysis of a thread of intranet postings from a Swedish web consultancy at the time of its pursuit of a tobacco company as a client. Prior to the data collection, the tobacco company was to launch a new brand of snus, or moist snuff, and invited online marketing proposals from various web consultancy firms. During the proposal writing process, the Creative Director from this study's focus company, hereafter referred to as WEB, posted on the company-wide intranet a brief announcement of the proposal work along with a 25-question survey concerning the habits and preferences of snuff-using colleagues. It was via this post that other employees learned of the company's intentions to pursue the tobacco company, hereafter referred to as SNUFF, as a client. While the original intranet post presenting the survey did not indicate or acknowledge any anticipation of conflict or debate, a number of employees immediately called into question, problematized or even vilified the pursuit of SNUFF as a potential client. Other employees posted in defense of WEB's decision to submit a proposal, and in this way a specific conflict about the ethical issues of pursuing a tobacco company unfolded, and a general debate over corporate vision and goals as well as moral responsibilities emerged.

This chapter presents an analysis of the intranet thread, focusing on the emergent conflict and debate between employees who supported the pursuit of SNUFF, and those who were against it. The application of discourse analysis methodology reveals that the participating WEB employees were able to exploit the digital medium to express opinion and negotiate conflict, aligning or disagreeing with colleagues to such an extent that the pursuit of SNUFF can be recognized as a corporate crisis. The analysis thus first addresses aspects of crisis communication, focusing on how potential collaboration with a tobacco company is perceived as a threat to WEB's reputation. Aspects of digital discourse are then highlighted, with an investigation of the role of mitigation and alignment techniques in relational communication. Throughout the analysis, the negotiation of personal vs. corporate identities and interests is considered. The chapter ends with a discussion of how intranets in general can be used as an equal-access forum for employees to participate to different degrees in internal corporate communication and debate.

At the time of data collection, WEB had 150 employees, including graphic designers, interactive designers, and web developers. The total of 55 intranet postings were authored by 26 individual employees, ranging in length from approval postings (i.e., "+1") to 350 words, and covering a 11-day period. At the time, the topic of the company's pursuit of SNUFF as a client generated more postings and greater employee participation than any other topic to date. The sections that follow present an analysis of these postings, focusing on the emergent conflict and debate between employees who supported the collaboration and those who were against it. To avoid unnecessary suspense, it can be revealed at this juncture that while WEB did ultimately submit a proposal, the company was not awarded the account.

In the next section, I establish the foundation for WEB's intranet conflict by providing a review of snuff use in Sweden, including statistics, current legislation, and possible health risks associated with snuff usage. This presentation is complemented by a brief summary of WEB's professional goals and history, including ongoing development of products and services that are diametrically opposed to SNUFF's corporate activity, and which contribute to a potential moral dilemma for WEB. Once the foundation for the conflict and debate is established, I present examples WEB's intranet postings, analyzed within a framework of crisis communication. I then focus on the use of mitigation and alignment techniques as discursive strategies typical of conflict management, but, significantly, practiced according to the parameters of the digital environment. I conclude the analysis by way of focusing on a recurring theme in the debate, namely, the negotiation and distinction of personal vs. corporate identities and interests.

The use of snus in Sweden

The Swedish word "snus" is related etymologically to the English word snuff, and, like snuff, also denotes a smokeless tobacco product. Snuff, in dry ground or powder form, predates snus, which originated in Sweden as a moist variant to snuff. Not to be confused with chewing tobacco, snus does not need to be chewed to activate or release the nicotine, nor does it create excess juices that need to be spat out.

Like all tobacco products in Sweden, snuff is available for legal purchase by anyone at least 18 years old. The European Union, however, has legislated that Swedish snus is not to be sold outside of Sweden; snus is therefore a uniquely Swedish product and contributes to the general national identity, although only approximately a quarter of the population are snuff users.

Swedish snuff contains nicotine and is addictive. It is a carcinogen and related to pancreatic cancer and increased risk of mouth cancer. Snuff damages mucous membranes in the mouth and causes receding gums and exposed dental roots (Public Health Agency of Sweden, 2013). Snuff usage results in short-term increased blood pressure and pulse rate, and is also believed to increase the risk of dying from heart disease (Cnattingius et al., 2005)

Finally, as a tobacco product, Swedish snus is often compared to cigarettes, and its usage is commonly hailed as being a safer alternative to smoking. However, reports on snuff usage in Sweden indicate that while it does not tend to serve as a gateway to smoking, smokers are more likely to use snuff than non-smokers (Holm Ivarsson, 2009; Statistics Sweden, 2007), and snuff usage is widely practiced as a strategy to quit smoking (Holm Ivarsson, 2009).

WEB

WEB is a digital consulting firm founded in 1993, which produces websites, apps, and intranets. The company's own intranet had been active for ten years prior to the recording of data, but only in recent years has it developed more distinct social media characteristics, such as a forum for individual announcements, status updates, informal inquiries or news sharing. The data on which this study is based were generated from an intranet posting in the Fall of 2011. This posting was written by a Creative Director (referred to as E1, the first employee to contribute to the thread) to announce the pursuit of SNUFF as a client for a mobile app. In the original posting (Table 7.1), E1 requested that "snuff using colleagues" complete a 25-question survey about snuff usage, so as to help with WEB's proposal to SNUFF, which wanted to develop an online marketing strategy to strengthen brand loyalty among snuff users 20–30 years old.

Table 7.1 Original post

We are currently working on a proposal for a mobile phone app for SNUFF. The target audience is snuff users 20–30 years old, the point is to strengthen the relationship between the user and the brand. We've been working a couple of weeks now and need a little help from our snuff-using WEB colleagues. We've put together 25 simple questions about snuff and snuff usage (most of which are yes/no). It would be a great help if you snuff users could take a couple of minutes to copy the questions below, paste them in a mail, answer then and then send them to E1@<u>WEB.se</u>. As usual it's a bit urgent and it would be excellent if I could get the answers by Thursday afternoon. Thanks in advance!

The questions included in the survey focused on snuff usage history and frequency, degree of enjoyment, activities associated with snuff usage, and brand familiarity and loyalty. Out of the 25 questions, only three suggested any problematic aspects of snuff usage, namely: Have you ever tried to quit using snuff and if so, did you use any assistance? Are you considering quitting using snuff? Would you consider a partial or complete transition to nicotine-free snuff? Significantly, in E1's original posting there was no admittance or indication of ethical issues in pursuing SNUFF. Instead, the language of the posting was declarative ("We are working on a proposal for SNUFF...") and revealed that work on a proposal had begun even before the survey was posted ("We have been working for a couple of weeks now..."). This gives cause to believe that no ethical issues were deemed prohibitive to the pursuit and, essentially, that the decision to pursue SNUFF was not subject to discussion. The only input being requested was data from employees, which could contribute to the proposal writing process. There was thus an implicit assumption of acceptance of the pursuit, which, as the analysis below will show, instigated inter-employee conflict.

Germane to the conflict and thus to the analysis is the fact that one of WEB's existing clients at the time of the intranet snuff debate was a public council (PC), in part responsible for contributing to and maintaining a national online health guide. WEB not only developed the web interface for this client, but was also commissioned to develop its "Smoke-free" mobile phone application (app). The online health guide includes pages devoted to establishing nicotine addiction as a sickness, presenting risk factors associated with using snuff, and providing guidance on quitting snuff usage. The "Smoke-free" app is aimed at helping smokers lead a nicotine-free lifestyle and thus by extension does not encourage snuff usage.

In the next section, I argue that the prospect of acquiring SNUFF as a client can be understood as a threat to WEB's reputation in that cooperating with a tobacco company is in conflict both with the personal beliefs of some employees and with the interests of some of WEB's current clients. This conflict is discursively constructed as a crisis throughout the intranet thread. Furthermore, the fact that other employees are not equally concerned about or are even explicitly in favor of pursuing SNUFF as a client compounds the crisis, as employees voice disparate ideas and aspirations with regard to WEB's corporate goals and social profile. By first establishing the pursuit of SNUFF as the root of a threat that ultimately can be understood as a crisis, I can then focus on how aspects of relational communication and the negotiation of personal vs. corporate identities and interests are embedded in digital discourse.

Crisis discourse and management

Coombs (2007, p. 64) proposes a crisis to be "a sudden and unexpected event that threatens to disrupt an organization's operations and poses both a financial and reputational threat." A crisis is thus normally understood as an external event that was beyond the control of the affected organization and that as a result threatens the organization's reputation and/or the ability to continue corporate activity. I do not propose that WEB's pursuit of SNUFF is, in and of itself, a crisis; it was neither sudden and unexpected, nor was it beyond the control of the organization. However, in this case study, the fact is that WEB's pursuit of SNUFF was, for the majority of WEB's employees, unknown, rendering the revelation sudden and unexpected. This in itself may be unsettling to employees, as it suggests ineffective internal organizational communication. Regardless of WEB's internal communication practices and how the pursuit of SNUFF was revealed, it was the decision to do so that proved to be divisive, as evidenced by the lengthy intranet thread in response to the announcement and snuff-usage inquiry. If we instead consider Coombs' (2007, p. 163) more general definition of a crisis as "a threat[s] to the organizational reputation," we can by reflexive extension consider any threat to the organizational reputation as a crisis. In other words, it is the threat that is perceived first, and which then develops into a crisis. Specifically, WEB employees see a potential collaboration with SNUFF as a threat to the company's reputation, and this threat is then discursively constructed as a crisis. Furthermore, as not all of WEB's employees perceive the collaboration as a threat, the emergent disparity of opinion compounds the crisis.

Crises bring about changes that "can affect how stakeholders interact with the organization" (Barton, 2001; Dowling, 2000), and thus if a WEB employee perceives the pursuit of a tobacco client as a threat to the company's reputation, then this is in effect a crisis that can furthermore affect the way in which that employee interacts with the company – perhaps ultimately leading to resignation or dismissal – and the way in which that employee interacts with colleagues, expressing alignment or distance according to their position *vis-à-vis* the crisis.

Throughout the intranet discourse, a number of WEB employees make statements that indicate their understanding of the pursuit of SNUFF as a threat to WEB's reputation and that confirm this threat as a crisis. Directly after WEB's Creative Director (E1) posted to the intranet information about the proposal to be submitted to SNUFF and the 25 questions about snuff usage, another employee responded with the following post (in all examples, employees (E) and posts (P) are identified by the order in which they appear in the intranet thread; e.g., E1 is the original poster and P1 is his/her first post. All postings are translated from Swedish):

Example 1
E2-P2: Personally I think working with a company like SNUFF diminishes WEB's brand.

While E2 clearly speaks for himself (the mitigation expressed by "personally" will be addressed further on), the focus is on the negative effect the collaboration would have on WEB; in other words, SNUFF is understood as a threat to the WEB's reputation. This opinion is echoed in the posts of another five employees, alternatively asserting that they "wouldn't want to work" (E13-P19) with a "company like SNUFF" (E3-P3) that "bases its operations on tobacco or alcohol" (E10-P12); claiming that a collaboration would be "iffy" (E7-P9) or "a really bad idea" (E8-P10). In contrast, two employees express explicit wishes to be included in the project if WEB were to win the account:

Example 2
E14-P21: E0 (non-participating employee) and I would work on the project if we got an unlimited supply of snuff :-P

Example 3
E16-P23: I would gladly work on the project since there is the potential of it being a really fun/different solution far removed from our usual information websites. (But I don't need any snuff supply) :)

While the two sets of postings represent contrasting opinions, they have in common the expression of similar focus: the potential collaboration either is or isn't personally or professionally appealing. While in none of the other 45 posts do any of the 20 remaining thread-active employees explicitly address their own willingness to be involved in a potential project with SNUFF, they do either align themselves as for or against a potential collaboration as a threat to WEB's reputation and financial prospects. Since Coombs' definition of crisis is a threat to the organizational reputation, it is worthwhile to investigate how the threat of SNUFF is asserted or challenged in the intranet discourse, and thereby discursively construed as a crisis. I therefore consider in the next sections the intranet discourse from the perspectives of threat as crisis and of crisis management.

Threat as crisis

Aspects of crisis discourse are evident in the postings by WEB employees who discursively construct the proposed collaboration with SNUFF as a threat to WEB's reputation. Employees initially focus on the physical threats of tobacco, including arguments in their discourse that are in line with what Coombs (2007, p. 165) identifies as ethical responsibility: "The first priority in any crisis is to protect stakeholders from harm." The term stakeholders refers to anyone who may experience ramifications of or otherwise be affected by an organization's actions (Agle et al., 1999; Bryson, 2004). Several WEB employees are quick to resist jeopardizing the health of the general public, that is, actual or potential stakeholders, by contributing to the production, sale or use of snuff. For example, in response to E2-P2 (see Example 1), E5 asks, "What has SNUFF done that is bad for our brand? I'm just curious..." (P5). In the next turn (P6), E4 responds with a link to the online health guide (the interface for which was developed by WEB for PC) where smoking and snuff usage are presented as sicknesses; E2 responds directly after (P7) that SNUFF produces "addictive products" and E8 echoes E2's response (P10), also accusing SNUFF of selling products that are "addictive and hazardous to one's health."

In addition to the physical threat SNUFF may impose on current or potential stakeholders, WEB employees argue that a collaboration with SNUFF ultimately threatens and compromises WEB's reputation with regard to current clients. As presented earlier, WEB has developed an online health guide for the public council (PC), as well as a mobile application, "Smoke-free." These projects are referred to throughout the intranet thread as an argument for seeing the collaboration with SNUFF as a threat, as SNUFF's aims to increase tobacco use are in opposition to the current clients' goals of helping people quit smoking and snuff usage, as pointed out by E8 in Example 4:

Example 4
E8-P10: [...] Then I think we might get burned as a company since we have developed [the] "Smoke-free" [app]. To do both just shows that we're only in it for the money, and we don't have any integrity to speak of.

Similar assertions of ethical responsibility (Coombs, 2007) can be found in subsequent postings by five other employees. These repeated expressions of concern for current customers ultimately develop into a discussion about WEB's corporate profile and the kind of client it aspires to acquire. The fact that WEB's employees differ in their perception of SNUFF as a desirable client also reveals aspects of a crisis. In the following example, E4, an active anti-SNUFF poster to the thread, addresses colleagues' previous arguments for the pursuit of SNUFF. The employee challenges the perceptions and assertions previously put forth by colleagues, and argues for a shared corporate vision:

Example 5
E4-P50: [...] It is not about moralizing over other individuals or corporate choices. Or trying to complicate the question to the extent that it seems meaningless to attack it. It is about knowing what kind of organization we want to be. And acting accordingly. It's rather simple. And as for accepting a challenge E24 and E13... Where is the challenge in developing a concept that strengthens the relationship between a consumer and a health-hazardous product? This isn't even a project we need. Why invest time and money in it? There's really so much else we can focus our energy on. Something that's positive for both WEB and for those who use our services. That is excellence for me. We don't need to work towards a better world, in small or grand gestures. But I don't think that we as a company should pursue projects that have negative consequences for people or the environment. And in this case, people's health. This is a rather simple principle.

Throughout the post, it is clear that conflicting opinions have emerged, and E4 both addresses attacks on threat perception ("it is not about

moralizing") and rejects counter arguments ("where is the challenge?").
Significantly, E4 appeals to her colleagues as a group and tries to align
with them by invoking a sense of solidarity through the use of the pronoun "we": "what kind of organization we want to be," "so much else
we can focus our energy on," "we as a company." In effect, E4 is practicing pre-crisis intervention. In the next section, I present examples from
the intranet thread authored by employees who post in defense of the
pursuit of SNUFF. The postings of these employees are analyzed from
the perspective of crisis management discourse, further suggesting that
the pursuit of SNUFF is perceived as a crisis.

Crisis discourse management

The perception of a collaboration with SNUFF as a threat to WEB's
reputation, and that this in turn is perceived as a crisis, is further suggested by examples of crisis discourse management. According to Fuchs-
Burnett (2002) and Patel and Reinsch (2003), stakeholders are expected
and even recommended to express concern about a crisis, but in terms
of a crisis management strategy, acknowledgment of and reciprocal
concern are not to be mistaken for an admission of guilt. At several
junctures (E6-P8, E11-P13 and P15, E1-P18), WEB employees directly
involved with the decision to pursue SNUFF acknowledge the emerging
conflict and defend their actions in ways discursively similar to crisis
management and image restoration. Two particularly illustrative examples of this include an additional post by the creator of the thread, E1,
and one by E11:

> Example 6
> E11-P15: [...] I wouldn't think that PC would have a problem with
> WEB having SNUFF as a client, but I may be wrong. Am fairly certain
> that there's nothing about this in the contract.

> Example 7
> E1-P18: [I] agree that this here is a little tricky, have myself had moral
> ponderings. I think further that a lot lies in how we solve the task
> and what is the core of our proposal. It can actually be the case that
> the proposal is based on attempts to increase the use of nicotine-free
> alternatives or to get as many as possible to stop smoking.

Coombs (2007) includes excuses and justifications among primary crisis
response strategies, while Benoit (1997) names evasion of responsibility

as a strategy of image restoration. In Example 7, E1 both excuses and justifies the pursuit of SNUFF by highlighting possible alternative proposals; the proposal can also be considered a corrective action, a discursive strategy associated with image repair (Benoit, 1997). In Example 6, E11 implies that because the pursuit does not represent a contractual breach with their current client (PC, which hosts the online health guide), WEB is not responsible for consulting with them before pursuing SNUFF.

A final example from the thread will furthermore illustrate crisis management and image repair discourse, this time from a framing perspective. In his Situational Crisis Communication Theory, Coombs (2007) cites framing strategies as factors that shape reputational threats. Communicators choose specific aspects to focus on when sending a message that receivers, ideally, will also focus on when developing their own opinions and judgments (Coombs & Holladay, 2002; Druckman, 2001). In Example 8, the proposed collaboration with SNUFF is framed in such a way as to minimize the threat by highlighting the legitimacy of SNUFF, the existence of snuff-using stakeholders, and the professional goal of WEB to serve both current and potential clients:

Example 8
E12-P17: I see no problem with WEB delivering services to both people who want to stop smoking/using snuff, and to people who want to continue smoking/using snuff. In some cases I think that it would be appropriate for WEB to take a moral position (for ex. weapons and pornography which were mentioned before) but in both this case and in the quit-smoking-app, the target audience is adults who make highly personal decisions about their own lifestyles, which don't affect other people to any significant extent. Imagine what kind of signal that would send if WEB actively refused to work with SNUFF. As far as I'm concerned, that would harshly call into question the highly personal choices of voluntary snuff users. We would in principle be saying, "we think you are wrong for using tobacco." I think that this would be more damaging to our brand and customer relations than a collaboration with SNUFF.

With this post, E12 takes a position that defends WEB's decision to pursue a collaboration with SNUFF, thereby not just effectively rejecting the threat of collaboration as it has been perceived and put forth by colleagues, but recasting the threat as a result of non-collaboration. Examples 1–8 thus illustrate how the proposed collaboration with

SNUFF, a producer of tobacco products, has divided WEB employees on the grounds of social and ethical accountability, with each side claiming a threat to WEB's reputation by endangering or alienating both actual and potential stakeholders. I have argued that the intranet thread represents a corporate crisis, by virtue of the aspects of discourse that are characteristic of crisis management and image repair. In the following sections, the focus is shifted from the content of the thread to the form of the contributions. In other words, I analyze not only what is contributed, but specifically how it is formulated and presented in the digital, intranet context. I thus consider the discourse from the perspective of computer-mediated communication, examining how the intranet posters partake in relational communication *vis-à-vis* the emergent conflict-cum-crisis while not only navigating but capitalizing on the digital environment.

Aspects of digital discourse: Emoticons

Examples 1–8 illustrate disagreement from a content point of view (Angouri & Locher, 2012), for example, that which constitutes the grounds for disagreement, namely, whether the pursuit of SNUFF threatens WEB's reputation. Kakava (1993, p. 36) defines disagreement as "an oppositional stance (verbal or non-verbal) to an antecedent verbal (or non-verbal) action." In the intranet thread, E2 is first to oppose the proposition of pursuit; colleagues thereafter either similarly oppose, agreeing with E2, or they establish another antecedent action, disagreeing with E2. Pomerantz (1984) proposes that disagreements can be strong or weak, the former type occurring more frequently among family, friends or other people of close social distance, while the latter occur between interlocutors who are less familiar with each other or who aspire to maintain neutralism in their interaction (Schnurr & Chan, 2011). It is weak disagreements that are more often mitigated (Jacobs, 2002; Myers, 1998).

In the workplace context, Angouri (2012) claims that disagreement in business meetings is more the rule than the exception. Furthermore, disagreement and problem-solving are unmarked activities in the workplace, and "opposing views" do not pose relational threats but rather contribute to the meaningful expression and recognition of one's own and others' identity and stance. Nevertheless, despite the potential for a culture of conflict, strong disagreements in business discourse are decidedly less common than weak, or mitigated, disagreements (Angouri, 2012; Schnurr & Chan, 2011).

Of the 55 intranet postings, only ten do not explicitly align with either side of the debate; these include exploratory questions ("Tricky subject. Where do we draw the line?" (E9-P11)), non-commented links (such as to the online health guide (E4-P4) or to SNUFF (E3-P45)), and appeals for face-to-face discussion ("I hope there will be a chance to discuss this question this weekend. It feels like something that needs to be discussed and is better discussed live than via comments" (E13-P42)). The remaining 43 postings clearly align with one side of the conflict, but are also overwhelmingly mitigated in terms of personal feelings and assessments. The underlined words in Example 9 each illustrate such mitigation:

Example 9
E7-P9: After a little discussion of the project I probably also think that it's iffy to work with a site "for snuff." An intranet would have been one thing, but an external campaign-site is another. I hadn't even thought about PC and the quit-smoking app but that actually just makes it even more doubtful in my view.

As Biber (2004) points out, such mitigations have been investigated from various perspectives, including "evaluation" (Hunston & Thompson, 2000), "intensity" (Labov, 1984), "affect" (Ochs, 1989), "evidentiality" (Chafe, 1986), "hedging" (Holmes, 1990; Hyland, 1998), and "stance" (Barton, 1993; Beach & Anson, 1992; Biber & Finegan, 1988; Conrad & Biber, 2000; Precht, 2000). Regardless of the label, they each refer to the same phenomenon, namely the grammaticalization or lexicalization of personal feelings or assessments, expressed in Example 9 by verbs such as "think," modals such as "would," minimizers such as "little," "just," and "even," and stance adverbials such as "in my view."

These instances of mitigation, however, are not unique to the digital environment, but can be found in examples of both written and spoken discourse. An example of a mitigation strategy that is specific to computer-mediated communication, on the other hand, is the use of emoticons. Emoticons, a blending of "emotion" and "icon" (Skovholt et al., 2014), were originally referred to as "relational icons" (Asteroff, 1987) and "pictographs" (Thompson & Foulger, 1996), and defined as "a sequence of ordinary characters [found] on [the] computer keyboard" (Sanderson, 1993, p. 1); "visual cues formed from ordinary typographical symbols that when read sideways represent feelings or emotions" (Rezabek & Cochenour, 1998, p. 201); and "icons for the expression of emotion, or for marking one's intent as non-serious" (Danet et al., 1997, n.p.). Walther & D'Addario (2001) note that the existing research on emoticons has focused on the additive, paralinguistic (Marvin, 1995, p. 326) value of emoticons, establishing "the notion that the computer-using society has attempted to incorporate surrogates for traditional types of interactive nonverbal cues."

At a total of 16 instances, the use of emoticons in the intranet thread corresponds to 30% of the total. They were distributed among 12 of the 26 contributing employees, with E23 and E2 using two each, and E4 using three. The varieties of emoticons included ten smileys in three versions: 8= :) 1= :-D and 1= :-P and six winks in two versions: 5= ;) and 1= ;-) . With the exception of one instance (:-P), the emoticons reveal distinct alignment or mitigation functions. Smileys were used six times to align and three times to mitigate; winks were used six times to mitigate and one time to align. Examples 10 and 11 illustrate aligning and mitigating functions:

Example 10
E12-P34: E20: +1
Was going to write what you wrote, but couldn't get the right formulation. Extremely well formulated! :)

Example 11
E20-P33: [...] Love and passion could also be classified as addictive and directly hazardous for one's health ;).

As presented earlier, the postings to the intranet thread consist largely of statements of alignment with one side of the debate and often in the form of aligning with one or more colleagues who have argued for or against the collaboration. The smiley emoticon is thus used mainly not to mitigate a disagreement, but to overtly align and agree with a colleague. The winking emoticon, on the other hand, functions predominantly as a mitigater or "softener" (Skovholt et al., 2014), accompanying statements that challenge a colleague's previous argument and, as evident in Example 11, connoting irony (Rezabek & Cochenour, 1998; Walther & D'Addario, 2001).

The single instance of :-P occurred in conjunction with a non-serious posting, E14-P21 (see Example 2), and was acknowledged in turn with an emoticon, E16-P23 (see Example 3). Interestingly, two other non-serious postings occur in the data: E21-P35, proposing that WEB establish a "Black Ops" group that could manage questionable accounts, and E20-P39, referring to a website that sorts beer by price and alcohol content; this posting included a winking emoticon. Appreciation of all three non-serious postings is implied by the subsequent use of emoticons by other colleagues in response. These subsequent usages thus show not only content appreciation, but also personal as well as stylistic alignment to a playful frame (Dresner & Herring, 2010). The use of emoticons thus contributes to comic relief in the midst of the developing conflict and perceived crisis with regard to the potential reputational threat of pursuing SNUFF as a client.

Aspects of digital discourse: Approval postings

As with emoticons, approval postings are unique to computer-mediated communication. Within social media contexts, approval postings can be in the form of a "like," such as is used in Facebook, a "favorite" as used in Twitter, or in the form of +1, as used in Google+. According to the Google+ online support page:

> +1 is how you signal your appreciation for anything that grabs your attention on Google+ or on your favorite websites. When you read a post that makes you want to cheer, +1 is your applause; when you watch a video that has you in stitches, +1 is your laughter; when you see a photo that perfectly captures that special moment, +1 is your 5-star review. ("About the +1 Button," n.d.)

The employees of WEB have appropriated the +1 approval posting into their intranet culture, and in the intranet thread, it is used according to the second example, that is, as a positive reaction to a post. Throughout the thread, +1 is used eight times by six employees (E20 and E22), twice in support of anti-collaboration postings, three times for pro-collaboration postings, and once in response to a non-serious posting. Approval postings are always preceded by a colleague's first name, such as in Example 10, repeated here:

> Example 10
> E12-P34: E20: +1
> Was going to write what you wrote, but couldn't get the right formulation. Extremely well expressed! :)

The +1 approval postings allow WEB employees to overtly align with other colleagues, cheering or applauding their postings and position in the debate. They are similar to feedback or back-channeling in face-to-face communication, but with the function of explicit agreement, as opposed to simply signaling continued participation in the interaction. Significantly, the +1 postings also seem to represent a possibility for less vocal employees to take part in the thread. Of the six employees who contributed with +1 postings, two of them wrote nothing more than "Name +1" and none of them posted more than this one instance.

Discussion

Although it was implied in the original post and made explicit in the ninth post that WEB would and ultimately did indeed submit a proposal to SNUFF, the intranet debate continued over ten more days and a total of 55 postings. The employees obviously found the issue compelling, and actively engaged in an intranet debate over whether the decision represented a threat to the company's reputation. The communication revealed inter-employee conflict, which in turn was discursively constructed as a crisis according to Coombs' 2007 definition as a "threat to the organizational reputation." Specifically, the intranet discourse focused not only on the social responsibility, moral accountability, and identity of WEB as a company, but also on the employees' own professional interests and identities. The decision to pursue SNUFF was made without a general consultation among staff, and the fact that management a priori deemed SNUFF to be an appropriate client fueled the conflict. The intranet thread thus suggests the importance of a forum not only for employees to discuss corporate actions but also, crucially, to have the opportunity to influence corporate decisions that may reflect on their own, shared, professional identities.

The application of discourse analysis methodology in the analysis of digital discourse serves to further the understanding of the communicative goals and how they are achieved. In this chapter, I have analyzed the use of discursive devices that are specific to the digital context such as emoticons and approval postings, focusing on their mitigation and alignment functions. However, a discourse analysis of the thread also reveals non-digital aspects of communication that are also meaningful: for example, throughout the approximately 4,000-word long thread, employees used the word "I" 70 times, an average of 1.3 times per post, and "we" 174 times, an average of three times per post. The intranet thread thus served as a forum for employees to ventilate their own interests, ideals, and identities as distinct from or in alignment with both those of their colleagues and those of the company as a whole.

There is thus reason to believe that the intranet is ideally used for pre-meeting purposes. First, the fact that the thread extended over 11 days suggests that employees needed time to read, consider, deliberate, and formulate responses. The first day of the thread generated 16 postings, the second day resulted in 24 postings, there were 11 postings on the third day, two on the fourth, then none until the tenth and 11th days, which each had one posting.

Second, compliments such as "Extremely well formulated!" in Example 10 and "Well formulated" (E24-P49) indicate that the written medium is appreciated, perhaps because it affords the employees an opportunity to think through, construct, and even edit their postings. Contributions that suggest attention has been paid to the written word are both noticed and overtly acknowledged.

Third, the length of some postings suggests that the written medium gives employees a chance to formulate and articulate their thoughts as well as hold the floor without interruption, seeing their turn through to completion; 21 of the 55 postings were within the range of 70–350 words.

Fourth, the intranet forum provides equal opportunity for employees to participate in discussion. As noted earlier, some participating employees posted minimally and only once. Considering the brevity of these postings, the contributors could just as well have opted out of participating. The fact that the intranet thread requires no minimum amount of participation can serve to encourage (more) employees to partake (more frequently) in discussions.

However, in contrast to these minimal, one-time contributions, E4 posted six times on four different days with initial posts of fewer than 30 words, but later posts ranging in length from 200 to 350 words. The intranet forum allows for such enthusiastic participation while minimizing the risk that a few employees will dominate the discussion in such a way that prevents others from participating.

A final reason for considering intranet discussions as pre-meeting activities is the indication of a general belief that decisions, ultimately, are best made in face-to-face communication. The appeal for a face-to-face continuation of the intranet thread presented earlier (E13-P42) was applauded in the next turn, "Good idea" (E23-P43, and garnered two approval postings (E13-P47 and E4-P50). A pre-meeting intranet discussion would allow employees to identify their position, formulate arguments, align with like-minded colleagues, and determine their own stakes and desired level of investment.

References

About the +1 Button. (n.d.) Retrieved January 29, 2014, from: https://support.google.com/plus/answer/1047397?hl=en.

Agle, B. R., Mitchell, R. K., & Sonnenfeld, J. A. (1999). Who matters to CEOs? An investigation of stakeholder attributes and salience, corporate performance, and CEO values. *Academy of Management Journal, 42* (5), 507–525.

Angouri, J. (2012). Managing disagreement in problem solving meeting talk. *Journal of Pragmatics, 44* (12), 1565–1579.

Angouri, J., & Locher, M. A. (2012). Theorising disagreement. *Journal of Pragmatics, 44* (12), 1549–1553.

Asteroff, J. F. (1987). Paralanguage in electronic mail: A case study. Unpublished dissertation, Columbia University.

Barton, E. L. (1993). Evidentials, argumentation, and epistemological stance. *College English, 55*, 745–769.

Barton, L. (2001). *Crisis in Organizations II.* Cincinnati, OH: South-Western College Publishing.

Beach, R., & Anson, C. M. (1992). Stance and intertextuality in written discourse. *Linguistics and Education, 4*, 335–357.

Benoit, W. L. (1997). Image repair discourse and crisis communication. *Public Relations Review, 23* (2), 177–186.

Biber, D. (2004). Historical patterns for the grammatical marking of stance: A cross-register comparison. *Journal of Historical Pragmatics, 5* (1), 107–136.

Biber, D., & Finegan, E. (1988). Adverbial stance types in English. *Discourse Processes, 11*, 1–34.

Bryson, J. M. (2004). What to do when stakeholders matter: Stakeholder identification and analysis techniques. *Public Management Review, 6* (1), 21–53.

Chafe, W. L. (1986). Evidentiality in English conversation and academic writing. In W. L. Chafe & J. Nichols (Eds), *Evidentiality: The Linguistic Coding of Epistemology* (pp. 261–72). Norwood, NJ: Ablex.

Cnattingius, S. Galanti, R., Grafström, R., Hergens, M., Lambe, M., Nyrén, O., Pershagen, G., & Wickholm, S. (2005). *Hälsorisker med svenskt snus.* Stockholm: Statens Folkhälsoinstitut.

Conrad, S., & Biber, D. (2000). Adverbial marking of stance in speech and writing. In S. Hunston & G. Thompson (Eds), *Evaluation in Text* (pp. 56–73). Oxford: Oxford University Press.

Coombs, W. T. (2007). Protecting organization reputations during a crisis: The development and application of situational crisis communication theory. *Corporate Reputation Review, 10* (3): 163–176.

Coombs, W. T., & Holladay, S. J. (2002). Helping crisis managers protect reputational assets: Initial tests of the situational crisis communication theory. *Management Communication Quarterly, 16* (2), 165–186.

Danet, B., Ruedenberg Wright, L., & Rosenbaum Tamari, Y. (1997). Hmmm... where's that smoke coming from? *Journal of Computer Mediated Communication, 2* (4).

Dowling, G. (2000). *Creating Corporate Reputations: Identity, Image, and Performance.* Oxford: Oxford University Press.

Dresner, E., & Herring, S. C. (2010). Functions of the nonverbal in CMC: Emoticons and illocutionary force. *Communication Theory, 20* (3), 249–268.

Druckman, J. N. (2001). The implications of framing effects for citizen competence. *Political Behavior, 23* (3), 225–256.

Fuchs-Burnett, T. (2002). Mass public corporate apology. *Dispute Resolution Journal, 57* (2), 26.

Holmes, J. (1990). Hedges and boosters in women's and men's speech. *Language & Communication, 10* (3), 185–205.

Holm Ivarsson, B. (2009). Vad vi vet om snus. Public Health Agency of Sweden/ Folkhälsomyndigheten. Retrieved from: http://www.folkhalsomyndigheten.se/ pagefiles/11953/Vad-vi-vet-om-snus-nytt%20ISBN.pdf.

Hunston, S., & Thompson, G. (Eds) (2000). *Evaluation in Text: Authorial Stance and the Construction of Discourse.* Oxford: Oxford University Press.

Hyland, K. (1998). *Hedging in Scientific Research Articles.* Amsterdam: John Benjamins. Jacobs, S. (2002). Maintaining neutrality in dispute mediation: Managing disagreement while managing not to disagree. *Journal of Pragmatics, 34* (10), 1403–1426.

Kakava, C. (1993). Negotiation of disagreement by Greeks in conversations and classroom discourse. Doctoral dissertation, Georgetown University, Washington, DC.

Labov, W. (1984). Intensity. In D. Schirin (Ed.), *Meaning, Form, and Use in Context: Linguistic Applications* (pp. 43–70). Washington, DC: Georgetown University Press.

Marvin, L. E. (1995). Spoof, spam, lurk, and lag: The aesthetics of text-based virtual realities. *Journal of Computer Mediated Communication, 1* (2).

Myers, G. (1998). Displaying opinions: Topics and disagreement in focus groups. *Language in Society, 27* (1), 85–111.

Ochs, E. (Ed.). (1989). *The Pragmatics of Affect: Special Issue.* Berlin: Mouton de Gruyter.

Patel, A., & Reinsch, L. (2003). Companies can apologize: Corporate apologies and legal liability. *Business Communication Quarterly, 66* (1), 9–25.

Pomerantz, A. M. (1984). Giving a source or basis: The practice in conversation of telling "how I know." *Journal of Pragmatics, 8* (5), 607–625.

Precht, K. (2000). Patterns of stance in English. Doctoral dissertation, Northern Arizona University.

Public Health Agency of Sweden/Folkhälsomyndigheten. (2013). Tobaksbruk. Retrieved from http://www.folkhalsomyndigheten.se/amnesomraden/livsvillkor-och-levnadsvanor/folkhalsans-utveckling/alkohol-narkotika-dopning-tobak-och-spel/tobaksbruk/.

Rezabek, L. L., & Cochenour, J. J. (1998). Visual cues in computer-mediated communication: Supplementing text with emoticons. *Journal of Visual Literacy, 18*, 201–215.

Sanderson, D. (1993). *Smileys.* Sebastopol, CA: O'Reilly.

Schnurr, S., & Chan, A. (2011). Exploring another side of co-leadership: Negotiating professional identities through face-work in disagreements. *Language in Society, 40* (02), 187–209.

Skovholt, K., Grønning, A., & Kankaanranta, A. (2014). The communicative functions of emoticons in workplace emails. *Journal of Computer Mediated Communication, 19*, 780–797.

Statistics Sweden/Centralbyrån (2007). *Alkohol-och tobaksbruk. Levnadsförhållanden,* Rapport 114.

Thompson, P. A., & Foulger, D. A. (1996). Effects of pictographs and quoting on flaming in electronic mail. *Computers in Human Behavior, 12*, 225–243.

Walther, J. B., & D'Addario, K. P. (2001). The impacts of emoticons on message interpretation in computer-mediated communication. *Social Science Computer Review, 19*, 324–347.

8

Sheer Outrage: Negotiating Customer Dissatisfaction and Interaction in the Blogosphere

Valerie Creelman

> *"To speak with a human voice, companies must share the concerns of their communities."* (Levine et al., p. xxiv)

Introduction

Corporate blogs have become one of many social media marketing tools organizations use daily to initiate, maintain, and strengthen relationships with customers and clients. As a two-way, asynchronous form of communication, corporate blogs offer customers an opportunity to broadcast their satisfaction and dissatisfaction with the products or services they receive in a dynamic public forum, where industry competitors and customers alike can view and respond to postings. Monitoring and tracking this type of computer-mediated communication has motivated marketing researchers to engage in a practice industry practitioners term *social media listening* (Tuten & Solomon, 2013). By listening to customers' voices in these online forums, companies use a variety of web-scraping tools and social media metrics to gain insight into what consumers have to report about their sentiments toward and experiences with an organization, its products, and/or its services (Deshpande & Sarkar, 2010; Godes & Myzlin, 2004; Harrison-Walker, 2001; Hong & Lee, 2005; Kozinets, 2009; Pang & Lee, 2008; Zabin & Jefferies, 2008).

In managing online relationships with customers, companies first regarded blogs as a unique way to communicate with customers in a humanized voice (Kelleher & Miller, 2006; Kelleher & Miller, 2009). Those in the public relations field, involved in managing corporate communication crises, saw these tools as an effective way to provide conversational human voices and to foster more direct connections and relationships with customers (Kelleher & Miller, 2006; Sweetser & Metzgar, 2007). Van Noort and Willemsen's (2011) study of online webcare interventions identified the presence of a perceived conversational human voice as having a favorable effect when managing negative word-of-mouth (NWOM). Indeed, blogs have offered companies a way to engage in conversation with their customers and stakeholders, creating an immediacy and authenticity, not achieved through more traditional, static forms of company publications such as press releases, newsletters, and annual reports. Companies can use their blogs to create online communities, build customer relations, and manage corporate crisis when it surfaces (Baxter & Connolly, 2013; Baxter et al., 2010; Cox et al., 2008; Guffey et al., 2013; Kent, 2008; Lee et al., 2006; Lee et al., 2008; Porter et al., 2009; Newman, 2015; Schultz et al., 2011; Sweetser & Metzgar, 2007).

The dialogic, conversational style that blogging, Facebook, and Twitter posts foster has helped engender that sense of company and customer in perpetual conversation with each other, and has proven critical to the generation of new relationships and the maintenance and, even enhancement, of existing ones. These social media platforms have become the digital marketplace where the give-and-take of conversation, at its best, takes on a cooperative aspect, as companies collaborate with their customers and clients to sustain, mitigate, and, in some cases, repair their relationships with customers through digital online conversations. The nature of these relationships and their effective management turn on the dynamic interplay that occurs in these online social interactions, and the conversations enacted by the various participants who decide to join the dialogue. Of the studies dedicated to corporate communication in this forum, most do not fully consider the role of language and its strategic use as a critical part of relationship management and image restoration practices. Nor do they subject this aspect of digital business discourse to rigorous analysis (Cho & Huh, 2010; Ki & Hon, 2006; Ko et al., 2008; Lee et al., 2006; Lee et al., 2008). This oversight is not entirely surprising given that the language of blogs in general has not been thoroughly studied (Myers, 2010).

In the face of customer dissatisfaction, businesses are now thrust into the awkward social situation of publicly responding to negative feedback, where their response to an individual customer is weighed and scrutinized, not only by the immediate correspondent but also by a community of consumers and potential respondents (Page, 2014). An ill-conceived response to a crisis situation can quickly spiral out of control, as it did for Applebee's and Amy's Baking Company when their social media missteps elicited an outpouring of negative feedback and public criticism (Burn-Callander, 2013; Thompson, 2013). This type of heightened scrutiny places the company representatives who respond to these posts and participate in these digital conversations under considerable pressure, as they publicly negotiate not only the immediate exchange at hand but also corporate identity, brand reputation, customer relations, loyalty, and trust. These digital conversations and their effective management constitute what Michael Hulme (2013) described as integral to an organization's "Reputational Resource" when building, cultivating, and controlling its brand and global image across social media channels (p. 6).

Corporate blogs as rhetorical artifact of online social interaction

As a marketing tool, company blogs offer marketers ample opportunity to glean customers' insights on their products and services. As a digital archive and rhetorical artifact of social interaction, however, corporate blogs offer business discourse researchers an irresistible opportunity to examine how customers respond and react to a company or an organization's public statements. More critically, the knowledge we gain from studying these online social encounters can inform the communication strategies of people working in the areas of public relations, marketing, and crisis response management, and help them develop the social scripts needed to deliver effective customer care and brand reputation management. As Steve Jones (1999), an early researcher of computer-mediated communication and culture, acknowledged, "we have the artifactual textual traces of interaction created instantaneously, at the moment of utterance" (p. 13). Analyzing the interactive elements of these preserved moments of language in use holds immense potential for marketers, communication managers, and customer or client care representatives responsible for preserving the public value and perception of a brand and its reputation. The viral spread of negative word-of-mouth (NWOM), and its potentially damaging effects to a brand's value, has heightened the need for proactive and reactive strategies in providing effective webcare (Van Noort & Willemsen, 2011). Only by studying actual examples of language in use and, then, in the context of primary and secondary responses to company crisis, by company and consumer, can we begin to piece together how consumer stakeholders engage with and respond to these messages. Analysis of this type will ultimately help social media, marketing, and communications managers develop creative strategies (and refine existing ones) for preventing, managing, or overcoming NWOM. Such analysis will likewise offer new ways for training employees who engage with customers online and who have a critical role to play in protecting a company's Reputational

Resource. A heightened attention to the role of language in social media communication will also equip corporate trainers and educators in the areas of business communication and professional writing to develop their students' online voice and build goodwill when speaking on behalf of the businesses and organizations they represent (Shwom & Snyder, 2014).

As part of this chapter's discussion, I examine a set of customer blog posts to explore the energetic, constitutive way in which customers' voices respond to and engage with the language of corporate communication in the more tension-filled context of a corporate crisis. To illustrate this dialogic interplay, I examine the specific case of lululemon, a popular athletic wear company that turned to its social media outlets to repair its image with customers, after it was publicly criticized for selling a batch of athletic pants many customers reported to be inappropriately sheer. As customers' discontent erupted, and questions about the company's quality control emerged, lululemon used its company blog to address its public relations crisis.

As a first step toward restoring its image and customer confidence, lululemon launched a recall of its popular black luon athletic pants and addressed its customers directly by posting a message to its blog on March 18, 2013, titled "a letter to our guests" (See Figure 8.1). While not an apology, the letter identified the steps lululemon was taking to replace the shipment and to exchange or refund customers' purchases. As a form of crisis communication, and a direct response to the rhetorical situation, the letter is a familiar public discourse type, immediately recognizable as a product recall message. Rather than satisfying customers and restoring confidence in the brand, however, this post ignited a firestorm among loyal lululemon customers as they quickly responded, using lululemon's blog to voice their dissatisfaction with its products, services, and efforts.

Rhetorical analysis of the artifact using a generative approach

To understand what features or characteristics of this message motivated lululemon's customers to respond in this vigorous way, I organized my analysis into two stages: the first focused on a close reading and coding of the letter, the second focused on a thematic or topic-based coding of customers' posted comments or responses to the company's image restoration discourse. The first stage was dedicated to a close textual analysis of the letter, reading the text as both a rhetorical artifact, written in response to a specific rhetorical situation, and as a type of image

a letter to our guests

At lululemon, our most important relationship is with our communities and our guests. We recently learned some information about some product that arrived in our stores and we wanted you to know right away.

At the beginning of March, our stores and ecommerce site received some black luon women's bottoms that didn't meet our high standards. The materials used in construction were the same but the coverage was not, resulting in increased sheerness. We want you to Down Dog and Crow with confidence and we felt these pants didn't measure up.

We keenly listen to your feedback and it is paramount to us that you know we're listening. We are 100% committed to doing the right thing for our guests and living our standards. It is with these intentions in mind that we've pulled the affected product from our floors and website.

We are working with our supplier to replace this fabric and other manufacturers to replenish the affected core items as fast as we can. What that means is there will be a shortage of these styles in our stores and online until our new stock arrives. We are also in conversation with our manufacturing partner to understand what happened during the period this fabric was made.

We are committed to making things right so if you purchased product from our store or on our website and you think it is too sheer, we welcome you to return it for a full refund or exchange. If you have any questions please click here for more information, visit any of our stores or contact our Guest Education Centre.

Tags: french, lululemon sheer luon, luon shortage, sheer lululemon pants, sheer luon

Figure 8.1   Original post, Letter to guests, March 18, 2013

restoration discourse. In doing so, I read the letter to identify what image repair discourse strategies – embedded within the rhetorical process of image restoration – were present and coded the text for words and phrases indicating the presence of each strategy. Here, my coding and textual analysis followed a top-down approach, using a predetermined set of codes based on Coombs' (1995) five image restoration strategies, a schema derived from Benoit's (1995) rhetorically based approach.

In contrast, I applied a generative, bottom-up approach to code the messages customers posted in response to the letter. For this stage, I wanted to know what textual elements of the letter (such as words, phrases, statements, and/or topics) might have triggered customers' responses and how the topics or themes present in those responses might indicate traces of customers' interactive engagement with and/

or response to the discourse repair strategies present in the crisis repair message. Treating their responses as rhetorical artifacts of their asynchronous online reaction to the image repair message, I enlisted a rhetorical method of analysis described as generative criticism (Foss, 2004). Derived, in part, from grounded theory (Birks & Mills, 2011), a generative approach to text analysis offers marketing and discourse researchers alike the opportunity to "listen" to customers' verbatims, and to mine those comments for recurring patterns and themes and formulate coherent categories accordingly. With this approach, the goal is not to apply an a priori, predetermined set of thematic codes and verify how many times they occur, a potentially limiting practice in that it can lead to interesting aspects of a text being overlooked or ignored because they don't fit a fixed coding framework. Instead, the goal is to subject the text to a series of close readings and manually code the text for recurring themes and patterns as they emerge. Based on the significance and importance attributed to the themes present within a corpus of texts, and the frequency with which they occur, they then become the central schema by which the text is coded, analyzed, and discussed. By taking this approach, it was possible to trace how, and to what extent, certain words, phrases, or topics in the letter prompted or triggered a direct response from customers to show the interplay between the primary and secondary communication and the critical role language and discourse strategy played in eliciting their reactions.

Using a corpus-based method of analysis, I treated the first 151 blog posts as my corpus and, using the generative approach, manually coded it once to discover what topics were addressed in each blog post. I then coded it a second time to organize the topics that appeared with some frequency and intensity into thematic categories and refine those categories as needed. To ensure intra-coder reliability, I let some time elapse and coded the corpus a third time to ensure the consistency of my coding and findings. While my coding focused on identifying the major topics addressed to generate theme categories, I also coded for instances of addressivity (for example, salutations, greetings, vocatives), intertexuality (referencing and direct quotation of words and phrases from the letter in a blog post, and/or to other posts), and speech activity (for example, advice-giving, praise, puns, reprimands). In this study, both the outgoing letter lululemon posted and customers' responding posts to it were analyzed in order to pinpoint the central themes featured in their comments and to thereby identify the critical points of tension or "cruces" motivating their responses (Fairclough, 1992, p. 230). Because the intent of this study was to capture customers' immediate reactive responses to lululemon's letter, the analysis

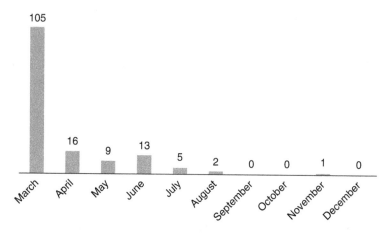

Figure 8.2   Number of blog posts, March to December 2013

and discussion that follows is limited to the comments customers posted from March 18, 2013 to December 2013. The majority of the excerpts I have incorporated in my discussion come from March to June 2013, the time period bearing the highest concentration of posts (Figure 8.2).

As my discussion of these posts will show, these combined methods of analysis proved highly effective in pinpointing the central themes present in customers' postings and in identifying the points of tension within these exchanges. In examining these themes, I will offer some insights into why the image restoration strategies present in this public statement, designed to repair a brand's reputation, did not elicit the positive response it might have anticipated and perhaps might have done more to damage than to repair it.

Impression management response strategies and lululemon's letter to its guests

In developing his rhetorically based theory of image restoration strategies, Benoit (1995) conceptualized communication as a "goal-directed activity" and asserted that "maintaining a positive reputation is one of the central goals of communication" (p. 63). Organizations have a repertoire of impression management response strategies they can draw from to mitigate the crisis, reassure stakeholders, and repair their image and reputation (Allen & Caillouet, 1994; Benoit, 1995; Coombs, 1995). Consolidating earlier response repertoires developed by Allen and Caillouet (1994) and Benoit (1995), Coombs (1995) delineated five main crisis response strategies organizations could integrate into their image restoration message: nonexistence, distance, ingratiation, mortification, and suffering. Of these strategies, my analysis revealed that the strategies of distance, ingratiation, and mortification figured prominently in the letter lululemon posted to its guests (see Table 8.1).

Distance

Distance strategies strive to reduce negative feelings or responses toward the organization by fully acknowledging that a problem or crisis exists but by "weakening the linkage between the crisis and the organization" (Coombs, 1995, p. 451). To create this distance, the organization attributes the problem causing the crisis to some third party external to the organization. By using this tactic, the organization attempts to minimize its involvement in, or level of control over, the action that sparked the crisis by holding some third party responsible for it. To underscore its lack of responsibility for a crisis, organizations can use *excuse*, a subvariant of this strategy commonly used in response to *accidents*, a common crisis type. "Accidents," Coombs (1995) explained,

> are unintentional and happen during the course of normal organizational operations. Product defects, employee injuries, and natural disasters are all examples of accidents. ... The excuse strategy is a perfect match for this weak link between the organization and the cause of the crisis. Excuses serve to reinforce the organization's lack of responsibility for the crisis. (p. 456)

At the beginning of its message (Figure 8.1), lululemon openly acknowledged the product quality problem, reporting they had "received some black luon women's bottoms that didn't meet [their] high standards" and "didn't measure up" to those high standards. Committed to "living [their] standards," they "pulled the affected product" from their inventory. However, in describing the problem, lululemon weakened its link as the cause or source of the product problem in two ways. First of all, the pronounced use of passive voice sentences enabled lululemon as the principal actor, at the syntactic level, to create a distancing effect from the action, removing itself from the events described (for example, "we learned some information about some product that arrived in our stores"; "our stores and ecommerce site received"). By doing so, the message characterizes lululemon as, much like its customers, the unwitting and unsuspecting recipient of a poor quality product, not the purveyor. Lululemon further distanced itself from the crisis by clearly

Table 8.1   Crisis-response strategies present in letter to guests, March 18, 2013

Crisis-response strategy	Characteristic	Example from letter
Distance	Minimize company's responsibility for crisis event	We recently learned some information about some product that arrived in our stores.
Excuse	Attribute problem, defect, or crisis to a third party	At the beginning of March, our stores and ecommerce site received some black luon women's bottoms that didn't meet our standards.
Ingratiation	Attempt to gain public approval	
Bolstering	Remind public of company's positive traits	[O]ur most important relationship is with our communities and our guests. We keenly listen to your feedback and it is paramount to us that you know we're listening. We are 100% committed to doing the right thing for our guests and living our standards.
Mortification		
Remediation	Compensate with money or goods; Offer product recall	We are committed to making things right for you so if you purchased product from our store or on our website and you think it is too sheer, we welcome you to return it for a full refund or exchange.
Repentance	Ask for forgiveness/ apologize	*Not present*
Rectification	Take action to solve problem and prevent event from happening again	It is with these intentions in mind that we've pulled the affected product from our floors and website. We are working with our supplier to replace this fabric and other manufacturers to replenish the affected core items as fast as we can. We are also in conversation with our manufacturing partner to understand what happened during the period this fabric was made.

Source: Crisis-response strategies from Coombs (1995).

attributing the fabric quality problem to third parties external to its organization, namely their supplier ("We are working with our supplier to replace this fabric") and their manufacturers ("We are also in conversation with our manufacturing partner to understand what happened during the period this fabric was made"). Collectively, these statements enabled lululemon to attribute responsibility for the affected product to the manufacturers, the external third party they entrusted to make their products and to meet their high standards.

Ingratiation

Ingratiation strategies try to restore an organization's positive face by reminding stakeholders of what they value or cherish about the organization (Coombs, 1995). By highlighting and reminding consumers of what they admire or like about a company, this strategy's goal is to activate or rekindle positive thoughts. This is achieved by bolstering existing positive attributions about the company and its products, and thereby diminishing any negative ones an action or event might have sparked. Lululemon attempted to ingratiate itself with its customers to this effect by using its message to remind them of its unequivocal commitment to delivering the same high-quality product and service they had come to expect in the past. As well, the company emphasized its relationship with its community and its guests as a unique and cherished one, and one it was and remained committed to preserving.

Mortification

Mortification involves those strategies designed to elicit stakeholders' forgiveness and restore their confidence in the company through some corrective action. Remediation (offering compensation), repentance (asking for forgiveness), and rectification (preventing future recurrence of the crisis event) represent the 3Rs of this strategy (Coombs, 1995). Lululemon attempted to remediate the situation by inviting its guests to return the product they purchased if they experienced it to be "too sheer," and by offering a full refund or exchange. While expressing its willingness to compensate its customers, lululemon did not apologize in this message for any potential dissatisfaction experienced by their guests. This lack of apology is interesting given that many service and retail providers often apologize in the face of customer dissatisfaction, usually as a polite and courteous gesture for whatever inconvenience or difficulty the customer might have experienced. This absence of the repentance strategy is, however, congruent with the excuse and distancing strategies present in this message. Because lululemon attributed the product quality problem to an external party outside of its organization, it may not have seen itself as culpable or responsible for the crisis and therefore not obligated to apologize for it. The company did, however, communicate its commitment to rectifying the problem to ensure their standards of quality were maintained in the future by meeting with their manufacturing partners to "understand what happened" in the making of this lot of luon fabric. Taken together, the remediation and rectification strategies present in lululemon's crisis response communication demonstrated its 100% commitment to "doing the right thing" for its guests and "making things right" for them.

Guests' or customers' responses to lululemon's letter

By incorporating these image restoration strategies, lululemon created a message designed to address an immediate rhetorical situation and to directly address its customers' potential concerns or doubts about product quality, to anticipate consumers' requests for compensation and corrective action, and to restore customer confidence. Evident in these restorative discourse strategies is a concerted effort to anticipate, address, and mitigate their publics' responses to this corporate crisis. This conscientious, strategic shaping of a public statement or utterance in response to a corporate crisis showcases the acute *addressivity* of this message genre and discourse type.

In his social discourse theory of language, Mikhail Bakhtin coined the term *addressivity* to describe how human statements or utterances are developed, whether strategically or not, in anticipation of a response. He explained:

> The utterance is constructed while taking into account possible responsive reactions, for whose sake, in essence, it is actually created. ... From the very beginning, the speaker expects a response from them, an active responsive understanding. The entire utterance is constructed, as it were, in anticipation of encountering this response. (1986, p. 94)

As Bakhtin described it, every spoken or written utterance has an explicit or implied author and addressee and that, at every step, writers and/or speakers develop their messages with the expectation and anticipation of their audience's active engagement with the language of their message. It is the anticipation of this active responsive reaction to our messages that Bakhtin conceptualizes as the intrinsic *addressivity* of human utterances. Traces of that addressivity were immediately apparent in those instances where customers introduced their responses to lululemon's letter using a variety of greetings, instantiating different levels of formality and relationship, addressing lululemon as a company ("Dear Lululemon"), a person ("dear lulu"), and, in some cases, as a friend ("Lulu"). Such *addressivity* is pronounced and marked in the epistolary language of letters in general, but it is especially heightened in the language of crisis communication letters where a company strategically uses the language and content of its messages to restore its public face and anticipate its publics' responsive reaction.

To locate the points of tension sparking customers' responsive reactions to the letter addressed to them, my thematic analysis of each blog post revealed that customers' comments clustered around six major themes: product recall information, time, product quality, price, customer service, and customer relationship. The frequency with which these themes were present in their posts and the image restoration strategies they appear to address or respond to are documented in Table 8.2.

Product recall information

For many customers, the message designed to alert and inform them about the product recall did not supply the information they needed to determine if the items they had purchased were included in the recall. This lack of clarity may well have stemmed from the imprecise, ambiguous phrasing (as in "some information"; "some product") used to describe the problem. Consequently, a number of their posts expressed uncertainty, suggesting that the letter was incomplete, not meeting their basic informational needs as readers and as customers. Customers therefore posted queries requesting a complete listing of what styles were affected and whether they could return the ones they had recently purchased. As one person asked, "I have a skinny will pant ... it is also see through..., so are these included in the return?" This query prompted another customer to concur: "I agree ... it would be nice if the letter included which specific product is being recalled." Some posts requested clarity about whether they could return clothing purchased before March 1.

For others, the lack of specific information about what products were included in the recall signified a lack of transparency and an attempt to hide the truth from customers. Several posts adopted a skeptical or accusatory tone, suggesting the company was "hiding" information and not being entirely honest and forthright with customers about the extent of the problem. As one customer demanded:

> Why are you being so secretive about which exact styles are "too sheer" – you need to be more forthcoming to say which exact styles are in this recall. ... You are hiding something about your product

Table 8.2   Themes present in customer blog posts, March to December 2013

Crisis-response strategy present in letter	Major themes present in customers' blog posts	Frequency
Distance	Time quality problem recognized and addressed	23
Excuse	Challenging company for not taking responsibility	6
Ingratiation		
Bolstering		
Commitment to standards	Product quality (negative)	65
	Sheerness of product	43
	Praise of past product quality introduces negative comments about present quality	18
	Product quality (positive)	9
Relationship with communities and guests	Product price (negative): Present dissatisfaction with high price for low quality	40
	Product price (positive): Past willingness to pay high price for previous high quality	16
Listening to feedback	Customer service and in-store treatment (negative)	42
	Customer care (negative)	7
	Relationship with brand	
	Love	23
	Ending relationship or "breaking up" with brand	14
	Moving to a competing brand	22
	Not listening, reading, or responding to feedback	21
Mortification		
Remediation		
Product recall	Product recall information incomplete	25
	Product recall not comprehensive enough, or insufficient as a remedy	20
Refund or exchange	Return policy (discontent with)	16
	General queries about how to refund or exchange	8
Rectification	Advice on how to rectify problem	43
Action to prevent problem in future		

quality, do you really care about your customers? If you do then you should be willing to release that information.

In this instance, neglecting to disclose information fully, or, at least, the perception of withholding information, was seen as undermining the company's claim in its message of being fully committed to its customers and its relationship with them. Such comments underscore that honesty is as much a foundation of personal relationships as it is in customer–company relationships and community.

Time, product quality issue noticed and addressed

Time, as it related to when the quality control issue was identified and when it was publicly addressed, was a recurring theme and a specific point of tension in customers' responding comments. Lululemon's letter created a sense of urgency in reporting that the company had "recently learned some information about some product" and wanted its "guests" to know "right away." The company also identified "the beginning of March" as the time it became aware of a quality problem with a shipment of athletic pants. As their responses indicated, these statements rang false for loyal lululemon customers. In particular, customers disagreed with lululemon's assessment and acknowledgment of when the quality issue had arisen and when they, as consumers, and product users, had observed and experienced a change in product quality. Indeed, customers were quick to correct the company, noting that they had observed and experienced a decline in quality that pre-dated March 1. As one customer forcefully argued,

> This problem did not start in March. ... I think you are insulting your customers by just acknowledging it now and pretending it's a new problem. The issue has been in the comments section of the products for a very long time.

Or, "By the way Lulu, your luon pants have been see through for much longer than this March." Echoing these statements, two other customers wrote the following:

> Lululemon please do not insult your customers further by announcing that the quality issue is a recent development! Your company has been well aware of its diminishing standards for a long while with your own disclaimer listed on the website with regard to the "sheerness" of your products.

I have noticed that the sheerness of your yoga pants in all colours has been a problem for close to one year. Surely you know this given that review after review on your website points this out. Suspicious and disappointing.

To add emphasis to their comments, some customers directly quoted key words from the original letter and incorporated the message's references to time in their responses: "It has been long before 'the beginning of March' that the quality has gone downhill." "I write this out of love for lulu. ... But people have been writing about this for a while now and it's disappointing to read that they 'recently' learned about it." In this way, customers strategically appropriated the language from the original message and accented it anew to bolster their statements expressing their disappointment, outrage, criticisms, and concerns.

Throughout these responses, customers used their comments to emphasize and reiterate that the quality problem was not a "new" discovery and that it had a history, fully documented by customers in their previous blog posts and product reviews. Customers' comments even directed the company and its representatives to read the blog's online archive of customers' past messages reporting their concerns about diminishing quality, as in this post: "Again and again, if you look at the comments in the blog and the customer reviews, you will see that the quality issues are not just since March 1, 2013." In doing so, customers like this one challenged the company's efforts to distance itself from the problem by reminding them that this is not a new event, but an ongoing one with a history chronicled by customers themselves, and one that had not been acknowledged or addressed publicly until now. In this way, customers successfully capitalize on the digital archive and permanence that computer-mediated communication affords as they strategically draw on previously archived messages to bolster their position. Such practices remind us that while online interaction resembles conversation in some ways, the technology nonetheless mediates those interactions and shapes how those exchanges emerge and unfold in the online realm.

From customers' perspectives, their posts articulate a frustration with the company's history of distancing itself from the problem (evident in their expression of being "disappointed" and "insulted") and their dissatisfaction with the *excuse* tactic. To some, the timing of the letter was not an announcement of a new problem, but a too little, too late attempt to address an ongoing one: "Finally addressing this issue after months and months of complaints is absurd and disrespectful to your customers. If you aren't going to fix the problem, at least fix your return policy." In a similar vein, "The quality of your products has taken a substantial nosedive in the last year. It's quite disgusting that this issue is being addressed only now and that you're only allowing luon items to be returned that were purchased after March 1st." For this consumer, the remediation strategy (product recall and refund) clearly wasn't extensive enough, given customers' claims that black luon pants were not, in their reported experience, the only styles affected. It is worth noting that many of the positive comments about the company's product quality were mostly oriented toward the past. In such instances, customers would begin their comment with a positive assessment of past product quality in order to introduce negative comments about the product quality they were experiencing in the present. Setting up this temporal comparison enabled them to underscore, in their estimation, how far the company had moved away from its past commitment to product quality. This pairing of positive with negative comments is characteristic of customer complaint discourse in online forums (Vásquez, 2011).

Product price

Frequently also paired with customers' discussions of declining product quality was product price. In discussing price, customers expressed their past willingness to pay a high price for lululemon clothing because of the high-quality fabrics used in their construction ("the price was steep, but worth every penny"), a product feature that distinguished the brand from its competitors in the athletic wear industry and a hallmark of its retail success. Customers expressed a sense of pride in the product that motivated them to pay more for a superior product: "I used to be a proud buyer and 'wearer' of Lululemon until about two years ago when I started to notice that the quality was declining while the prices were not. In fact, I would say that in the last year, the poor quality has been much more evident." In the absence of this quality, a number of customers reported they planned to, or had already begun to, buy their yoga wear from competing companies, since the lower price reflected the lower product quality they affiliated with those alternative brands (for example, "I think I'm going to switch to [competing brand] ... they aren't nearly as expensive!"). As one customer reported:

> Sadly, it looks like the quality has suffered and like another commenter said, I can't justify the costs when the product is not acceptable. ... Time to shop elsewhere ladies.

These sentiments and reflections were echoed by other customers and illustrated how the company's genuine efforts to ingratiate itself with its customers, by reminding them of their commitment to quality, only served to remind customers of the extent to which quality had declined and how the brand no longer signified a quality product for them, deserving of the high price they were willing to pay for it in the past.

Customer service and treatment

As part of its remediation strategy and its efforts to remedy the problem and effect the product recall, lululemon rightly offered its guests the opportunity to return their purchase for a full refund or exchange, and expressed in its letter a commitment to "doing the right thing for their guests," reminding them that "[their] most important relationship is with our communities and our guests." Instead of soothing disgruntled customers, this mention of their commitment to customer service sparked a negative response from customers as they recalled a litany of difficulties they had experienced when trying to seek refunds and exchanges in the past. Instead of successfully *ingratiating* customers by reminding them of lululemon's commitment to and appreciation of them, these statements seemed to trigger, for a number of lululemon customers, a recollection of negative experiences with lululemon's return policies when trying to exchange or refund past purchases. Where one person described it as an "unfriendly return policy," another advised that if the company wasn't going to fix its product quality problems it might "at least fix [its] return policy." Others recalled and shared a similar experience when trying to return items:

> [I] agree with the other comments on customer service in stores being less than friendly when you are returning something unworn.

Some went so far as to caution and discourage other customers from trying to receive compensation:

> Don't waste your time going to a Lulu store and requesting some type of compensation for faulty products. ....I vowed this day on NEVER to shop at Lulu again!

In addition to a decline in product quality, customers also expressed concern about a perceptible decline in customer service and treatment. As one customer reflected, "I, too, have noticed a change in attitude at the stores. It seems no matter what complaint someone walks in with, the customer is always wrong. That's not the way it should be, I heard." Besides an "unfriendly" returns policy, customers frequently expressed their reluctance to return any product, describing their previous exchanges with in-store customer service representatives as equally unfriendly: "I wasn't going to try to return them because their return policy is so bad and the sales people there are so rude to you." The decline in customer care motivated some customers to challenge ("You say you care") and question ("Do you really care about your customers?") the company's commitment to them on this front.

Some customers expressed their outrage at purportedly being asked to perform in-store tests to determine the coverage of the "sheer" clothing they tried to return. As one customer confessed,

> I never felt so humiliated and embarrassed /violated in my life. You know the product has issues and to ask that question is completely unacceptable. ... I was fine with quality issues that's normal things happen but to be asked to bend over to see if they can see my underwear was the last straw.

This reported experience prompted the following response from another customer:

> I read another 'Guest' wanted to return 'transparent' pants, and she was asked to bend over so the educator could assess the sheerness. Seriously?

The palpable disbelief customers expressed in these and other comments at being asked to participate in these actions to have their claims validated by customer service representatives reveals how customers left these encounters feeling emotionally distressed and victimized by their in-store experience. Indeed their comments collectively confirm that their in-store experiences did not make them feel they were valued, part of a community, or that the company was fully committed to preserving their relationship.

Customers' relationship with lululemon

Beyond the in-store customer service relationship, customers' resounding disappointment with the brand they valued and loved for its quality products led many customers to use the discourse of personal relationships to express how their relationship with the company and its brand had changed. When describing the brand and its products, customers frequently used the word *relationship* to describe their connection with and allegiance to the lululemon brand. Frustrated with the lack of response in addressing customers' concerns, one customer expressed how that relationship had changed:

> We went *unheard* and received no explanation nor response. ... I'm a bit miffed now. Mostly, I'm losing my allegiance to the only brand of athletic wear I felt I had a *personal relationship* with. [emphases added].

In the face of declining product quality and customer service, customers described their relationship with the brand as having changed, and passionately enlisted the language ordinarily associated with failed personal relationships to express their disappointment. A common sentiment expressed was *sadness*:

> I am sad to discontinue my relationship with Lulu, but I have to carefully save for each item I purchase, and to have this kind of quality let down isn't worth it.

> It makes me very sad as I was such a devotee of lululemon.

> It's a sad day for what used to be loyal lulu lovers.

Especially remarkable was how frequently customers also used the word *love* to describe their past passion for the brand and the regret they experienced at having to "break up" with a brand they once loved, valued, and championed. Two customers traced their "love stories," explaining how their respective relationships with the brand fell apart in the face of deteriorating quality, continued high prices, and/or poor treatment:

> When I first walked into a Lululemon store five years ago, I instantly fell in love with everything you had to offer ... the price was steep, but worth every penny. ... Sorry Lulu years of falling in love with your brand and promoting the clothing to all my friends is over!.

> Dear lululemon,
> I'm breaking up with you. Well, I actually broke up with you months ago but now I just want to get some things of my chest because quite honestly I'm still hurting.
> When we first fell in love, I would spend all my money on you. And it was a pleasure to do so because you were worth it! ... I was proud of you and I couldn't wait to show you off everywhere we went. ... But as time

wore on, things changed. You changed. First you started squeezing me for my money. I took notice but didn't care. At the time, my love for you was greater than my love for my hard earned disposable income.... Goodbye lover. It hurts me just as much as it hurts you. Ugh and I still have hundreds of reminders of you in my closet. Literally. Hundreds.

Customers nonetheless remained hopeful that once lululemon fully addressed its product quality issues, the relationship might be repaired and restored, at some future time. Some customers petitioned lululemon to address their concerns to ensure the relationship was maintained:

Please please please fix this right lululemon!! I really don't want to break up with you but really it's not me, it's you.

In this case, the customer enacted the familiar scripts used to soften bad news when ending a personal or romantic relationship. This same trope featured in other posts, often tinged with sarcasm: "Sorry lulu, but we are breaking up. It's you, not me." Some customers, however, offered the company advice, suggesting that once they addressed their issues they might want to return to and restore the relationship. One customer urged lululemon to follow a course of rehabilitation before she would return to the relationship:

Check yourself into manufacturing rehab, find yourself again, and redeem yourself. When you're ready, I'll meet you on the sweaty side of the mat again.

Here, the customer recommends a more rigorous mortification strategy, offering a set of corrective actions that would, perhaps, make the company a worthy partner again.

That customers regarded themselves as in a unique relationship with this organization and part of a community sharing similar values, at least where good quality and design are concerned, is reflected in the language they use to identify themselves and their roles in relationship to lululemon. Within lululemon's organizational culture, customers are assigned the role of "guests" who "experience" lululemon culture when they buy their clothing, visit their stores, interact with their staff of "Guest Educators," and attend their community events or classes. On one hand, the word "guest" elevates the status of their customers, promising them superior treatment when they visit and shop at their various outlets. On the other, its formality creates a distancing effect.

Lululemon's customers, however, describe themselves as "devotees," "loyal followers," "diehard fans," "core Lulu customers," and as part of "the lululovers community." One customer described herself as "a hard core Lululemon fan." One self-described "core Lulu customer," however, challenged the labelling lululemon uses to describe its customers as irksome, patronizing, and an inaccurate way to characterize the buyer–seller relationship:

> [M]aybe this is just me, but I really hate being called a 'guest.' 'Guests' do not pay for things, but customers do. It's okay, just call us customers. We know how stores work.

Here, a customer invites the company to use a more human voice, to speak to customers more authentically in a language that resonates with them as a member of this community and culture.

Reflection and summary

Although lululemon's admirable effort to speak directly to customers through their company blog post would appear to have followed best practice in terms of crisis communication and image restoration theories, my analysis of how customers responded to their message illustrates the extent to which the company underestimated the *addressivity* of its message and the responsive reaction such public utterances can potentially initiate. A prevailing concept in Bakhtin's discussion of a message's addressivity is the level of influence a writer or speaker can assert in shaping the addressee's or audience's response. "When constructing my utterance," Bakhtin explained, "I try actively to determine this response" (p. 95). To determine that response fully, Bakhtin underscored the importance of assessing and calculating "the apperceptive background" of the intended audience, "the extent to which he is familiar with the situation, whether he has special knowledge of the given cultural area of communication, his views and concerns" (pp. 95–6).

My analysis of the predominant themes present in the language of customers' responding statements revealed that the image-restoration strategies present in lululemon's message did not fully take into account the *apperceptive background* of its intended audience, and their acute awareness, and knowledge of, a decline in product quality that pre-dated the March 1 discovery by, to many of their observations, about a year. A failure to fully anticipate and acknowledge the intended audience's apperceptive background in the composition of this crisis repair message resulted in a resounding backlash that flared, rather than soothed, customer discontent. As Coombs (1995) noted in his assessment of crisis repair strategies, distance and ingratiation strategies work best if the company has a history of positive performance in the mind of its targeted audiences. In the absence of that positive performance history, statements that attribute product defect to a third party will be unconvincing. Customers' tracking of what they perceived as a decline in lululemon's performance history, both in terms of product quality and customer service, made it difficult for them to be persuaded that lululemon was fully unaware of the product quality issue or that it was beyond its control.

Likewise, a company's attempts to ingratiate itself with customers by bolstering its brand's positive attributes and commitment to customers will be unsuccessful if the company's credibility has grown unstable in the minds of its publics. In the case of lululemon, we observed how customers' statements revealed their skepticism about the company's level of commitment to them, and their unacknowledged concerns about product quality before the incident was made public did not convince them their feedback was taken seriously. A critical part of delivering effective customer service is listening and responding to customer feedback. In its letter, lululemon characterized itself as taking customers' concerns seriously, emphasizing its commitment to "listening" to customers. However, the allegedly unacknowledged and unaddressed customer comments concerning product quality posted long before March led customers to doubt the company and its representatives were truly listening to them. Not surprisingly, their statements expressed their outrage at the incongruity between the company's stated intention and action and their experiences as customers:

> Dear lulu – so you pulled what you had on the shelves at your store – but *listen* [emphasis added] to us now – what about what was already sold and are now in our closets.

Other comments challenged the company's ongoing failure to listen to its customers' complaints, challenging the "head in the sand approach" to customer service they were observing.

> It is a shame [one customer argued] lululemon is still putting their head in the sand and not acknowledging die hard customer complaints related to ongoing quality issues.

As one customer forcefully advised,

> You need to start *listening* [emphasis added] to your customers, not your shareholders. Cutting corners is not profitable ... and your loyal fan base is disappearing fast. We see right through you Lululemon, literally this time.

Here critique also gives way to irony as the writer engages in wordplay to address the decline in product quality. And, finally, a customer advised:

> I really hope your company actually *listens* [emphasis added] to the sentiment expressed by so many over the last few years.

As displayed and heard in these examples, customers intentionally repeated the word "listening" and its variants from the original message, and accented it, often to harsher effect, in their responses. The echoing effect displayed here, and in other examples I have highlighted throughout this chapter's discussion, illustrates how customers' statements or utterances are, as Bakhtin would characterize them, "filled with the echoes and reverberations" of not only language from the original message but also from each other's posts and comments (p. 91). The "echoes and reverberations" that infuse customers' responses, as they incorporate key words and phrases from the original message and reference other customers' comments in their responses, showcase how customers' statements in online environments respond to and are shaped by the utterances and statements that precede them, and how this practice can be used to reinforce or corroborate the sentiments expressed in their messages. "Each utterance," Bakhtin underscored, "refutes, affirms, supplements, and relies on the others" (p. 91).

In discussing the themes customers' comments clustered around, I have also demonstrated how customers effectively referenced and quoted aspects of the original letter into their responding statements to heighten the rhetorical impact of their messages. The iterative way customers intentionally appropriated the language from lululemon's letter and accented it anew to express their disappointment, indignation, complaints, advice, and recommendations vividly illustrates the pivotal and precarious way the language present in a message designed to repair a company's image can potentially do further damage to it, if its intended audience chooses to use elements of it to bolster a negative responsive reaction to it. The potential for this type of appropriation and reinterpreting of key words and phrases thus serves as important reminder to communications practitioners, strategists, educators, and students alike why language selection cannot be overlooked as an integral part of the process in composing crisis communication messages.

The purpose of this chapter's study was to determine what prompted the vigorous and overwhelmingly negative response to lululemon's well-intended message of repair and reparation in response to its public relations crisis. My analysis of these postings has shown how a generative approach to text analysis proved highly effective in locating the central themes present in customers' responding blog posts and in identifying the major points of tension or cruces within these exchanges. My rhetorical analysis of customers' responses to lululemon's message also indicated a high level of engagement with the language used in this message, evident in the prevalent and strategic use of reference and quotation within their responses. Indeed, corporate blogs and the complex strands of social interaction they house capture the dynamic and dialogic nature of speech communication in ways that Bakhtin, in developing his social theory of language, perhaps had not fully imagined. The burgeoning archive of voices and conversations that blogs preserve makes them a fascinating example of one type of digital business discourse that will continue to hold our interest as we observe the vital, yet frequently overlooked, role of language in negotiating the digital marketplace where companies and consumers meet.

References

Allen, M. W., & Caillouet, R. H. (1994). Legitimation endeavours: Impression management strategies used by an organization in crisis. *Communication Monographs, 61,* 44–62.

Bakhtin, M. M. (1986). The problem of speech genres. In C. Emerson & M. Holquist (Eds), (tr. V. W. McGee) *Speech Genres & Other Late Essays* (pp. 60–102). Austin, TX: University of Texas Press.

Baxter, G. J., & Connolly, T. M. (2013). The "state of art" of organisational blogging. *The Learning Organization, 20* (2), 104–117.

Baxter, G. J., Connolly, T. M., & Stansfield, M. H. (2010). Organisational blogs: Benefits and challenges of implementation. *The Learning Organization, 17* (6), 515–528.

Benoit, W. L. (1995). *Accounts, Excuses, and Apologies: A Theory of Image Restoration Strategies.* Albany, NY: State University of New York Press.

Birks, M., & Mills, J. (2011). *Grounded Theory: A Practical Guide.* Thousand Oaks, CA: Sage.

Burn-Callander, R. (2013). Top ten corporate social media blunders. Retrieved from http://www.telegraph.co.uk/finance/10473523/Top-ten-corporate-social-media-blunders/.

Cho, S., & Huh, J. (2010). Content analysis of corporate blogs as a relationship management tool. *Corporate Communications: An International Journal, 15* (1), 30–48.

Coombs, W. T. (1995). Choosing the right words: The development of guidelines for the selection of the "appropriate" crisis-response strategies. *Management Communication Quarterly, 8* (4), 447–476.

Cox, J. L., Martinez, E. R., & Quinlan, K. B. (2008). Blogs and the corporation: Managing the risk, reaping the benefits. *Journal of Business Strategy, 29* (3), 4–12.

Deshpande, M., & Sarkar, A. (2010). BI and sentiment analysis. *Business Intelligence Journal, 15* (2), 41–50.

Fairclough, N. (1992). *Discourse and Social Change.* Cambridge: Polity Press.

Foss, S. K. (2004). Generative criticism. *Rhetorical Criticism: Exploration & Practice* (pp. 411–459) (3rd edition). Long Grove, IL: Waveland Press.

Godes, D., & Myzlin, D. (2004). Using online conversation to study word-of-mouth communication. *Marketing Science, 23* (4) 545–560.

Guffey, M. E., Loewy, D., Rhodes K., & Rogin, P. (2013). *Business Communication: Process and Product* (4th brief Canadian edition). Toronto, Canada: Nelson.

Harrison-Walker, L. J. (2001). E-complaining: A content analysis of an Internet complaint forum. *Journal of Services Marketing, 15* (5), 397–412.

Hong, Y., & Lee, W. (2005). Consumer complaint behaviour in the online environment. In Y. Gao (Ed.) *Web System Design and Online Consumer Behavior* (pp. 90–105). Hershey, PA: Idea Group Publishing.

Hulme, M. (2013). The rise of the Linguarati. Retrieved from: http://www.linguarati.com.

Jones, S. (1999). Studying the net: Intricacies and issues. In S. Jones (Ed.), *Doing Internet Research: Critical Issues and Methods for Examining the Net* (pp. 1–27). Thousand Oaks, CA: Sage.

Kelleher, T., & Miller, B. M. (2006). Organizational blogs and the human voice: Relational strategies and relational outcomes. *Journal of Computer-Mediated Communication, 11*, 395–414.

Kelleher, T., & Miller, B. M. (2009). Conversational voice, communicated commitment, and public relations outcomes in interactive online communication. *Journal of Communication, 59*, 172–188.

Kent, M. L. (2008). Critical analysis of blogging in public relations. *Public Relations Review, 34*, 32–40.

Ki, E., & Hon, L. C. (2006). Relationship maintenance strategies on Fortune 500 company web sites. *Journal of Communication Management, 10* (1), 27–43.

Ko, H., Yin, C., & Kuo, F. (2008). Exploring individual communication power in the blogosphere. *Internet Research, 18* (5), 541–561.

Kozinets, R. V. (2009). *Netnography: Doing Ethnographic Research Online.* London: Sage.

Lee, S., Hwang, T., & Lee, H. (2006). Corporate blogging strategies of the Fortune 500 companies. *Management Decision, 44* (3), 316–334.

Lee, S., Park, S. R., & Hwang, T. (2008). Corporate-level blogs of the Fortune 500 companies: An empirical investigation of content and design. *International Journal of Information Technology and Management, 7* (2), 134–148.

Levine, R., Locke, C., Searls, D., & Weinberger, D. (2001). *The Cluetrain Manifesto: The End of Business as Usual.* New York: Basic Books.

Lululemon athletica (March 18, 2013). Letter to our guests [blog post]. Retrieved from: http://www.lululemon.com/community/blog/a-letter-to-our-guests/.

Myers, G. (2010). *The Discourse of Blogs and Wikis.* London: Continuum.

Newman, A. (2015). *Business Communication: In Person, in Print, Online.* Stamford, CT: Cengage.

Page, R. (2014). Saying "sorry": Corporate apologies posted on Twitter. *Journal of Pragmatics, 62*, 30–45.

Pang, B., & Lee, L. (2008). Opinion mining and sentiment analysis. *Foundations and Trends in Information Retrieval, 2* (1–2), 1–135.

Porter, L., Sweetser, K., & Chung, D. (2009). The blogosphere and public relations: Investigating practitioners' roles and blog use. *Journal of Communication Management, 13* (3), 250–267.

Schultz, F., Utz, S., & Göritzb, A. (2011). Is the medium the message? Perceptions of and reactions to crisis communication via Twitter, blogs, and traditional media. *Public Relations Review, 37*, 20–27.

Shwom, B., & Snyder Gueldenzoph, L. (2014). *Business Communication: Polishing Your Professional Presence* (2nd edition). Boston, MA: Pearson.

Sweetser, K. D., & Metzgar, E. (2007). Communicating during crisis: Use of blogs as a relationship management tool. *Public Relations Review, 33*, 340–342.

Thompson, H. (2013). 6 examples of social media crises: What can we learn? Retrieved from: http://oursocialtimes.com/6-examples-of-social-media-crises-what-can-we-learn/.

Tuten, T. L., & Solomon, M. R. (2013). *Social Media Marketing*. Boston, MA: Pearson.

Van Noort, G., & Willemsen, L. M. (2011). Online damage control: The effects of proactive versus reactive webcare interventions in consumer-generated and brand-generated platforms. *Journal of Interactive Marketing, 2*, 131–140.

Vásquez, C. (2011). Complaints online: The case of TripAdvisor. *Journal of Pragmatics, 43*, 1707–1717.

Zabin, J., & Jefferies, A. (2008). *Social Media Monitoring and Analysis: Generating Consumer Insights from Online Conversation*. Aberdeen Group Benchmark Report.

Part III
Theoretical and Methodological Approaches to Digital Business Discourse

9
What Did I Just Tweet?!: The Need to Address Digital Emotional Literacy in Corporate Communications

Steven A. Edelson, Philip Kim, Ron Scott, and Julie M. Szendrey

Introduction

Digital culture is quickly becoming a saturated term. The vast array of media, platforms, and audiences, all have their own specific languages, rituals, and purposes. Highly targeted and specific markets are ready to digitally engage, but poorly thought-out public relations campaigns, moments of weakness among CEOs and other high-ranking officers remind us we live in a reputation economy (Schawbel, 2011). Using a term like digital culture as a stand-in for such a varied environment establishes boundaries that are fluid and dynamic at best.

What, then, can organizations do to negotiate this ever-changing world? In appearance at least the culture seems to mimic computer games, offering a landscape strewn with monsters and land mines (public relations fiascos, poorly understood opportunities) while also providing clear pockets of gold (rich, ready markets) as rewards. Some great ideas fail or find, at best, marginal usefulness and profitability – file-sharing, crowdsourcing, knowledge sharing, virtual environments – while other far more seemingly limited concepts become huge money-makers. Facebook, for instance, starts out as a way for a social recluse to meet women and becomes essential to maintaining an organization's presence on the Web (Kirkpatrick, 2011), and Twitter begins as a location device designed to help friends direct meet each other to a publicly held enterprise with over 270 million active users (Twitter, 2014). Mobile devices open up markets in lesser-developed countries that are previously only foreseen in science fiction novels. Even if all of these activities fall within the confines of digital culture, they spread the definition of this culture so far that attempts to connect these border points feel futile.

Of all the rapid changes brought on by this culture perhaps none is more fraught with organizational peril than the possibilities of open communication. The gatekeepers of information and media access can quickly be walked around or leapt over by the immediacy of newsfeeds, and forums like Reddit or news aggregators like Digg. News organizations fly to Twitter in order to be the first to post information about the crisis-of-the-moment, and editors responsible for maintaining the veracity and integrity of their media outlets have to confirm or refute conclusions drawn up with faulty or incomplete information. All of the openness of digital culture can be threatening on multiple levels, as major retailers lose millions of records to hackers, even while companies highly regulate their employees' social media usage. On the other hand, companies can pinpoint potential customers in ways never before possible. Executives can converse directly with new and existing customers to address concerns or complaints immediately. The possibilities for communication in this culture are powerful and organizations often struggle with making these communications work.

Of course, there are many organizations that are successfully negotiating and exploiting digital culture. Some of these organizations take data-driven approaches, and this method has generated a billion-dollar industry (Ranii, 2014), as the success of Google analytics (and the industry that has grown up around it) attests. On one hand, quantitative data-driven approaches yield targeted advertising that merely extends a form of marketing that is over a hundred years old (Ohmann, 1998), but on the other, they result in the invention of new forms of external communication such as viral videos and social media campaigns. Organizations that successfully negotiate digital culture often develop new rules around the use of older technologies like email and newer ones such as social media platforms, and they have also figured out how to manage projects more efficiently by using wikis and other forms of collaborative software, often eliminating the need for expensive travel and enabling organizational units to communicate in productive ways. Through online collaboration websites, labor and talent resources have become available 24 hours a day for entities both within and outside the organization.

The notion of a communications revolution triggered by the rise of digital culture has been around since Marshall McLuhan's musings in the 1960s (McLuhan, 1962, 1964), but its pace has quickened with the ubiquity of digital culture. While analytical approaches to understanding how communication occurs in the digital age are important, we argue that other approaches are now necessary. Thinking about digital culture in terms of digital literacy offers organizations a way of understanding how to communicate, and is critical to organizations that want to prosper in this economy. The term we have labeled "digital emotional literacy" combines the components of digital literacy and emotional intelligence within the context of business communications. Both concepts (digital literacy and emotional intelligence) have been actively researched for a number of years, but now is the time for those concepts to be joined and studied together.

The demands of today's digital literacy are subtly different than those of previous media, as Buckingham (2006, p. 268) in particular argues. He defines digital literacy as involving a systematic awareness of four components:

- the actual construction of digital media
- the unique rhetoric of interactive communication
- an understanding of exactly who is communicating to whom
- an awareness of one's own position as an audience, and how that position fits within the larger digital communication environment.

While Buckingham's (2006) definition is a useful starting point, it responds specifically to parameters that organizations are familiar and comfortable with – media platforms and environments, senses of audience and purpose, and analyses of communication contexts. The new world of digital literacy requires even more from organizations, and in this chapter we establish the need to consider that digital emotional literacy is important for organizations needing to navigate the bounds of its digital culture.

Digital literacy and business communications

As we extend Buckingham's 2006 definition of digital literacy, analyzing the intersections of this new form of literacy and the business communications skills required helps us make the business case for digital emotional literacy. The belief that "creating and publishing information" is strictly a technical skill does not fully account for just how much of this ability depends upon nuanced senses of rhetorical skills such as audience awareness, previous context, and strategic sensitivity.

Digital literacy can be described as the ability to use, access, edit, create, and share information utilizing a variety of digital technology platforms. Internet users have come to expect and demand immediacy of information. The importance of digital literacy skills becomes more evident as the "older" formats of print media and even television news are quickly becoming a secondary source of information (Gilster, 1997); the Web and specifically social networking platforms are more frequently being used for communications, both internal and external to organizations (Correa et al., 2010; Purcell et al., 2012).

While there are multiple definitions and interpretations of the term digital literacy (e.g., Bawden, 2008; Eshet-Alkalai, 2002, 2004; Gilster, 1997; Lanham, 1995), a growing number of studies point to the importance of being able to skillfully interact with digital media (e.g., Lee & Hsu, 2002; Mundrof & Laird, 2002). Skills that are particularly valuable in becoming digitally literate include the ability to assemble information from various sources, make informed judgments as to the validity of sources, and create and publish information as well as consume it (Bawden, 2008). Bawden's list speaks to the need to combine analytics (information assembling, the technical aspects of creating and publishing) with skills that require more emotional literacy (making informed judgments). To that end, we now present a brief review of emotional intelligence as it applies in the context of digital literacy. This review is followed by our development of a construct we refer to as digital emotional literacy, reflecting a combination of these two fields.

Emotional intelligence

The development of the emotional intelligence (EI) construct initially evolved from the works of Gardner (1983, 1998) and Wagner and Sternberg (1985), who suggested that intelligence be studied as a broader concept than exclusively academic intelligence or IQ. Multiple intelligences are noted to exist, including those categorized as "intrapersonal" – the ability to understand one's own emotions, and "interpersonal" – the ability to appreciate the emotions of others (Gardner, 1983, 1998), as well as "school smarts" – academic intelligence and "street smarts" – practical intelligence (Wagner & Sternberg, 1990).

From Gardner's research a working definition of emotional intelligence was developed: "a type of social intelligence that involves the ability to monitor one's own and others' emotions, to discriminate among them, and to use the information to guide one's thinking and actions" (Mayer & Salovey, 1993, p. 433). Subsequently, emotional intelligence was further defined in dimensional format: the intrapersonal dimensions of self-awareness, managing emotions, and self-motivation, and the interpersonal dimensions of relating well and emotional mentoring.

Goleman (1995, 1998) introduced the connections between EI and organizational success by addressing the importance of EI in effective business careers and group performance. Those individuals with leadership positions in an organization typically had higher EI than average performers. Additionally, groups with members showing appropriate social behavior typically had higher "group intelligence" than those with members lacking socially appropriate behavior (Williams & Sternberg, 1988).

More recently, Goleman's findings about the success of those with EI has led to more detailed examinations of how EI can be applied to the business world, including the development of business communication, curriculum, leadership development, and conflict management strategies (Abraham, 2006; Ashkanasy & Dasborough, 2003; Myers & Tucker, 2005; Rahim et al., 2002; Tucker et al., 2000). Emotional intelligence is needed within the work environment in both the intrapersonal and interpersonal contexts.

The interpersonal dimensions of EI are specifically essential to successful business communications by providing the link to "how well do we interact with others?" Weisinger's (1998) EI dimension of "relating well" focuses on relationship building and the communication skills and practice one uses to build those relationships. "Emotional mentoring" focuses on helping others develop their "relating well" skills to the best of their abilities through their own emotions, communication, and problem-solving abilities. Rahim et al. (2002) expands on Goleman's (1998) interpersonal dimensions of empathy and social skills by understanding the importance of feelings transmitted, providing support, and understanding the linkage between emotions and behavior. Dealing with problems and addressing conflict without demeaning others can be associated with strong social skills (Rahim et al., 2002).

Having strong interpersonal skills in the corporate environment is essential to effective communication. In the digital communication world the proper medium selection, word usage, and tone are just a few critical elements in successful business communication. The question still remains however: how emotionally literate do employees need to be in digital culture in order to make the right choice in conveying messages?

We believe the answer to this question is very. As organizations become immersed in digital culture, the importance of EI becomes even more apparent. It extends beyond business into the world of digital communication and social media, focusing on the traits of the senders and receivers and elements of conversation within the corporation. Groysberg and Slind

(2012) note the importance of employee engagement and "emotional proximity" in today's digital organization.

Emotional intelligence within business communication

Those who have become immersed in digital culture understand that simply using social networking sites and related digital media is not enough to effectively communicate; business communicators must move beyond dated metaphors of technological revolutions and information societies. Communicating solely in the context of these metaphors results in a reliance on technology as a product rather than a tool, and depersonalizes communications; by attributing communicative failures to a digital origin, communicators in business organizations attempt to escape responsibility for their actions (Martin, 2008), which is particularly troubling in an environment in which many organizations are effectively getting their message out. Business communicators with digital emotional literacy adopt technological tools to further their ability to perceive, understand, and manage the emotions of their audience. The pace of technological development challenges business communicators to use an assortment of technical, cognitive, and sociological skills requisite to communicate effectively (Eshet-Alkalai & Amichai-Hamburger, 2004).

Digital literacy is necessary but an insufficient prerequisite to digital emotional literacy. With the influx of a younger generation of employees who have grown up with digital tools, the technology-adoption gap in organizations is narrowing; the spread of digital literacy in companies is often resisted, but irrespective of the pace of adoption, digital literacy progresses (Efimova & Grudin, 2008). We posit that the challenge in organizations is no longer technological adoption or proficiency, but rather combining that technical skillset with emotional intelligence, enabling business communicators to go beyond use of technology to effective mastery of technological tools for effective corporate communications.

A challenge business communicators – particularly public relations (PR) professionals – face is the scrutiny that comes with their communications. The ability to manage and understand emotions has been suggested to be a key trait for PR professionals (Walton, 2011). Managing a message to create an emotional appeal has been suggested as an important capacity for brand managers (Karaosmanoglu & Melewar, 2006), as brands can create an emotional bond with their loyal users, facilitating emotional selling propositions (Fan, 2006). Corporate reputation, managed through digital communications, is facilitated through emotionally triggered awareness (Barnett et al., 2006; Schwaiger, 2004).

The reliance of business communications to external constituents but also the processes involved in communicating internally within an organization is increasingly necessary (Heath, 1994). Managing corporate communications is thus a dually oriented challenge, one in which digital emotional literacy becomes paramount. Still, simply noting this truism does not guarantee an organization success in the digital culture, and attempting to learn how to define success can become a problem that corporations fail to overcome.

Emotional intelligence as a learned capability

If the challenges in communication are so potentially overwhelming, then, how can organizations embrace them in productive, efficient ways? If the connector is digital emotional literacy, can it be learned? Organizations can best decide this by looking closely at the components thereof – emotional intelligence (EI) and digital literacy. We first address the component of emotional intelligence with the premise that even if business communicators are currently lacking in EI, then this trait may be further developed within the corporate environment. Business communicators needn't worry if employees do not currently possess such skills because they can be learned (Salovey & Sluyter, 1997).

An empirical study by Nelis et al. (2009) supports the argument that emotional intelligence can be learned. "Overall, the results are promising as they suggest that, with a proper methodology relying on the latest scientific knowledge about emotion and emotional processing, some facets of EI can be enhanced " (Nelis et al., 2009, p. 40). These findings are significant because emotional intelligence influences other positive outcomes in life, including the ability to effectively communicate within the corporate environment.

Expanding digital literacy with development of a digital emotional literacy construct

Digital literacy skills might well be a basic necessity to function in digital culture, but, as Eshet-Alkalai noted as early as 2004, the term digital literacy is too vague and even suggests there is too much of an emphasis on technical skills as opposed to cognitive and socio-emotional aspects of the digital world. A resource-based view (Barney, 1991, 1996, 2001) of the firm requires a more holistic approach to utilizing technology resources within the organization to achieve competitive advantage. These resources include how well their employees are utilizing information most effectively to increase their knowledge, skill, and production (Zhuang & Lederer, 2005). This highlights the instrumentality of competencies of rhetorical skills such as audience awareness and strategic sensitivity in effective business communications.

Another limitation of our understanding of digital literacy occurs as the notion of the workplace itself is changing. In a recent study, nearly half of the respondents do at least some work from home, and workers are more likely to use the Internet constantly at work than at home (Madden & Jones, 2008). The study goes on to report that nearly all those employed (96%) are utilizing new communication technologies in their work environment, including going online, telecommunications, and electronic communication. While the worker is online, it is unclear where the delineation between personal work life lies. Social networks and telecommuting have merged and intertwined the lines between the workplace duties and responsibilities and personal interests. To complicate things further, many organizations have strategically integrated their business into the social networking world. In fact, employees often use social networks for personal purposes while at work (Blank, 2010). While social networks may provide new opportunities to market to new customers and sell products and services, they can also make it difficult to determine the source of a message. Questions arise in digital culture that previous employee handbooks did not face; among these are: whether a given posting belongs to the individual or the organization; whether using organizational resources changes that relationship; and how organizational policies on electronic communications interact with organizational culture. Individuals have shown less inhibition and appear to be less reserved when using various forms of Internet communication (Joinson, 2003). In this new digital world how do organizations draw boundaries around work and personal life?

Researchers are examining these questions. Marwick and boyd (2010) have coined the term "context collapse" to explain the difficulty of imagining audiences in digital culture. They argue that intra-organizational tensions are created as organizations' attempts to present a singular identity are challenged by the diverse groups of people using social networks on behalf of those organizations. This context collapse results in the construction of authenticity in digital culture, and that construction causes particular issues for organizations as they attempt to navigate it (Marwick & Boyd, 2010). Organizations embracing the notion of digital emotional literacy will be better positioned to understand just how questions of identity – ones not often addressed in pre-digital culture days – now have become critical to digital success.

The difficulties in thoroughly understanding what audiences actually consist of leads to many of the difficulties seen in communication in digital culture. In today's environment in which we are always connected, online postings can be visible and available to the world instantly. The risk of communication errors and employee misuse continues to rise, and as organizations wrestle with what their authentic persona is in an environment in which representation and identity are tricky concepts. The need for organizations to focus their efforts on developing digital and emotional communication skills that encompass not only digital literacy but emotional intelligence as well is clear.

Digital emotional literacy involves the cognitive and socio-emotional aspects of working in and with a digital environment, behaving correctly and sensibly in cyberspace (Bawden, 2008; Eshet-Alkalai, 2004); the socio-emotional focus we present follows how the meaning of "literacy" has extended from a mere ability to read and write to refer to "the ability to understand information however presented" (Lanham, 1995, p. 198), and that digital literacy involves "being skilled at deciphering complex images and sounds as well as the syntactical subtleties of words" (Lanham, 1995, p. 199). We build upon this by focusing on the intersection of digital literacy and emotional intelligence. By moving to a digital context, we define digital emotional literacy as the ability to perceive, understand, and manage the emotions of both senders and receivers in a digital media context.

Our focus on digital emotional literacy corresponds to the concept of socio-emotional literacy within the digital literacy framework proposed by Eshet-Alkalai (2004). Furthermore, it aligns with the conceptualization of a plurality of digital literacies considered appropriate because, among other reasons, there are many accounts and different concepts represented in the many ways of understanding digital literacy (Lankshear & Knobel, 2008). Literacies can become a more appropriate term, one that encompasses the multiple constructions of identities, authenticity, and self- and organizational presentations as well as the skills required to negotiate these constructions.

Being digitally emotionally literate requires an individual to move beyond mere comprehension of a given communicative effort, instead proceeding to a deeper understanding of the emotions within digital culture – and how those emotions are expressed, perceived, and managed. Digital communications are filling the need to balance audience reach and cost considerations, especially with the use of social networking. The effective use of electronic media, however, is not as universal as its general use. Effective use of social networking sites from a business communications perspective necessarily requires digital emotional literacy from both the senders and receivers. As Bawden (2008) suggests with respect to digital literacy:

> The "integrative" aspect also silences many unproductive arguments. Digital literacy touches on and includes many things that it does not claim to own. It encompasses the presentation of information, without subsuming creative writing and visualization. It encompasses the evaluation of information, without claiming systematic reviewing and meta-analysis as its own. It includes organization of information but lays no claim to the construction and operation of terminologies, taxonomies and thesauri. And so on. (p. 26)

Understanding digital literacy in this way, then, leads to an envisioning of how digital emotional literacy can encompass a similar integrative viewpoint as well; digital emotional literacy touches on and includes many concepts that are not exclusive to the domain of digital emotional literacy. It encompasses the perception of emotions, without incorporating all the affect-driven responses. It covers emotion management, without embodying emotional labor (Mann, 1997). It embraces understanding emotions without asserting the need to be a context-free analytical tool.

Martin (2008) suggests: "We live in a society permeated by the digital, where our actions are frequently mediated by digital tools, and the objects we encounter are frequently shaped by digital intervention" (p. 151). It is this permeation that both enables corporate communications to flow with heretofore unknown speed but also challenges business communicators to encapsulate digital emotional literacy in their communications to ensure messages are understood by receivers as intended – "the advent of the digital, offering instant communication to one or many disassembled from a face-to-face situation requires the user to be more aware of the nature and implications of the medium" (Martin, 2008, p. 162). The ubiquity of digital communication media presents corporate communicators with the challenge of employing sociological and emotional skills in order to communicate effectively (Eshet-Alkalai & Amichai-Hamburger, 2004) both synchronously and asynchronously (Merchant, 2007).

Digital emotional literacy is a skillset that organizations need to develop in employees who are constantly within digital culture, both inside and outside of the organization that employs them. The prevalence of electronic means of communication means effective business communication within a digital environment is crucial to the organization's ability to disseminate information across the company, and digital literacy is no longer simply a concern for those who interact with customers, vendors, and other partners who inhabit a landscape previously seen as external to a company. "Internal [business] communication is understood here as the strategic management of interactions and relationships between stakeholders at all levels within organizations" (Welch & Jackson, 2007, p.183), but digital communication technologies have flattened the organization and have increased both customer and supplier intimacy. The importance of understanding the requirements of such close relationships is vital, as these impact a broad array of organizational activities that stretch beyond what was previously considered internal (Welch & Jackson, 2007) such as customer relationship management, human resource management, and supply chain management. As such, this requires a new understanding of digital literacy and the significance of the emotional elements thereof.

As consumers and customers become better attuned to and trained in the vagaries of communication in digital culture, the demand for digitally emotionally literate organizations increases. While customers and employees are adopting new communication technologies at a startling rate, there is little empirical evidence to suggest that this has increased effective communication skills (Crumpacker & Crumpacker, 2007; Martin, 2005). Surprisingly, the contrary may be occurring. As millennials are entering the multi-generational workforce, they have more skills and experience with digital technologies than the previous generation of employees, yet there is a growing criticism of their ability to effectively connect and communicate with others inside and outside of the organization (Dittman, 2005; Fogg, 2009; Twenge & Campbell, 2008). While some may view this ineffectiveness as disconcerting, organizations that take seriously the task of training their employees in digital emotional literacy will be better positioned to navigate the extremes of digital culture.

Developing digital emotional literacy within organizations

A process for developing EI has been created by focusing on the steps of preparation, training, transfer and maintenance, and evaluation (Cherniss et al., 1998). The same process was modified and shown to be successfully implemented within a business curriculum (Tucker et al., 2000).

We propose that the training and development of digital emotional literacy can follow a similar format within organizations with combining opportunities for practice, monitoring progress, providing frequent feedback, using models, and avoiding relapse. Cherniss et al. (1998) also noted that more practice is required with "emotional learning ... because old, ineffective neural connections need to be weakened and new, more effective ones established" (p. 8).

If digital emotional literacy can indeed be learned, then its importance within organizations should follow a similar course as the importance of EI in the workplace, especially as the boundaries of digital culture become increasingly diffused. Subsequently, research focusing on the conceptual integration of emotional intelligence into business education curriculum has more recently evolved. Myers and Tucker (2005) utilized the inclusion of student-centered assignments focusing on self-assessment and journaling, in-class role-play and discussion, and an interview with the development of a case analysis to cultivate students' knowledge of EI. Abraham (2006) recognized the importance for well-developed EI in the workplace, particularly for accountants, and encouraged accounting faculty at business schools to integrate EI in the teaching of leadership. She noted that "active personal involvement," as noted by Ashkanasy and Dasborough (2003, p. 21), and self-awareness of one's own emotions (Brown, 2003) are critical in the learning process.

Applicability of a digital emotional literacy framework across functional business areas

While we have examined digital emotional literacy specifically in the context of social networking sites, the applicability and importance of digital emotional literacy crosses organizational functional boundaries. In the following section, we highlight some of the areas where the importance of digital emotional literacy can make the difference between organizational success and failure, and how social and other digital media need to be considered in the context of an organization. The following section is not meant to be an exhaustive list of the organizational units where digital emotional literacy is applicable, but rather to provide the reader with some representative examples in a framework of the broad applicability of the digital emotional literacy construct we have proposed.

Marketing. The first area we examine for applying digital emotional literacy is in the functional area of marketing. This ties naturally in with our existing examination of DEL use in social networks, as well as in the context of a unified or integrated marketing communications (IMC) platform. Initially defined as the coordination of promotional marketing activities used to communicate with an organization's customers (Fawcette, 1993; Schultz, 1993), the definition of IMC has expanded to the following:

> Integrated marketing communication is a strategic business process used to plan, develop execute and evaluate coordinated, measureable, persuasive brand communications programs over time with consumers, customers, prospects, employees, associates and other targeted relevant external and internal audiences. The goal is to generate both short-term financial returns and build long-term brand and shareholder value. (Schultz, 2004, pp. 8–9)

The IMC environment provides an avenue for evaluating the construct of digital emotional literacy by capturing the elements of "coordinated communications with employees and associates" (Schultz, 2004, p. 9) using the marketing communication channels of digital and social media.

Understanding and managing emotions includes responding to them in an appropriate manner; managing digital word of mouth (e.g., Qualman, 2013) along with other public relations and advertising activities (e.g., Kaplan & Haenlein, 2010) requires digitally emotionally literate professionals.

Management Information Systems. The effective use of management information systems (MIS) extends beyond the traditional view of digital literacy (Gilster, 1997; Kerka, 1999; Lanham, 1995) as a set of technical skills to include other competencies in the areas of effective communications, problem-solving, team-building, and collaboration (Eshet-Alkalai, 2004; Mundrof & Laird, 2002). As both internal and external stakeholders become more digitally connected their network of relationships become increasingly useful, creating what some researchers call value networks (Allee, 2000), which can be defined as a "set of relationships between firms involving multiple two-way interaction in bringing increasingly complex products and services to the market" (Rajala & Westerlund, 2007, p.117). The proliferation of MIS across organizations – both for use internally, and to connect internal and external stakeholders – requires users to navigate a variety of digital environments with a greater understanding of the information being shared and the emotional context that may be more difficult to ascertain across digital lines.

Human Resource Management. The recruitment and selection function is one where the antecedents to digital emotional literacy have been prominently featured. For instance, the use of social media in recruitment has been examined in a variety of studies (e.g., Davison et al., 2011; Madera & Chang, 2011), highlighting the importance of digital literacy for both job seekers and organizational recruiters. The role of social media in new employee orientation has also been examined (Arthur, 2012). Concerns related to the emotional intelligence element of this field have also been raised; for instance, developing trust in an organization from both job seeker and organizational perspectives can be tricky (Klotz et al., 2013), while organizations face potential legal ramifications in monitoring employees and potential employees' personal social networking activities (Sprague, 2011–12). Beyond recruitment and selection, the use of computer- and online-based training programs for organizational purposes continues to rise, both in terms of skill-based training such as business process improvement (Börner et al., 2012) and development as well as legal compliance, such as occupational health and safety programs and evaluations of their effectiveness (Papelo et al., 2013). More specialized training in delivery of effective digital communications is being provided, often focusing on particular areas such as public relations (e.g., Verhoeven et al., 2010), though training is clearly still an area in which organizations can improve their focus. According to a recent study over two-thirds of Australasian and nearly three-quarters of European organizations do not provide any training to their staff for using social media (Macnamara & Zerfass, 2012), highlighting the need for development.

Conclusion and discussion

Digital emotional literacy might well be a key consideration in corporations staying competitive as digital culture continues to evolve. While the importance of analyzing data will certainly not be surpassed by the need to become more digitally emotionally literate, the combination of pitfalls and opportunities that exist in digital culture can only encourage organizations to become better versed in just what success in digital culture means. Digital culture is where the vast majority of the industrialized world will reside in the foreseeable future.

What, then, does this future look like? We conclude our chapter by challenging organizations to think differently about the skillsets that those who negotiate this space successfully will need to possess. Buzzwords – resiliency, flexibility, and openness to change – abound, but organizations will need to understand the implications behind these terms to become successful. The true challenge lies in understanding how to encourage organizational thinking that is able to respond to what might from a quantitative perspective appear to be a faintly whimsical and definitely confusing communication environment. Understanding the skills necessary to navigate the electronic seas of cyberspace will mark organizations ready to succeed. Those same organizations that go beyond navigation and actually forge paths that create the products and relationships that make them leaders will be ones that comprehend what digital emotional literacy can bring.

References

Abraham, A. (2006). The need for the integration of emotional intelligence skills in business education. *The Business Renaissance Quarterly, 1* (3), 65–79.

Allee, V. (2000). Reconfiguring the value network. *Journal of Business Strategy, 21* (4), 36–41.

Arthur, D. (2012). *Recruiting, Interviewing, Selecting & Orienting New Employees.* New York: AMACOM .

Ashkanasy, N. M., & Dasborough, M. T. (2003). Emotional awareness and emotional intelligence in leadership teaching. *Journal of Education for Business, 79* (1), 18–22.

Barnett, M. L., Jermier, J. M., & Lafferty, B. A. (2006). Corporate reputation: The definitional landscape. *Corporate Reputation Review, 9* (1), 26–38.

Barney, J. (1991). Firm resources and sustainable competitive advantage. *Journal of Management, 17* (1), 99–120.

Barney, J. (1996). The resource-based theory of the firm. *Organization Science, 7* (5), 469.

Barney, J. (2001). Is the resource-based view a useful perspective for strategic management research? Yes. *Academy of Management Review, 26* (1): 41–56.

Bawden, D. (2008). Origins and concepts of digital literacy. In C. Lankshear & M. Knobel (Eds), *Digital Literacies: Concepts, Policies and Practices* (pp. 17–32). New York: Peter Lang.

Blank, A. (2010). On the precipice of d-discovery: Can litigants obtain employee social networking website information through employers? *18 Commlaw Conspectus, 18,* 487–495.

Börner, R., Moorman, J., & Wang, M. (2012). Staff training for business process improvement: The benefit of role-plays in the case of KreditSim. *Journal of Workplace Learning, 24* (3), 200–225.

Brown, R. B. (2003). Emotions and behavior: Exercises in emotional intelligence. *Journal of Management Education, 27* (1), 122–134.

Buckingham, D. (2006). Defining digital literacy: What do young people need to know about digital media? *Digital Kompetanse, 4* (3), 263–276.

Cherniss, C., Goleman, D., Emmerling, R., Cowan, K., & Alder, M. (October 1998). *Bringing Emotional Intelligence to the Workplace.* Technical Report Issued by The Consortium for Research on Emotional Intelligence in Organizations. Retrieved from: http//www.eiconsortium.org/_report.htm.

Correa, T., Willard, A., & Gil de Zúñiga, H. (2010). Who interacts on the Web? The intersection of users' personality and social media use. *Computers in Human Behavior, 26,* 247–253.

Crumpacker, M., & Crumpacker, J. M. (2007). Succession planning and generational stereotypes: Should HR consider age-based values and attitudes a relevant factor or a passing fad? *Public Personnel Management, 36,* 349–369.

Davison, H. K., Maraist, C., & Bing, M. N. (2011). Friend or foe? The promise and pitfalls of using social networking sites for HR decisions. *Journal of Business Psychology, 26,* 153–159.

Dittman, M. (2005). Generational differences at work. *Monitor on Psychology, 36,* 54–55.

Efimova, L., & Grudin, J. (2008). Crossing boundaries: Digital literacy in enterprises. In C. Lankshear & M. Knobel (Eds), *Digital Literacies: Concepts, Policies and Practices* (pp. 203–226). New York: Peter Lang.

Eshet-Alkalai, Y. (2002). Digital literacy: A new terminology framework and its application to the design of meaningful technology-based learning environments. *Proceedings of EDMEDIA, 2002,* World Conference on Educational Multimedia, Hypermedia, & Telecommunication, pp. 493–498.

Eshet-Alkalai, Y. (2004). Digital literacy: A conceptual framework for survival skills in the digital era. *Journal of Educational Multimedia and Hypermedia, 13* (1), 93–106.

Eshet-Alkalai, Y., & Amichai-Hamburger, Y. (2004). Experiments in digital literacy. *CyberPsychology & Behavior, 7* (4), 421–429.

Fan, Y. (2006). Ethical branding and corporate reputation. *Corporate Communications: An International Journal, 10* (4), 341–350.

Fawcett, A. W., (1993). Marketers convinced: Its time has arrived. *Advertising Age* (Integrated Marketing). *64* (7), S1–S2.

Fogg, P. (2009). When generations collide. *Education Digest, 74,* 25–30.

Gardner, H. (1983). *Frames of Mind: The Theory of Multiple Intelligences.* New York: Basic Books.

Gardner, H. (1998). Are there additional intelligences? The case for natural, spiritual, and existential intelligences. In J. Kane (Ed.), *Education, Information, and Transformation* (pp. 111–132). Englewood Cliffs, NJ: Prentice Hall.

Gilster, P. (1997). *Digital Literacy.* New York: John Wiley.

Goleman, D. (1995). *Emotional Intelligence: Why It Can Matter More Than IQ.* New York: Bantam Books.

Goleman, D. (1998). *Working with Emotional Intelligence.* New York: Bantam Books.

Groysberg, B., & Slind, M. (2012). Leadership is a conversation. *Harvard Business Review,* June, 76–84.

Heath, R. L. (1994). *Management of Corporate Communication: From Interpersonal Contacts to External Affairs.* Hillsdale, NJ: Lawrence Erlbaum Associates.

Joinson, A. (2003). *Understanding the Psychology of Internet Behavior.* New York: Palgrave Macmillan.

Kaplan, A. M., and Haenlein, M. (2010). Users of the world, unite! The challenges and opportunities of social media. *Business Horizons, 53* (1), 59–68.

Karaosmanoglu, E., & Melewar, T. C. (2006). Corporate communications, identity and image: A research agenda. *Journal of Brand Management, 14* (1/2), 196–206.

Kerka, S. (1999). Consumer education for the information age. *Practice Application Brief, 4,* 12–15.

Kirkpatrick, David (2011). *The Facebook Effect: The Inside Story of the Company that is Connecting the World*. New York: Simon & Schuster.

Klotz, A. C., da Motta Veiga, S. P., Buckley, R. M., & Gavin, M. B. (2013). The role of trustworthiness in recruitment and selection: A review and guide for future research. *Journal of Organizational Behavior, 34* (S1), S104–S119.

Lanham, R. A. (1995). Digital literacy. *Scientific American, 273* (3), 198–199.

Lankshear, C., & Knobel, M. (2008). Introduction: Digital literacies). cy. kley, R. M., & Gavin, M. B.. In C. Lankshear & M. Knobel (Eds), *Digital Literacies: Concepts, Policies and Practices* (pp. 1–16). New York: Peter Lang.

Lee, J. J., & Hsu, Y. (2002). Web navigation: The role of metaphor, concept map and individual differences. *In Proceedings of ED-MEDIA, 2001. World Conference on Educational Multimedia, Hypermedia & Telecommunications* (pp. 1000–1001). Norfolk, VA: Association for the Advancement of Computing in Education.

Macnamara, J., & Zerfass, A. (2012). Social media communication in organizations: The challenge of balancing openness, strategy and management. *International Journal of Strategic Communication, 6*, 287–308.

Madden, M., & Jones, S. (2008). Most workers use the internet or email at their jobs, but they say the technologies are a mixed blessing. *Pew Internet & American Life Project*. Retrieved from: http://www.pewinternet.org/~media//Files/Reports/2008/PIP_Networked_Workers_FINAL.pdf.

McLuhan, Marshall (1962). *The Gutenberg Galaxy: The Making of Typographic Man*. Toronto: University of Toronto Press.

McLuhan, Marshall (1964). *Understanding Media: The Extensions of Man*. New York: McGraw-Hill.

Madera, J. M., & Chang, W. (2011). Using social networking sites to investigate employees in the hospitality industry. 2011 International Conference on Hotel, Restaurant and Institutional Education, Amherst, MA.

Mann, S. (1997). Emotional labor in organizations. *Leadership & Organization Development Journal, 18* (1), 4–12.

Martin, A. (2008). Digital literacy and the rainingmaintenan." In C. Lankshear & M. Knobel (Eds), *Digital Literacies: Concepts, Policies and Practices* (pp. 151–176). New York: Peter Lang.

Martin, C. A. (2005). From high maintenance to high productivity. *Industrial & Commercial Training, 37*, 39–44.

Marwick, A., and boyd, d. (2010). I tweet honestly, I tweet passionately: Twitter users, context collapse, and the imagined audience. *New Media Society, 2011* (13), 114. Originally published online July 7, 2010. Retrieved from: http://nms.sagepub.com/content/early/2010/06/22/1461444810365313

Mayer, J. D., & Salovey, P. (1993). The intelligence of emotional intelligence. *Intelligence, 17*, 433–442.

Merchant, G. (2007). Writing the future in the digital age. *Literacy, 41* (3), 118–128.

Mundrof, N., & Laird, K. R. (2002). Social and psychological effects of information technologies and other interactive media. *Media effects: Advances in Theory and Research* (2nd edition) (pp. 231–255). Mahway, NJ: Erlbaum.

Myers, L. L., & Tucker, M. L. (2005). Increasing awareness of emotional intelligence in a business curriculum. *Business Communication Quarterly, 68* (1), 44–51.

Nelis, D., Quoidbach, J., Mikolajczak, M., & Hansenne, M. (2009). Increasing emotional intelligence: (How) is it possible? *Personality and Individual Differences, 47*, 36–41.

Ohmann, R. (1998). *Selling Culture: Magazines, Markets, and Class at the Turn of the Century.* London: Verso.

Papelo, B., Cangiano, G., & Calicchia, S. (2013). Occupational safety and health professionals' training in Italy: Qualitative evaluation using T-Lab. *Journal of Workplace Learning, 25* (4), 247–263.

Purcell, K. Rainie, L., Heaps, A., Buchanan, J., Friedrich, L., Jacklin, A., Chen, C., & Zickuhr, K. (2012). How teens do research in the digital world. Retrieved from: http://www.pewinternet.org/Reports/2012/Student-Research.aspx.

Qualman, E. (2013). *Socialnomics: How Social Media Transforms the Way We Live and Do Business* (2nd edition). Hoboken, NJ: John Wiley and Sons.

Rahim, M., Psenicka, C., Polychroniou, P., Zhao, J., Yu, C., Chan, K., Susana, K., Alves, M. G., Lee, C., Rahman, M., Ferdausy, S., & van Wyk, R. (2002). A model of emotional intelligence and conflict management strategies: A study in seven countries. *International Journal of Organizational Analysis, 10* (4), 302–326.

Rajala, R., & Westerlund, M. (2007). Business models – a new perspective on firms' assets and capabilities: observations from the Finnish software industry. *The International Journal of Entrepreneurship and Innovation, 8* (2), 115–126.

Ranii, David (2014). SAS revenue topped 3 billion in 2013. Retrieved from: http://www.newsobserver.com/2014/01/23/3555436/sas-revenue-topped-3-billion-in.html.

Salovey, P., & Sluyter, D. J. (Eds) (1997). *Emotional Development and Emotional Intelligence: Educational Implications.* New York: Basic Books.

Schawbel, D. (2011). The reputation economy is coming – Are you prepared? *Forbes.* Retrieved from http://www.forbes.com/sites/danschawbel/2011/02/28/the-reputation-economy.

Schultz, D. E. (January 18, 1993). Integrated marketing communications: Maybe definition is the point of view. *Marketing News,* 17.

Schultz, D. E. (September 15, 2004). IMC receives more appropriate definition. *Marketing News,* 8–9.

Schwaiger, M. (2004). Components and parameters of corporate reputation – an empirical study. *Schmalenbach Business Review, 56,* 46–71.

Sprague, R. (2011–12). Invasion of the social networks: Blurring the line between personal life and the employment relationship. 50 U. Louisville L. Rev. 1.

Tucker, M. L., Sojka, J. Z., Barone, F. J., & McCarthy, A. M. (2000). Training tomorrow's leaders: Enhancing the emotional intelligence of business graduates. *Journal of Education for Business, 75* (6), 331–337.

Twenge, J. M., & Campbell, S. M. (2008). Generational differences in psychological traits and their impact on the workplace. *Journal of Managerial Psychology, 23,* 862–877.

Twitter (2014). *About Twitter.* Retrieved from: https://about.twitter.com/company.

Verhoeven, P., Tench, R., Zerfass, A., Moreno, A., & Verčič, D. (2010). How European PR practitioners handle digital and social media. *Public Relations Review, 38* (1), 162–164

Wagner, R. K., & Sternberg, R. J. (1985). Practical intelligence in real-world pursuits: The role of tacit knowledge. *Journal of Personality and Social Psychology, 49* (2), 436–458.

Wagner, R. K., & Sternberg, R. J. (1990). Street smarts. In K. E. Clark & M. B. Clark (Eds), *Measures of Leadership* (pp. 493–504). West Orange, NJ: Leadership Library of America.

Walton, S. B. (2011). EQ is the new IQ: The vital role of emotional intelligence in public relations. *Public Relations Tactics, 18* (4), 14.

Weisinger, H. (1998). *Emotional Intelligence at Work.* San Francisco, CA: Jossey-Bass.

Welch, M., & Jackson, P. (2007). Rethinking internal communication: A stakeholder approach. *Corporate Communications: An International Journal, 12* (2), 177–198.

Williams, W. M., & Sternberg, R. J. (1988). Group intelligence: Why some groups are better than others. *Intelligence, 12* (4), 351–377.

Zhuang, Y., & Lederer, A. L. (2005). A resource-based view of electronic commerce. *Information & Management, 43* (2), 251–61.

10
Recovering the Human in the Network: Exploring Communicology as a Research Methodology in Digital Business Discourse

Craig T. Maier and David Deluliis

Introduction

In 2012, the British cellphone company SecurEnvoy (2012) reported that as many as 66% of the United Kingdom's population suffered from what it called *nomophobia*, the irrational, persistent fear of losing access to their smartphone. Short for "no-mobile-phone phobia," nomophobia has been reported to induce stress levels comparable to those felt when going to the dentist or getting married (Moran, 2012), and is apparently so strong that it induces 75% of smartphone users to operate their devices while in the bathroom (SecurEnvoy, 2012). Similarly, Middleton (2007, p. 169) has observed that smartphones like the BlackBerry – affectionately called the "CrackBerry" by many users – possess an addictive, even "Pavlovian" quality. BlackBerries, she contends, intensify the experience of work by enabling people to complete small tasks in moments of downtime, lengthening the duration of the work day well into evenings and weekends, and expanding the location of work to anywhere on the globe, even on vacation. Yet, even as the participants in her study almost universally praise their devices as helping them to negotiate an increasingly intense workplace, Middleton (2007, p. 165) worries that the unreflective and addictive usage of these "always-on, always connected" devices is ironically sustaining the very workplace cultures that cause workers to feel such stress.

Researchers and practitioners of digital business discourse can view something like nomophobia in a number of ways. Psychologists, for instance, may see it as an example of the addictive power of communication technologies, while critical scholars may see it as a sign of how technology is enabling ever more oppressive organizational cultures. But we can also see nomophobia as reflecting what the German philosopher Martin Heidegger (1927/1996) describes as *idle talk*: an inattentive, thoughtless, forgetful way of communicating in which an overemphasis on empirical elements like functionality, effectiveness, and efficiency distracts from the lived experience and meaning of communicating itself. In light of Heidegger's concerns, we propose defining digital business discourse differently, as *the embodied experience of using technology to communicate within organizations*. We suggest that digital business discourse research needs to find ways to pay attention to the thoughts and feelings that persons have when using communication technologies – the frustration of receiving a confusing text message, the anxiety of hearing the cell phone vibrate at 3:00 in the morning – that are often more meaningful and important than the use of language itself.

In this chapter, we will adapt a branch of communication research known as *communicology* to develop a research methodology that can help us attend to the "human," experiential element in the technological systems that increasingly define our working lives. Richard Lanigan (1984, p. 2), perhaps the greatest proponent of this area of scholarship, contends that communicology deepens our understanding of communication by "refocusing attention on the performance and practice of persons communicating." Until now, Lanigan and other communicologists have often taken a deeply philosophical and autoethnographic approach, thereby limiting communicology's relevance to applied communication research. Here, we propose to extend communicology's line of inquiry in a new direction by developing it into a qualitative methodology that can rediscover digital business discourse as a *human practice*, instead of a purely *technological process*. Using Lanigan's work as a foundation, we begin by providing an introduction to the field of communicology and establishing its applicability to digital business discourse, using the case of smartphone usage in the workplace as a point of entry. Then, we describe the communicological methodology of *description, reduction,* and *interpretation* as it could relate to digital business discourse. Finally, we discuss practical ways of incorporating communicology into the research and practice of digital business discourse and offer a case study illustrating its applicability.

Communicology and the study of digital business discourse

The case of smartphones in the workplace and the sense of nomophobia that they seem to spark provides a particularly telling example of how attending to the experience of digital business discourse has become increasingly important. Even before the advent of the iPhone and similar devices, Fortunati (2001) referred to mobile phones as *charismatic technologies* whose protean nature enables them to be used in a variety of ways and gives birth to new styles of communicating. Reinsch et al. (2008) and Stephens (2012) describe how smartphones foster what they call *multicommunicating*, a form of business discourse in which workers participate in multiple conversations simultaneously, both in person and online. Reinsch et al. note how multicommunicating workers come to experience a new sense of being-in-the-workplace that they call *connected time*. "Multiple persons described being connected and available for text messaging as 'like breathing,'" they observe. "We heard many persons speak about 'living,' 'being,' or 'working' either 'on' or 'in' a special form of time – connected time" (2008, p. 398). Ivarsson and Larsson (2011) observe that such intense connectivity blurs the boundaries between home and work and places unique pressures on employees, encouraging employees to turn *toward* and not away from their devices as a means of recovering from these tensions. Connected time thus becomes a self-perpetuating cycle, with smartphones and other devices serving as both a cause of stress for employees and a means of alleviating that stress. Soon, workers find that their devices demand ever-greater attention, establishing expectations for communication that take on the appearance of an imperative.

Phenomena like nomophobia raise important issues for practitioners, as well. Indeed, while some may view multicommunicating and "connected time" as signs of an engaged, active workplace, research has found that the productivity benefits of multitasking are often illusory (see, for instance, Jeong & Hwang, 2012; Wang & Tchernev, 2012). Beyond the sense of omnipresent distraction, however, nomophobia also calls attention to how the emotional and relational tolls that communication technologies take on workers contribute to broader issues like organizational communication climates (Jablin, 1980), organizational cultures (Schein, 2010), incivility in the workplace (Fritz, 2013), and what Edelson et al. (2015) in this volume call *digital emotional literacy*. Though these factors may not be measurable or quantifiable or directly contribute to an organization's bottom line, they can point to problems that, if left unaddressed, contribute to employee dissatisfaction and burnout, organizational conflict, problematic working relationships, and numerous other problems that require intervention. These issues suggest the need for a new dimension of applied scholarship and professional practice that helps workers and organizations to look beyond the "how" of digital business discourse and think more critically about "what" they are doing with their technologies and "why" they are doing it.

Middleton and Cukier (2006) use Morgan's (1997) metaphor of the *psychic prison* to describe how workers can trap themselves into particular ways of thinking that encourage them to accept or do things that outside observers would find unacceptable. Employees dwelling in psychic prisons often have no idea that they are holding themselves captive, nor do they understand that the behaviors that confine them and cause them such stress are of their own creation. For card-carrying nomophobes like the BlackBerry users interviewed in Middleton's (2007, p. 169) study, smartphones are not intrusive but heroic devices, and only the technology's liberating power and "efficiency, immediacy, accessibility, and flexibility" are apparent to them. But in making devices the heroes of their working lives, employees can easily lose sight of ways in which the quality of their workplace communication has suffered. They come to assume that responses to emails must be instantaneous, that answering a routine text message in the middle of their daughter's school play is a form of freedom, and that everyone must have a smartphone to be a competent employee, ignoring the ways in which these behaviors cause them stress, harm their relationships with others, and diminish their effectiveness. In response, Middleton and Cukier call for a shift in research and practice away from what they see as a singular focus on functionality toward approaches that encourage us to think more broadly and differently about digital business discourse to make its practice less technological and more humane.

We contend that *communicology* provides such a perspective. Communicology, as a branch of communication research, joins two complex and rigorously philosophical disciplines: *phenomenology*, the philosophical study of conscious experience, and *semiotics*, the study of signs in the context of the sign systems that give those signs meaning. As this lineage suggests, communicology represents a complex and difficult body of literature. But in a nutshell, it comes down to a single, koan-like research question: *How can we understand the experience of communicating?* This deceptively simple question illustrates why communicology brings phenomenology and semiotics together. Phenomenology can help us describe our experience of the world around us, but describing the experience of communicating presents an odd and paradoxical case: *describing the experience of using language requires us to use the very thing that we are attempting to describe.* Communicologists therefore look to semiotics to help break through this cycle. In important ways, this realization distinguishes communicology from Gee's (1999) understanding of discourse analysis. While Lanigan (1988) certainly recognizes the importance of studying language-in-use, he nevertheless describes communication as both *centrifugal* and *centripetal*: the centrifugal movement describes how our expressions shape the social context that defines communicative choices we make, while the centripetal movement emphasizes how that broader social context reflects back upon us, defining our perception of experience and influencing our discourse anew. This reflexive relationship between expression and perception allows us to discover something fundamental: that communication is much more than a one-way transfer of information but is instead a co-relational transaction between persons and the world in which they are embedded.

Though communicologists draw from many influences, Lanigan's pioneering work is perhaps the most important, and so understanding his contribution is essential if we are to adapt communicology to the study of digital business discourse. From Lanigan's (1972) early work on the French phenomenologist Maurice Merleau-Ponty, the field of communicology has sought to add depth to the experience of communication in a world where the influence of science and technology is both ubiquitous and unquestioned. For Lanigan and the communicologists he has influenced, every discursive act – whether it is a gesture, a voicemail or a text message – is both *empirical* and *existential* in nature. In other words, communicology contends that digital business discourse always begins with a living body who breathes, feels, and thinks and whose actions of pointing, speaking or typing are just as important to the message as the message itself. To focus exclusively on the empirical elements of communication – particular bits of information or conversational turns, for instance – at the expense of the existential is to forget that every discursive act begins with a person attempting "to convey his unique humanity to another person" (Lanigan, 1972, p. 22). Within digital business discourse, then, communicology invites us to recognize that the ultimate "back end" of any communication technology is the person who is using it, and it challenges us to account for and attend to this mysterious influence.

Consequently, Lanigan and other communicologists move away from theories of communication that view discourse primarily as the exchange of information or use of language to achieve particular goals. While he recognizes the potential value of such theories, Lanigan (2013, p. 78) nevertheless believes that they represent only the first level of human discursive life. Focusing primarily on the technical problems of information *transmission* ("How accurately can the symbols of communication be transmitted?"), they gloss over higher-level questions regarding *semantics* ("How precisely do the transmitted symbols convey the desired meaning?") and *pragmatics* ("How effectively does the received meaning affect conduct in the desired way?"). Human beings, he contends, naturally integrate the informational, semantic, and pragmatic dimensions of discourse when they communicate in a way that machines and animals cannot. Information-based theories, he argues, ignore this complexity. Such theories, in other words, can establish *that* information is being exchanged, but they cannot give insight into *what* that information means to those participating in that exchange or *how* those participants are using those meanings to create and sustain a shared lived world. In privileging digital business discourse as a *technological process* concerned with the clarity, efficiency, and repeatability with which information is transmitted from senders to recipients, they cannot affirm digital business discourse as a *human practice*.

For communicologists, seeing communication as a technological process reduces the act of communicating to an assemblage of functions and skills. Catt (2010, p. 132) in particular warns that such skill-driven and functionalistic approaches reduce communication to a simplistic process of "self-assertion, control of image, and compliance gaining," and encourage persons "to develop, hone, weigh, and measure these skills and to direct them consistently in the mirror image of the sedimented norms of society" without stopping to consider what those norms actually are. As a result, even as the contemporary marketplace and society demand that employees "express themselves" and "make their voice heard," workers can find that the possibilities for expression have been defined in advance by the inscrutable rules and regulations of an economic system that transforms communication from a living event into "a mere commodity and a form of capital in an exchange system" (Catt, 2010, p. 134). Over time, Catt contends, communication becomes increasingly narcissistic, desensitizing persons not only to other people but also to themselves. Communication becomes merely a means of getting our message across or completing our agenda at the expense of conveying our humanity to others.

This brings us to a fundamental theoretical, methodological, and ethical question that has profound implications for the study and practice of digital business discourse: do we view digital business discourse as providing purely objective data for our dissection, prediction, and control? Or do we see it as an embodied experience, in which we see the empirical presence of data is inextricable from the existential act of communicating? For communicologists, answering "yes" to the first question threatens to transform digital business discourse into a form of technological implementation, a form of idle talk that loses its power to inform and transform organizational life for the better. However, answering "yes" to the second question brings its own challenges because it requires us to acknowledge the mysterious, ambiguous, and unquantifiable depth of our own communicative experiences. In revealing communication as a reflexive, living encounter between persons, communicology invites us to understand digital business discourse as a human encounter that occurs through our use of technology in the workplace. By shifting our focus to the experience of using technology to communicate – and the unique sense of being-in-the-workplace that emerges from this usage – it offers a way of inquiring into digital business discourse that can help scholars and practitioners attend to the process of creating meaning, critique their assumptions regarding communication, and perhaps break free of the psychic prisons that incarcerate them. The next section discusses the particulars of this form of inquiry.

Communicology as a digital business discourse methodology

Finding ways to account for and appreciate the experience of communicating can give both scholars and practitioners the insight and awareness necessary to attend to the practice of digital business discourse and establish a new sense of agency in organizational contexts that are increasingly dominated by communication technologies. As Taylor (1993) reminds us, communication problems that look at first like straightforward technological issues – the adoption of a new smartphone app does not result in the promised productivity gains, for instance, or meetings are disrupted because multicommunicating employees are constantly checking their devices – have their roots in the people who are using them. Understanding and addressing these problems requires researchers and practitioners to go deeper. In this section, we will condense the conceptually challenging work of Lanigan (1988, 1992) and other communicologists into a methodology anchored in a three-fold process of *description, reduction,* and *interpretation* that can explore the experiential aspects of digital business discourse.

By extending the research of Lanigan and other communicologists into the context of digital business discourse, we hope to create a qualitative methodology that researchers and practitioners can use in focus groups or workshops that are part of larger organizational intervention strategies. Consequently, this methodology can be seen as a form of what Argyris et al. (1985) call *action science*, a research paradigm in which researchers work alongside organization members to solve problems and shed light on to the assumptions and habits of thought that give rise to those problems in the first place. In expanding the scholarly understanding of workplace dynamics, action researchers aim to increase the agency of workers and assist them in meeting the challenges they face. In framing communicology as a methodology for understanding digital business discourse, we hope to give rise to a similar sort of interaction and double learning that deepens researchers' and practitioners' understanding of how digital interactions take place while encouraging workers to attend more closely to their own experiences of using communication technology.

Because it emerges from the human sciences, communicology brings a set of assumptions that differentiates it from social scientific research. These differences begin in communicology's selection of the unit of analysis. Catt and Eicher-Catt (2010) observe that communicology privileges *capta* – that is, the perceptive and intuitive dimensions of communication – over the collection of *data*. As a result, they contend, communicological research is undertaken "not with the goal of accumulating more and more social science facts, continuously pouring more sand on the beach, but with the goal of deciphering how the meanings of our lives are intersubjectively constituted through communicative practices" (Catt & Eicher-Catt, 2010, p. 17). Within the context of digital business discourse, the shift from *data* to *capta* requires a different approach to research that views the entire experience of a particular encounter as the unit of analysis. Where Gee's (1999) understanding of discourse analysis emphasizes breaking interactions into lines and stanzas, communicology strives to remain holistic, recognizing that the meaning of any experience is always more than the sum of its individual parts.

Communicology's holistic approach also calls into question the emphasis on objectivity that has long been a part of social scientific research. Lanigan's (1992) emphasis on the reflexivity of the experience of communication suggests that communicology is a mode of inquiry best experienced *with* participants, not a set of procedures done *to* them (Catt, 2010). As a research methodology, communicology is therefore allergic to approaches that would see communication research as anything other than a living, reflecting, human practice between persons. In contrast to discourse analysis (Gee, 1999), in which critical investigation takes place separately from the interactions being studied, communicology places researchers and participants together as co-inquirers and allows participants to correct and guide researchers' observations as the process unfolds. The validity of the research findings emerges in the complex negotiation between the researcher and the participant.

Communicology's project of co-relational inquiry begins with *description*. In this initial phase, participants in the research study recount, without judgment and in as much detail as possible, a particular experience of communicating and generate the text that will become central to the analysis that follows (Lanigan, 1992). While it seems simple, the task of description can often be more difficult than it looks. As Middleton and Cukier (2006) observe, persons trapped within psychic prisons may not fully understand the depth of their imprisonment. In these cases, their descriptions of their experiences of digital business discourse can easily become functionalistic and strategic, focusing solely on explaining how particular technologies work, how they can serve organizational ends, or how they have "saved" the day. Consequently, participants need to be encouraged not only to relate what they have done but also attend to the broader context that informs and gives rise to those actions.

In the context of research into the business use of smartphones, for example, descriptions would include things like the emotions workers feel (e.g., stress, anxiety or excitement), the thoughts they have, the sights and sounds they experience, the physical strains they experience on eyes and fingers, the weight and smoothness of the devices in their hands, or the ways using their devices affects or appears to affect others around them. Of course, not every description will include all of these elements, and some elements will be more predominant than others. Participants will describe their experiences in different ways and may even describe the same experience differently in different situations. What matters most here, though, is that researchers and practitioners look for ways to invite participants to attend to their usage of their devices more fully and to explore aspects of their experience that they would have otherwise missed.

In the next step of the communicological method, *reduction*, researchers ask participants to return to the descriptions they have just produced and highlight – or "bracket" – the elements that they believe are most important, evocative or meaningful (Lanigan, 1992). Through this process, participants discover *revelatory phrases*, "the words and phrases of the person, words that nominate what the discourse is about as a conscious experience" and that "signify the lived-meaning of the discourse as a life-event" (Lanigan, 1988, p. 147). As with description, what matters most is that participants focus on highlighting the words and phrases that are most significant *to them*, not to the researchers involved in the study. In recounting an episode of checking email during her child's school play, for instance, a worker may be drawn to any number of parts of the description: experiences of boredom or embarrassment, feelings of stress and pressure or guilt (or lack of it) in regard to her role as a parent, and so on. In isolating these parts of her experience, she gathers insights that launch her into the final part of the methodology.

The third step, *interpretation*, brings the work of the first two phases together. In this phase, Lanigan (1988) notes that the investigator often rejoins the process to work alongside participants and discover the relationships between participants' descriptions of their experiences and the revelatory phrases they highlighted as significant. In some cases, the meaning might be readily apparent. In others, researchers and participants may need to work together, with researchers taking care to suspend their own prejudices or predispositions and focusing instead on helping participants to clarify and deepen their thinking. This give-and-take sets the stage for breakthroughs and insights. "Confirmation," Lanigan (1988, p. 147) writes, "is often readily at hand with such respondent reactions as 'that's what I meant, but I didn't know I said it' or the reaction to the analyst's proposition, 'that's what I was trying to say.'" But such "A-ha!" moments are only the beginning. Communicology is always an *iterative* endeavor that can (and should) be repeated over and over again, just as perception itself is a continuous process: description leads to reduction, which leads to interpretation, which leads to another description. Within the context of digital business discourse research, this does not necessarily mean working over the same episode again and again, but it does suggest a long-term collaborative relationship between researchers and practitioners. The next section outlines three approaches that can allow this relationship to unfold.

Incorporating communicology in digital business discourse research

As a research approach, communicology's iterative methodology of description, reduction, and interpretation invites both researchers and participants to undertake several research projects together. In this section, we draw from the communicology literature to develop three possible methodologies – what we call *life-event methodology, reflective interviewing*, and *generational storytelling* – that demonstrate what this research could look like in practice. Because these methodologies originate in contexts outside of the scope of applied communication research, we will focus on defining these approaches more formally and connecting them more clearly to digital business discourse.

Life-Event Methodology. In describing a classroom project, Lanigan (1988) suggests a research approach that invites participants to tell narratives about significant events in their lives. "As these persons express their life experiences, as they tell their story," he writes, "the narration of the life-event instantiates the existential value and phenomenological meaning of society, of the lived-world of others" (1988, p. 144). As an illustration of this approach, he invites participants to write a short, autobiographical account (description) about a meaningful moment in their lives in which they learned an important moral or social value. The intent here is to give participants an opportunity to attend to practices they often take for granted. Then, participants examine the document for key words and revelatory phrases that "signify the lived-meaning of the discourse as a life-event" (reduction) (Lanigan, 1988, p. 147). After highlighting these phrases, participants work closely with researchers to produce a statement suggesting the event's meaning or significance (interpretation).

When applied to digital business discourse, Lanigan's life-event methodology offers a simple way to explore a variety of communication experiences and situations in the workplace. Researchers can assemble a group of participants (e.g., "Crackberry" addicts, casual users, non-users or a mixed group) and ask them to reflect on and write a short narrative about a key moment in their use of communication technology at work (e.g., using mobile email, experiences of connected time, multicommunicating) and interpret that text. When repeated over time, participants can reflect on different types of encounters and explore how they experience digital business discourse differently depending on the situation and the technology they use.

This methodology emphasizes direct relationships between researchers and participants. In a focus group, for instance, researchers can assign this task and then follow up with each participant individually to help them through the process of interpretation, or (as in the case study below) they can ask participants to relate their stories aloud for the group to discuss. For practitioners, this approach seems highly amenable to executive coaching, in which workers who have bad habits that inhibit their productivity or experience high levels of stress or burnout can work one-on-one with a coach to uncover and address problem areas. Finally, a life-event methodology can also be used as an initial relationship building or diagnostic tool that can highlight issues – multicommunicating, for instance – for further inquiry.

Reflective Interviewing. In her communicological analysis of human sexuality, Martinez (2011) suggests a small-group methodology that could be highly applicable to research in digital business discourse. In her approach, groups of three to four participants begin by deciding to explore a particular type or category of experience, such as moments in which they felt powerful, humiliated, anxious or fulfilled. Once the group decides on the focus of the research, each member of the group interviews another member of the group about a particular experience in which they experienced this emotion. Following the interview, both the interviewer and interviewee write a narrative describing the experience (description). Participants then read their interviewer's more impartial account of the interaction and compare it with their own. After pinpointing and prioritizing revelatory phrases in their interviewer's narrative (reduction), the participants discuss the similarities and differences between the accounts and work together to reflect on why the particular revelatory phrases are so meaningful (interpretation). As they do, they shed light on broader issues or cultural norms that would have otherwise gone unnoticed.

Reflective interviewing differs from life-event methodology in two important respects. First, reflective interviewing focuses on the emotions that arise while using technology, while life-event methodology emphasizes particular situations as the point of departure. Second, where life-event methodology focuses solely on the experiences of individuals, reflective interviewing includes additional observers who can elaborate upon or even challenge participants' accounts, which may be clouded by self-justifications and rationalizations. For persons whose nomophobic addiction to their devices blinds them to the costs that usage demands, an outside assessment may be sobering. If a person feels anxious or powerless when she is away from her smartphone, why does she feel that way? If he feels free, from what does he feel free?

In raising these questions, this approach can respond to Middleton and Cukier's (2006) call for research that sheds light on the walls of the psychic prisons that may hold workers captive and helps them to learn ways of thinking about and using technology that are more humanly sustainable. For instance, a practitioner whose job description includes responding to social media feeds may experience unusually high amounts of frustration, anxiety, and anger when performing those tasks. The opportunity to describe these emotions to another person – a co-worker or impartial bystander – and to hear his or her response can be both liberating and illuminating. The worker may come away from the experience confirmed – yes, people can indeed say hurtful and frustrating things – but may also learn to place those emotions in context and to see online encounters in a new light, deepening what Edelson et al. (2015) describe as her digital emotional literacy and helping her to respond with greater professional civility (Fritz, 2013).

Generational Storytelling. How do the psychic prisons that so often characterize the contemporary workplace form and sustain themselves? Drawing on McFeat's (1974) work on small-group cultures, Lanigan (2013) outlines a methodology that accounts for how cultures develop and shift over time and how communication constitutes culture across generations. In this methodology, a group of ten participants reads an unfinished novel and is asked to invent the ending. Then, the researcher replaces one of the members of the original group (the first generation) with a newcomer unfamiliar with the ending (the second generation). After the group explains the novel's ending to the newcomer, a second newcomer replaces a second original member. The group, now consisting of eight original members and two newcomers, must describe and teach the ending of the novel once again. Group members repeat this process until no original members remain, and the group represents a completely new generation. By recording the discussion and development of the narrative in its various stages, researchers create a complex text that allows them to explore how the group completes the narrative (a form of description), analyze the details of that narrative that group members isolate and choose to pass on to newcomers (reduction), and inquire into participants' rationales for telling the story in the way that they do (interpretation).

While Lanigan's initial approach focuses on novels, researchers of digital business discourse who adopt a generational storytelling approach can instead present participants with unfinished case studies or scenarios that focus participants' attention on the use of communication technology in the workplace. As they *tell* the story, participants begin to generate a myth complete with its own terminology that reflects a particular set of interests, values, and assumptions. And as they *retell* the story to newcomers, they begin to embody the sign system it represents. This type of approach seems particularly useful in examining the ways in which digital business discourse intersects with organizational culture. As Schein (2010) observes, we can understand organizational cultures on the level of the artifacts that members create and use, the values that define members' corporate understanding of the world, and underlying assumptions that shape how members think. In situations where an organization appears resistant to the adoption of a particular technology, for instance, generational storytelling can be helpful in exposing the values and assumptions that can easily lie hidden beneath the technical implementation. As organization members come together to tell and retell the story – and debate why the story needs to end as it does – they can begin to reveal the human network that communicology seeks to recover and explore.

Case study: Life-event methodology

In this section, we illustrate how this approach can drive empirical research through an example of research conducted during a workshop given by one of the authors (Maier) in which life-event methodology played an important role. Halfway through a two-hour workshop, which took place in a large Roman Catholic organization in the United States, participants were provided with a single sheet of lined paper with a short prompt asking them to think of a particular communication incident that they believed to be especially memorable or illustrative of their working life. The protocol requested that participants tell the story of that event in as much detail as possible: *What led up to the encounter? Who was involved? What occurred? What were the outcomes?* After reading the prompt aloud and answering questions, participants were given 15 minutes to reflect and write (description). Then, after the time was up, participants were given three minutes to reread their story and circle what they took to be the most important or evocative words or phrases that captured the significance or meaning of the story (reduction). The group then spent the next 45 minutes talking about and interpreting their stories (interpretation). Detailed notes were taken throughout the process, yielding two sets of texts: the stories produced by the participants, and the notes of the facilitator and participants' joint effort to interpret the stories.

During the workshop, one of the participants, a journalist and editor, provided the following story that shed light on her own practice of digital business discourse. The words that she highlighted are represented in **bold**:

At the time of the papal election [of Pope Francis], I was sending out tweets on our [organizational] accounts. A mom without a TV, a sick child, and other kids running around asked me to DM [direct message] her when there was white smoke. When that happened, I did as she asked. She started asking questions, some which were **answered** by our stories, some which went unanswered. It was very nice to **communicate** with someone who had a lot of interest. ... We included her in a story. But this is so **different** than any **contact** that I [in my professional capacity] would have had before since I am always trapped in my office.

When asked to elaborate on the event to the rest of the group, the participant emphasized the ways in which using her smartphone created an unexpected experience of transcendence, in which she was able to overcome numerous obstacles that were between her and the woman with whom she was communicating. Overall, technology set the stage for an exchange in which she believed that she made a connection – a moment of authentic "contact" – with another person that was professionally meaningful. Yet, the facilitator suggested to her that this experience of connection and transcendence also seemed to have a dark side: the feeling of being "trapped" and distanced from others, an experience that she indicated was actually quite normal for her given the way that her job was constructed. Suddenly, she provided a glimpse into the organizational and personal context that added depth and resonance to her practice of digital business discourse. While her smartphone may have been a heroic device in this case, this insight encouraged her and everyone else to wonder why she needed "saving."

Though this story represents only a single experience, it can nevertheless lead to broader insights. For the participant who related the story, for instance, the realization of her need to escape feelings of being "trapped" gave her a new awareness of her own practice of digital business discourse and experience of being-in-the-workplace. When placed alongside other accounts, this individual experience can contribute to a broader picture of her co-workers' experiences and of deeper communication and organizational problems that require intervention: Do other organization members feel "trapped" in their working lives, and if so, why do they feel so distanced and alienated from others? What traps them? How can they redefine their working lives in more sustainable ways? As researchers and participants answer these questions together, they can attend to the practice of digital business discourse more completely and find ways to improve their practice of digital business discourse and their organizational culture, as well.

Conclusion: New directions

In this chapter, we sought to reframe a highly philosophical branch of research known as communicology for use in digital business discourse. As a methodology, communicology invites us to ask: *What do we experience when we use technology to communicate with others in organizations?*

Are we using language, processing bits of information, or standing enthralled by the dance of pixels on a screen? Or are we experiencing something more? We began this chapter with the case of persons whose forgetful and inattentive use of smartphones had transformed the use of their devices into an addiction. For these workers, technology had become the hero of their discursive lives, and their focus on the empirical over the existential dimensions of communication encouraged them to communicate in inattentive, distracted ways. In response, we framed communicology as a research methodology that could help researchers and practitioners to account for the lived experience of technology and recover digital business discourse as a human practice. Through a disciplined effort of describing particular experiences, reducing these experiences to their essential elements, and then interpreting their meaning, communicology invites persons to encounter digital business discourse differently, not as a technologized process of information exchange but as an embodied and profoundly human experience.

Communicological research can transform the study and practice of digital business discourse in a number of ways. Certainly, inviting persons to explore the experience of using communication technology in organizations may prompt them to acknowledge and challenge practices – texting while driving, constantly multicommunicating during meetings or repeatedly checking for messages during nonworking hours – that may seem essential in an always-on, always-connected world but may, in actuality, be extremely harmful both to productivity and to relationships outside of work. This research could help to address addictive and stressful communication behaviors, reveal social and cultural pressures on workers, and perhaps inform more critically oriented studies seeking to transform workplaces to make them more ethical and humane. But alongside its potential to help workers break out of the psychic prisons they have created for themselves, we also suggest that communicology may be helpful in generating other, more fundamental insights into and awareness of the ways in which technology is changing the experience of communicating in the workplace itself. As the influence of technology on our working lives becomes increasingly pervasive, communicology can help researchers and practitioners to rediscover the human in the human network.

References

Argyris C., Putnam R., & Smith, D. M. (1985). *Action Science: Concepts, Methods, and Skills for Research and Implementation*. San Francisco, CA: Jossey-Bass.

Catt, I. (2010). Communication is not a skill: Critique of communication pedagogy as narcissistic expression. In D. Eicher-Catt & I. Catt (Eds), *Communicology: The New Science of Embodied Discourse* (pp. 131–150). Madison Teaneck, NJ: Fairleigh Dickinson University Press.

Catt, I., & Eicher-Catt, D. (2010). Communicology: A reflexive human science. In D. Eicher-Catt & I. Catt (Eds), *Communicology: The New Science of Embodied Discourse* (pp. 15–29). Madison Teaneck, NJ: Fairleigh Dickinson University Press.

Edelson, S., Kim, P., Scott, R., & Szendrey, J. (2015). What did I just tweet?!: The need to address digital emotional literacy in corporate communications. In E. Darics (Ed.), *Digital Business Discourse* (pp. 189–207). Basingstoke: Palgrave Macmillan.

Fortunati, L. (2001). The mobile phone: An identity on the move. *Personal and Ubiquitous Computing, 5* (2): 85–98.

Fritz, J. M. H. (2013). *Professional Civility: Communicative Virtue at Work*. New York: Peter Lang.

Gee, J. P. (1999). *An Introduction to Discourse Analysis: Theory and Method*. New York: Routledge.

Heidegger, M. (1996). *Being and Time* (tr. Joan Stambaugh). Albany, NY: SUNY Press (original work published 1927).

Ivarsson, L., & Larsson, P. (2011). Personal Internet usage at work: A source of recovery. *Journal of Workplace Rights, 16* (1): 63–81.

Jablin, F. M. (1980). Organizational communication theory and research: An overview of communication climate and network research. *Communication Yearbook, 4*, 327–347.

Jeong, S., & Hwang, Y. (2012). Does multitasking increase or decrease persuasion? Effects of multitasking on comprehension and counterarguing. *Journal of Communication, 62* (4): 571–587.

Lanigan, R. (1972). *Semiology and Speaking: Maurice Merleau-Ponty's Phenomenological Theory of Existential Communication*. The Hague: Mouton.

Lanigan, R. (1984). *Semiotic Phenomenology of Rhetoric: Eidetic Practice in Henry Grattan's Discourse on Tolerance*. Washington, DC: University Press of America.

Lanigan, R. (1988). *Phenomenology of Communication: Merleau-Ponty's Thematics in Communicology and Semiology*. Pittsburgh, PA: Duquesne University Press.

Lanigan, R. (1992). *The Human Science of Communicology: A Phenomenology of Discourse in Foucault and Merleau-Ponty*. Pittsburgh, PA: Duquesne University Press.

Lanigan, R. (2013). Information theories. In Peter J. Schulz & Paul Cobley (Eds), *Handbook of Communication Science: Theories and Models of Communication* (pp. 59–60). The Hague: De Gruyter Mouton.

Martinez, J. (2011). *Communicative Sexualities: A Communicology of Sexual Experience*. Lanham, MD: Lexington.

McFeat, T. (1974). *Small-Group Cultures*. New York: Pergamon Press.

Middleton, C. (2007). Illusions of balance and control in an always-on environment: A case study of BlackBerry users. *Continuum: Journal of Media and Cultural Studies, 21* (2): 165–178.

Middleton, C., & Cukier, W. (2006). Is mobile email functional or dysfunctional? Two perspectives on mobile email usage. *European Journal of Information Systems, 15* (3): 252–260.

Moran, A. (2012). Study: Two-thirds suffer from nomophobia, fear of losing a phone. Retrieved January 27, 2014 from: http://digitaljournal.com/article/319921.

Morgan, G. (1997). *Images of Organization*. Thousand Oaks, CA: Sage.

Reinsch, L., Turner, J., & Tinsley, C. (2008). Multicommunicating: A practice whose time has come? *Academy of Management Review, 33* (2): 391–403.

Schein, E. H. (2010). *Organizational Culture and Leadership* (4th edition). San Francisco, CA: Jossey-Bass.

SecurEnvoy. (2012). 66% of the Population Suffer from Nomophobia, the Fear of Being without their Phone. Retrieved January 27, 2014 from: http://www.securenvoy.com/blog/2012/02/16/66-of-the-population-suffer-from-nomophobia-the-fear-of-being-without-their-phone/.

Stephens, K. (2012). Multiple conversations during organizational meetings: Development of the multicommunicating scale. *Management Communication Quarterly, 26* (2): 195–223.

Taylor, J. R. (1993). *Rethinking the Theory of Organizational Communication: How to Read an Organization*. Norwood, NJ: Ablex.

Wang, Z., & Tchernev, J. (2012). The "myth" of media multitasking: Reciprocal dynamics of media multitasking, personal needs, and gratifications. *Journal of Communication, 62* (3): 493–513.

11

Identification of Rhetorical Moves in Business Emails Written by Indian Speakers of English

María Luisa Carrió-Pastor

Introduction

Digital communication has become increasingly important for the everyday exchange of information (Crystal, 2001; Darics, 2014; Skovholt & Svennevig, 2006; Thurlow & Mroczek, 2011). My specific interests lie in the study of the use of emails for international communication and in the role of the linguistic background of speakers of English as a foreign language when communicating. Email has replaced traditional communication in the form of a letter, and it is important to consider the effect this has from a linguistic point of view. In this chapter, the focus is on the rhetorical moves undertaken by Indian businessmen when communicating digitally in English as a second language.

In professional contexts it is essential to communicate effectively, and this chapter sets out to explore how this effectiveness is achieved. The chapter provides a model that identifies the steps involved in naturally occurring interactions between the managers of an international export company. Analyzing emails written by English speakers who belong to the Outer Circle, as shown in Figure 11.1 (Kachru, 2005) may enable new features to be detected and thus allow the identification of rhetorical moves in business digital discourse, raising awareness of the implications of digital communication.

English speakers can be placed in different circles that imply their proximity to the cultural conventions of English depending on the use and the importance of this language in a country. In this respect, Kachru (2005) identified three circles in which he placed the different speakers of English. The Inner Circle includes speakers of English as a native language (Great Britain, USA and Australia); the Outer Circle comprises speakers of English as a second language (India, Pakistan, Nigeria, etc.)

and the Expanding Circle contains speakers of English as a foreign language. A representation of the concentric circles of Kachru (2005) can be observed in Figure 11.1.

Also of interest is the identification of the rhetorical moves employed by speakers of English as a second language in order to determine the variation that exists in digital communication. Rhetorical moves represent the choices speakers make when they are using language for specific purposes. Speakers of a language move systematically through a thinking process that leads them to explain their ideas in a given way. In this sense, identification of the rhetorical moves used in genres is useful to understand the way speakers organize language.

In this vein, Swales (1990) proposed the CARS Model, which identified three moves in the introductions of academic research papers. The first move entails establishing a territory: the writer defines the field in which he/she is interested. The second move establishes a niche: the researcher delves further and identifies a gap in current knowledge. The third move is to occupy the niche: the researcher details the specific aspects the study will consider. Another approach to the moves of academic papers was suggested by Dudley-Evans (1994), who identified information move, statement of result, finding, expected outcome, reference to previous research, explanation, claim, limitation and recommendation. Further studies have built on these classifications of moves, adding other elements depending on the medium of communication, but still mainly with reference to academic English and grant proposals (Biber et al., 2007;

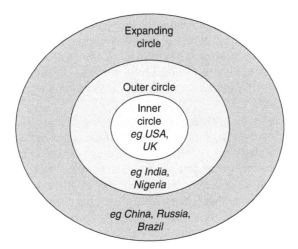

Figure 11.1   The three concentric circles of speakers of English (Kachru, 2005)

Connor, 2000; Del Saz Rubio, 2011; de Vries & van der Meij, 2003; Henry & Roseberry, 2001; Kanoksilapatham, 2005; Lim, 2012; Peacock, 2002; Ren & Li, 2011; Sun, 2004; Upton & Connor, 2001). The above authors have put forward different models or made further proposals for moves and steps, focusing on, for example, research papers and other specific fields of communication.

Moves analysis has also been applied to a wider range of written genres; for instance to professional communication and email communication (Kankaanranta, 2005; Skovholt, 2009; Skovholt & Svennevig, 2013). With regard to the structures of emails, Jensen (2009) analyzed the use of specific discourse strategies in email communication, focusing on relations between the participants. More recently, Economidou-Kogetsidis (2011) also analyzed types of supportive moves used in emails, concentrating on the lexical/phrasal modifiers used by students. Focusing on moves in business correspondence, Bhatia (1993) proposed several moves that may be applied to email messages: establishing credentials, introducing the offer, offering incentives, enclosing documents, soliciting response, using pressure tactics and ending politely. More recently, Zarei and Darani (2013) identified the following rhetorical moves in spam emails: capture attention, establish credentials, welcome prospect, introduce the offer, use pressure tactics, solicit response and give a polite way out. These moves are specific for spam emails and in this sense might not be applied to general emails. A more recent study has focused on the rhetorical moves of business emails specifically: Carrió-Pastor and Muñiz-Calderón (2013, pp. 60–1) have identified the moves for the body of business emails, based on a study of such texts written by Chinese businesspeople, as follows: reporting about the company visited, reporting about the participants in the meeting, reporting about the local agent, reporting about the representative of a company in the meeting, establishing the negotiation description and summarizing or concluding the outcome of the negotiation.

Two key aspects of business interaction in English as a lingua franca are that it involves communication between speakers of different nationalities and that it is important for the message to be properly understood. Business interaction and the rhetorical features used in international business letters have been studied by such authors as Bargiela-Chiappini and Nickerson (2002), Bremmer (2008), Carrió-Pastor and Muñiz-Calderón (2010a, 2010b, 2012), Flowerdew and Wan (2010), Nickerson (2005), Okamura and Shaw (2000), Pinto dos Santos (2002), and Yeung (2007). Although business communication has been the focus of such research, not many of these studies have focused on the rhetorical moves employed in business emails for successful effective communication to occur.

Nowadays, it is a fact that digital communication plays an important role in the exchange of information between native and non-native speakers of a language. As Economidou-Kogetsidis (2011, p. 3193) explains,

> [...] there are as yet no established conventions for linguistic behavior in e-mail communication [...] most academic syllabi lack explicit instruction in e-mail writing. As a result, both native and non-native speakers are often faced with uncertainties regarding style and politeness strategies in e-mail interaction.

For this reason, the main aim of this chapter is to further the research of rhetorical moves in professional genres, as described above. In particular I aim to identify the moves followed in emails written by non-native speakers of English.

The language used in business emails has been analyzed by several researchers, given the importance of digital communication in trade transactions: examples include Baron (2000, 2002, 2003), Biesenbach-Lucas (2005), Crystal (2001), Evans (2012), Gains (1999), Giménez (2000, 2006), Kankaanranta (2005), and Skovholt (2009). Furthermore, some of these authors point out that the standard communication patterns followed in business emails display variation when comparison is made between speakers with different cultural backgrounds.

The present work studies the moves employed in digital communication by non-native users of English language in a business environment. This chapter seeks to test and examine the moves proposed by the different authors by applying them to the corpus compiled in this study, consisting of emails written by Indian businesspeople.

Despite its obvious importance in an era of globalization and the increasing number of multinational companies, little empirical research has been carried out on this genre. The following points are of particular interest for this study on rhetorical moves in business emails:

1. The identification of rhetorical moves.
2. The patterns in the rhetorical moves used by non-native speakers of English.
3. The variations in the use of different moves that do not prevent successful digital business communication.

The study of the rhetorical moves undertaken by Indian businesspeople when communicating digitally in English as a foreign language is addressed here to show that the linguistic backgrounds of the speakers play an important role in communication. The influence of the mother tongue of the speakers may produce variations in the patterns previously established in the same genre, and this fact may be taken into account to be conscious that language changes and adapts to the purpose of the speakers and to the mental sets previously established when learning the mother tongue.

Method

Contextual background of the corpus

India has become a country with great economic power and many business transactions are now carried out. Indian businessmen mainly use English to communicate in international settings, but sometimes, as a result of the wide variety of languages used in this huge country, they also use English to communicate in the same country, something which is widely attested in the literature (Kachru, 2005, 2011; Kirkpatrick, 2007; Sailaja, 2009). In this sense, English is the language of commerce and administrative affairs. Jenkins (2009, p. 46) describes the functions of English as follows: "[...] a function of the unifying role it [English] plays as a neutral language of communication across a people of diverse mother tongues and, as a result, the way in which it has become bound up with Indian national consciousness and identity". English has an important role in India, as it is used daily by millions of people from different cultural and social backgrounds. Indian English is a variety of English, as Jenkins (2009, p. 152) explains: "The Indianisation of English essentially involves on the one hand adaptations of existing features of British English and on the other, the use of transferred mother-tongue items where British English lacks the scope to express a particular concept."

Method

The data used in this study were drawn from 30 email messages written by Indian business managers working in an export company, who were sending these messages to the company head office, located in Spain. The workers had to send emails to report their activity in India to the head office, and they followed identifiable patterns to be understood. The messages were selected randomly, with the only criterion being that each one should contain more than 200 words. The resulting corpus contains a total of 7,372 words.

The emails were analyzed manually in order to identify the rhetorical moves employed by the Indian email writers. In order to identify and analyze the different moves, the moves identified by Bhatia (1993), written by native speakers of English, and Carrió-Pastor and Muñiz Calderón (2013)'s moves, identified in emails written by Chinese and Indian businesspeople, were taken into account. As the intention of this analysis was to identify the rhetorical moves used by speakers of English as a second or foreign language, the first step was to consider moves that had previously been identified in other studies in which speakers with different linguistic backgrounds were analyzed, enabling the existence of other possible rhetorical moves to be determined and contrasted. Therefore, the organization of the emails compiled in this study, written by Indian businesspeople, and the way these L2 writers used different rhetorical strategies to communicate with their counterparts were compared with the different rhetorical functions outlined by Bhatia (1993) for native English speakers and Carrió-Pastor and Muñiz Calderón (2013) for Chinese and Indian speakers of English, as described below.

A quantitative and qualitative study of the corpus was performed. The frequency of the moves was considered as well as factors not reported in previous studies. Bhatia (1993)'s classification of moves taken into account in this study is as follows:

Move 1. Referencing
Move 2. Greeting/establishing credentials
Move 3. Introducing the offer
Move 4. Offering incentives
Move 5. Using pressure tactics
Move 6. Enclosing documents
Move 7. Soliciting response
Move 8. Ending politely.

These steps were suitable for the purpose of this study, given that digital business communication might include moves 3, 4 and 5, typical in business negotiations. Therefore, as stated above, this classification was taken as a starting point in this study to identify the moves altogether with another classification, suggested by Carrió-Pastor and Muñiz Calderón (2013, p. 61), for emails sent by Chinese and Indian businesspeople, as follows:

Move 1. Reporting about the client/company visited
Move 2. Reporting about the participants (customers)

Move 3. Reporting about the agent participant
Move 4. Reporting about the X company representative
Move 5. Establishing the negotiation/description
Move 6. Summarizing/concluding the outcome of the negotiation
(follow up).

As can be observed, the moves established by Bhatia (1993) and referring to native speakers of English are not the same as those reported by Carrió-Pastor and Muñiz Calderón (2013). The emails analyzed in this latter study were written by non-native speakers of English and the writers focused more on negotiation than on being polite. These two classifications were taken into account as the researchers identified different moves, and perhaps this chapter will show a further aspect to be taken into account.

Once the moves identified by other researchers were taken into account, the emails were analyzed to identify and tag the moves. Finally, the different examples of the rhetorical features of the emails written by Indian businesspeople were identified. The moves that coincided and the ones that diverged from the previously established classifications were then also identified. Specifically, the results were compared with the moves identified by Bhatia (1993) in native speakers of English and by Carrió-Pastor and Muñiz Calderón (2013) in non-native speakers of English to identify the different stages and features that Indian speakers of English employed to communicate digitally with their counterparts.

The implications of and conclusions drawn from this study are twofold: one concerns the use of English by non-native speakers of English and would thus benefit ESP teachers; the other relates to the identification of the rhetorical moves in digital business discourse and would provide a comparable, easily outlinable structure for further research, teaching and training.

Results

Following the analysis of the corpus, several moves were identified. Some were the same as those identified by Bhatia (1993) in the communication of native speakers of English, but others varied. In the results identified after the analysis of the corpus, the rhetorical moves may differ because the purpose of these emails was to explain meetings and business with other companies. Most of the emails were sent by Indian workers who were explaining the actions undertaken in India while also referring to future needs or meetings. The moves found in the emails analyzed are shown in Table 11.1.

If we compare the moves identified in this analysis with those established by Bhatia (1993) and Carrió-Pastor and Muñiz Calderón (2013), we can see that moves 1, 2, 4, 7 and 9 coincided with Bhatia's proposal (1993), but none coincided with Carrió-Pastor and Muñiz-Calderón (2013)'s proposal.

Table 11.2 summarizes the quantitative results of the moves identified in this study. The first and second columns show the different moves and their descriptions, and the third column displays the occurrences and corresponding percentages, taking into account that the total number of emails analyzed was 30 and that each move was identified once in each email.

There was one case in the occurrences found in this analysis of another possible move, but it was disregarded as it was not mentioned in previous studies and there were too few occurrences for it to be included

Table 11.1   Moves in business emails written by Indian businesspeople

Moves in business emails	
Move 1	Referencing
Move 2	Greeting/establishing credentials
Move 3	Thanking and referring to previous business
Move 4	Introducing an offer
Move 5	Establishing facts of the offer
Move 6	Giving details of business
Move 7	Enclosing documents
Move 8	Giving positive feedback/inviting
Move 9	Ending politely

Table 11.2   Occurrences and percentages found in the corpus of emails written by Indian workers

Moves		Occurrences (percentage)
Move 1	Referencing	30 (100.0%)
Move 2	Greeting/establishing credentials	30 (100.0%)
Move 3	Thanking and referring to previous business	16 (53.3%)
Move 4	Introducing an offer	20 (66.6%)
Move 5	Establishing facts of the offer	16 (53.3%)
Move 6	Giving details of business	22 (73.3%)
Move 7	Enclosing documents	2 (6.6%)
Move 8	Giving positive feedback/inviting	24 (80.0%)
Move 9	Ending politely	30 (100.0%)

as a move. In this case, the email writer requested some pictures from the receiver, as can be seen in Example 1:

Example 1
"Be kind to send them as per our request by email" (em02).

This move was not included in the proposal, as the significance of this finding could not be established in this study.

Table 11.3 includes a comparison of the moves identified in business letters written by native speakers (Bhatia 1993), in business emails as reports written by non-native speakers from the Outer Circle (India) and the Expanding Circle (China) (Carrió-Pastor and Muñiz Calderón, 2013) and in business emails written by non-native speakers of English from the Outer Circle (India) (this chapter).

It can be observed in Table 11.3 that the emails written by Indian businesspeople include more moves than the letters written by native speakers of English and the reports as emails written by non-native

Table 11.3 Comparison of the identification of moves in business correspondence

Moves (Bhatia, 1993)	Moves (Carrió-Pastor & Muñiz Calderón, 2013)	Moves (this study)
Move 1 Referencing	Move 1 Reporting about the client/company visited	Move 1 Referencing
Move 2 Greeting/establishing credentials	Move 2 Reporting about the participants (customers)	Move 2 Greeting/establishing credentials
Move 3 Introducing the offer	Move 3 Reporting about the agent participant	Move 3 Thanking and referring to previous business
Move 4 Offering incentives	Move 4 Reporting about the X company representative	Move 4 Introducing an offer
Move 5 Using pressure tactics	Move 5 Establishing the negotiation/description	Move 5 Establishing facts of the offer
Move 6 Enclosing documents	Move 6 Summarizing/concluding the outcome of the negotiation (follow up)	Move 6 Giving details of business
Move 7 Soliciting response		Move 7 Enclosing documents
		Move 8 Giving positive feedback/inviting
		Move 9 Ending politely

speakers of English. Indian writers of business emails are polite as they include positive feedback and end their emails politely. It can be observed in Table 11.2 that Indian writers always include referencing, greetings and a polite ending in their mails as a courtesy, which may be considered an important aspect in business interaction. The politeness and positive expressions used by Indian businesspeople can be observed in the examples detailed below; included here to provide evidence of the variation found when the corpus was analyzed.

As a qualitative analysis of the corpus, examples of the moves found in the corpus are shown below in Examples 2–10 to illustrate the discursive features detected and analyzed in this study. The examples are numerated and the number of the move detected is included at the beginning of the example; the number of the email in which the example was found is also included at the end of the example in brackets:

Example 2
M.1 "Team arrow clothing-Ahmedabad meeting" (em01).

All the emails analyzed included the references or topic of the message; this aspect is almost compulsory in an email, with this being one of the fields to be filled.

Example 3
M.2 "Greetings for the week" (em01). "Greetings for business" (em02). "Kind attn Mr. Abhijit Gohil-President- Team soma textiles" (em06). "Greetings Enrique" (em11).

This move was included in all of the emails, although the way the writers greet or establish credentials varies.

Example 4
M.3 "Many thanks for the Saturday meeting" (em01). "It was indeed pleasure meeting last week Friday/Saturday" (em03). "Many thanks for time and association last week two interactions. It was indeed pleasure meeting on both occasions" (em14).

This move was not included in previous studies, but almost 54% of the writers included this move in their emails. I consider this to be a discursive feature typical of Indian English, as the tendency of Indian writers is to be polite.

Example 5
M.4 "As a taste of customer delight-Mr. Enrique has made special offer including one week training" (em01). "We are sincere and keen to supply G2 technology in your esteemed plant in Ahmadabad" (em27).

This move is used to introduce the offer of business, and it is employed by almost 67% of the writers. The discourse features used are frequently positive and polite, as in: "are sincere and keen to", "special offer" etc.

Example 6
M.5 "Spain was closed from Thursday till Monday- local holidays. We can expect all details from tomorrow" (em04). "Mr. Jose Maria, please, add this in green target" (em07). "I just happened to make a call to Brandix about one of the technical issue we had there and enquired them about the G2 again to Jayampathi" (em18).

In this move, the writer establishes facts that are important for the negotiation, with the information included in this move being issues that need to be taken into account; the writer uses the imperative form as no answer is required.

Example 7
M.6 "Jayampathi had already called the technical head of Hiradaramni Susiri to visit and see the machine but not yet visited them. I told him I'll be coming down to Sri Lanka next month and will visit him" (em08). "The LC draft copy of Canara Bank can be marked to Ms. Carle attention in Spain. Be rest assured after the EPCG license is obtained we will ship the machine" (em10).

This move is used by the writers to give details of the business trans-actions: the intention is to report a deal and the style of discourse is direct; few polite strategies are used. The writer explains facts that need to be clearly understood, and the rhetorical function of this move is to explain the details of the business. In the corpus analyzed, almost 74% of the Indian writers used this move, suggesting its high importance in business communication.

Example 8
M.7 "The attachment has the details of machine CATLOG" (em10). "Find attached the info" (em29).

This move was seldom used by the writers analyzed, as they used emails to give details or explain an offer. The reason for this may be that the receiver and the sender worked in the same company and shared documents in a virtual file system. In this study, this move was not important for the writers, but it was included in the model, as it was in Bhatia's (1993) proposal.

Example 9
M.8 "We value our business association" (em06). "We are keen to meet again to develop this opportunity given" (em15). "I also take the opportunity to invite to visit our demo-centre in Bangalore" (em28). "HAPPY TO START business with this group again" (em21). "MANY THANKS TO SPAN FOR THE SUPPORT" (em15).

This move was used by 80% of the writers analyzed. Indian speakers of English take the view that they should be polite and pleasant with other businesspeople, using polite forms and capital letters to achieve this. They are grateful, and they want to communicate this to the receiver. Before finishing the emails, they always give positive feedback and their appraisal of all the work done; they even invite the receivers to visit their offices. It is my view that this move expresses feelings to the reader, which is quite unusual in business negotiations. The writer wishes to be polite and interact with the reader to create a friendly atmosphere, engaging the reader in the message. This might be a cultural aspect of the corpus being analyzed and of Indian English in general. Other studies (Bhatia, 1993; Carrió-Pastor & Muñiz, 2013; Gains, 1999) have not included this move, not specific to Indian speakers of English. In this regard, this trait might be characteristic of Indian communication in business as they wish to be polite and to empathize with their counterparts.

Example 10
M.9 "Best regards" (em13). "Warm regards" (em20).

The same formula is used in almost all the emails to end politely. The farewells used by Indian writers are short and repetitive. As they have shown their politeness in moves 3 and 8 and have already explained their intentions in previous parts of the emails, the end of the mail is not an important section for them and is merely a formulaic aspect of the communication.

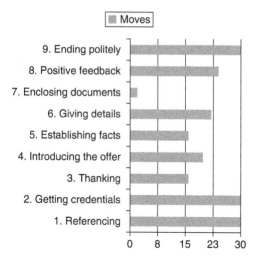

Figure 11.2   Comparison of occurrences of the moves identified in the emails

In order to compare the results obtained and provide greater context for the above comments, the frequency of the moves is shown in Figure 11.2.

Figure 11.2 shows that the emails analyzed started and finished in the same way and that the senders did not consider it important to attach files. In the same way, most of the Indian writers gave positive feedback or finished with a positive reference to the business in a friendly manner, giving details of the business transactions.

Conclusions

This chapter focused on the rhetorical moves contained in business emails, in this case written by Indian businesspeople. The different rhetorical moves used to communicate effectively in business communication were identified and detailed in the examples discussed in the Results section. The patterns that coincided with previous studies (Bhatia, 1993; Carrió Pastor & Muñiz Calderón, 2013) were recognized after the analysis of the corpus. The moves that coincided were: M.1 Referencing, M.2 Greeting and establishing credentials, M.4 Introducing the offer, M.7 Enclosing documents and M.9 Ending politely. The moves that differed from other studies were: M.3 Thanking and referring to previous business, M.5 Establishing facts, M.6 Giving details of business, M.8 Giving positive feedback and inviting. The non-native speakers of English, Indian businesspeople in this case, used moves that reflected

Indian English. The Indian businessmen thanked and gave positive details to the readers to empathize with them; these two moves were not identified by previous studies. In the words of Jenkins (2009, p. 46), mentioned in the Introduction, Indian English involves adaptations of existing features of British English and the use of transferred mother-tongue items. Thus, Indian businessmen express politeness in business texts and use positive expressions as a result of their linguistic background.

Occurrences of moves other than the ones proposed in previous studies indicate variation in the way Indian writers of the data sample communicate. The authors of the collected emails seem not to be interested in using pressure tactics or soliciting responses, preferring to thank their interlocutors and to be positive in their negotiations, using rhetorical features that reflect their intentions – to be friendly with their counterparts. The positive tone used in these Indian emails can probably be attributed to the writers' intentions not only to provide information, but also to recommend action and to propose business deals. We can see this in certain expressions in the corpus: "This is super special price" (em02), "Many thanks for the excellent dinner meeting" (em04), "We are keen to meet again to develop this opportunity given" (em09), "CONGRATULATIONS for meeting with team Soma yesterday" (em08), etc. The use of positive adjectives (boosters) and superlatives or capital letters to emphasize the positive aspects of the negotiation are quite evident in most of the emails analyzed. The writers tended to include positive adjectives or expressions at the beginning or at the end of the email, to empathize with the readers and to communicate in a friendly manner. Actions to be carried out are predominantly expressed as imperatives, but the preceding sentence softens the tone used.

They use these tactics to achieve the rhetorical aim of persuasion, creating an impression of a positive atmosphere. For this reason, they use positive adjectives, thanking expressions and friendly constructions. The rhetorical moves of business emails show a pragmatic structure, which begins with greeting and thanking the reader (subjective discourse), then moves on to identifying problems and giving details (objective discourse) Finally, the email finishes in the same way as it began, giving positive feedback and extending an invitation to the reader (subjective discourse). The moves followed in the corpus are mainly persuasive, since they do not consist of commands or instructions; rather, they recommend solutions and adopt a positive tone to inspire confidence and optimism in the negotiation. The rhetorical mood used by the Indian writers is more positive than negative in order to persuade readers that they can resolve all the problems.

Some of the moves identified in this study appeared in Bhatia (1993), but other moves have been identified. These may be attributed to changes in communication arising from the use of emails or perhaps to the fact that the linguistic background of the writers influences the way they structure the moves. Other studies on digital communication have obtained different results, one example being the study by Carrió-Pastor and Muñiz-Calderón (2013), analyzing reports written by Chinese nationals. The different moves identified in this latter study were a result of the fact that the purpose of these texts was to report on business issues and explain the negotiation, and so the rhetorical moves varied to match the writers' intentions.

At a more general level, this study provides support for the idea that the content and style of business emails varies when used by non-native speakers of English: our linguistic and cultural backgrounds play a role when we communicate in a given language. Language not only transmits the ideas of writers, but also their cultural and linguistic background. Thus, when English is used in a discourse community, although the writers share the same medium of communication, this does not mean that they employ the same rhetorical moves, as they are individuals with different conceptions of reality and ways to communicate.

References

Bargiela-Chiappini, F., & Nickerson, C. (2002). Business discourse: Old concepts, new horizons. *International Review of Applied Linguistics in Language Teaching, 40* (4), 273–286.

Baron, N. (2000). *Alphabet to e-mail. How written English evolved and where it's heading.* New York: Routledge.

Baron, N. (2002). Who sets e-mail style? Prescriptivism, coping strategies, and democratizing communication access. *The Information Society, 18,* 403–413.

Baron, N. (2003). Why e-mail looks like speech: Proofreading pedagogy and public face. In J. Atchison & D. M. Lewis (Eds), *New Media Language.* New York: Routledge, 85–94.

Bhatia, V. K. (1993). *Analysing Genre: Language use in professional settings.* London: Longman.

Biber, D., Connor, U., & Upton, T. (2007). *Discourse on the move: Using corpus analysis to describe discourse structure.* Amsterdam: John Benjamins.

Biesenbach-Lucas, S. (2005). Communication topics and strategies in e-mail consultation: Comparison between American and international university students. *Language Learning &Technology, 9* (2), 24–46.

Bremmer, S. (2008). Intertextuality and business communication textbooks: Why students need more textual support. *English for Specific Purposes, 27,* 306–321.

Carrió-Pastor, M. L., & Muñiz-Calderón, R. (2010a). International communication: Certainty and uncertainty terms in business e-mails written by non-native English speakers. *Proceedings of the 9th International Conference of AELFE.* Hamburg: University of Hamburg.

Carrió-Pastor, M. L., & Muñiz-Calderón, R. (2010b). Variations in business English letters written by Spanish learners. *Lenguas para Fines Específicos, 15* (16): 39–56.

Carrió-Pastor, M. L., & Muñiz-Calderón, R. (2012) Lexical variations in business e-mails written by non-native speakers of English. *LSP Journal – Language for special purposes, professional communication, knowledge management and cognition, 3* (1), 4–13.

Carrió-Pastor, M. L., & Muñiz-Calderón, R. (2013). Variation of English business e-mails in Asian countries. *Ibérica*, Special Issue, *26*, 55–76.

Connor, U. (2000). Variation in rhetorical moves in grant proposals of US humanists and scientists. *Text, 20* (1): 1–28.

Crystal, D. (2001). *Language and the Internet.* Cambridge: Cambridge University Press.

Darics, E. (2014). The blurring boundaries between synchronicity and asynchronicity: New communicative situations in work-related instant messaging. *International Journal of Business Communication*, April 11, 2014. doi: 10.1177/2329488414525440.

Del Saz Rubio, M. M. (2011). A pragmatic approach to the macro-structure and metadiscoursal features of research article introductions in the field of agricultural sciences. *English for Specific Purposes, 30*, 258–271.

Dudley-Evans, T. (1994). Model for research article discussion sections. In M. Coulthard (Ed.), *Advances in written text analysis* (pp. 224–228). London: Routledge.

Economidou-Kogetsidis, M. (2011). Please answer me as soon as possible. Pragmatic failure in non-native speakers' e-mail request to faculty. *Journal of Pragmatics, 43*, 3193–3215.

Evans, S. (2012). Designing email tasks for the business English classroom. Implications from a study of Hong Kong's key industries. *English for Specific Purposes, 31*, 202–212.

Flowerdew, J., & Wan, A. (2010). The linguistic and the contextual in applied genre analysis: The case of the company audit report. *English for Specific Purposes, 29*, 78–93.

Gains, J. (1999). Electronic mail – A new style of communication or just a new medium?: An investigation into the text features of e-mail. *English for Specific Purposes, 18* (1): 81–101.

Giménez, J. C. (2000). Business e-mail communication: Some emerging tendencies in register. *English for Specific Purposes, 19*, 237–251.

Giménez, J. C. (2006). Embedded business emails: Meeting new demands in international business communication. *English for Specific Purposes, 25*, 154–172.

Henry, A., & Roseberry, R. L. (2001). A narrow-angles corpus analysis of moves and strategies of the genre: "Letter of application." *English for Specific Purposes, 20*, 153–167.

Jenkins, J. (2009). *World Englishes.* London: Routledge.

Jensen, A. (2009). Discourse strategies in professional e-mail negotiation: A case study. *English for Specific Purposes, 28*, 4–18.

Kachru, B. B. (2005). *Asian Englishes today: Asian Englishes beyond the canon.* Hong Kong: Hong Kong University Press.

Kachru, Y. (2011). World Englishes: Context and relevance for language education. In E. Hinkel (Ed.), *Handbook of research in second language teaching and learning*, volume II (pp. 155–172). New York: Routledge.

Kankaanranta, A. (2005). *"Hej Seppo, Could you pls comment on this!" Internal email communication in lingua franca English in a multinational company.* Jyväskylä: University of Jyväskyla.

Kanoksilapatham, B. (2005). Rhetorical structure of biochemistry research articles. *English for Specific Purposes, 24,* 269–292.

Kirkpatrick, A. (2007). *World Englishes: Implications for international communication and English language teaching.* Cambridge: Cambridge University Press.

Lim, J. M.-H. (2012). How do writers establish research niches? A genre-based investigation into management researchers' rhetorical steps and linguistic mechanisms. *Journal of English for Academic Purposes, 11,* 229–245.

Nickerson, C. (2005). English as a lingua franca in international business contexts. *English for Specific Purposes, 24,* 367–380.

Okamura, A., & Shaw, P. (2000). Lexical phrases, culture, and subculture in transactional letter writing. *English for Specific Purposes, 19,* 1–15.

Peacock, M. (2002). Communicative moves in the discussion section of research articles. *System, 30,* 479–497.

Pinto dos Santos, V. B. M. (2002). Genre analysis of business letters of negotiation. *English for Specific Purposes, 21,* 167–199.

Ren, H., & Li, Y. (2011). A comparison study on the rhetorical moves of abstracts in published research articles and master's foreign-language thesis. *English Language Teaching, 4* (1), 162–166.

Sailaja, P. (2009). *Indian English.* Edinburgh: Edinburgh University Press.

Skovholt, K. (2009). Email literacy in the workplace. A study of interaction norms, leadership communication, and social networks in a Norwegian distributed work group. PhD Dissertation, University of Oslo, Norway.

Skovholt, K., & Svennevig, J. (2006). Email copies in workplace interaction. *Journal of Computer-Mediated Communication, 12,* 42–65.

Skovholt, K., & Svennevig, J. (2013). Responses and non-responses in e-mail interaction. In S. Herring, D. Stein, & T. Virtanen (Eds), *The Pragmatics of Computer-Mediated Communication* (pp. 589–612). Berlin: De Gruyter Mouton.

Sun, H. (2004). Opening moves in informal Chinese telephone conversations. *Journal of Pragmatics, 36,* 1429–1465.

Swales, J. M. (1990). *Genre analysis: English in academic and research settings.* Cambridge: Cambridge University Press.

Thurlow, C., & Mroczek, K. (2011). *Digital discourse.* Oxford: Oxford University Press.

Upton, T., & Connor, U. (2001). Using computerized corpus analysis to investigate the textlinguistic discourse moves of a genre. *English for Specific Purposes, 20,* 313–329.

Vries, de, B., & Meij, H. van der (2003). Using e-mail to support reflective narration. *International Journal of Educational Research, 39,* 829–838.

Yeung, L. (2007). In search of commonalities: Some linguistic and rhetorical features of business reports as a genre. *English for Specific Purposes, 26,* 156–179.

Zarei, G. R., & Darani, P. A. (2013). A comparative study of the rhetorical moves in spam emails: A cross-linguistic investigation between English and Persian spammers. *English for Specific Purposes World, 40* (14), 1–13.

12
Deconstruction–Analysis–Explanation: Contextualization in Professional Digital Discourse

Erika Darics

Instant messaging in business

It is already a truism that emerging communication technologies have changed the landscape of communication in every aspect of our lives, but this is specifically true for how we communicate at work. Advances in communication technologies have enabled a wide range of digital communication modes to be utilized for both internal and external business communication; including audio and visual communication and voice-over protocols, as well as text-based channels, such as email, forums, instant messaging and social media. In spite of the wide range of available audio-visual channels, and despite the ever-increasing popularity of email, real-time text-based communication technologies (instant messaging or IM) are also on the rise (see Mak, 2014; Pazos et al., 2013; Radicati & Levenstein, 2013; and Markman in this volume). The prominence of IM is evident in the rise of this mode of communication, not only as a tool for internal business communication, but as a front-stage channel, particularly for customer service encounters or professional–client conversations (Makarem et al., 2009; Pearce et al., 2013; L. Zhang et al., 2011).

The reason for its popularity is perhaps that, for both internal and external interactions, IM allows for an almost synchronous channel for interactions when both conversational partners are online (Nardi et al., 2000). In the workplace, for example, IM allows for colleagues to contact each other for quick questions and clarifications, thus creating the notion of a shared working environment (Cameron & Webster, 2005; Nardi et al., 2000), when the "line" is left open indefinitely, allowing participants to query one another infrequently on an as-needed basis

(Garrett & Danziger, 2008). For front-stage encounters, from a business perspective, "live chats" are appealing because of their low running costs and the opportunities they present for synchronized interactions (L. Zhang et al., 2011), as well as, from the customer's perspective, the anonymity they create (Pearce et al., 2013).

The increased usage of IM for professional or business purposes, however, has brought to the foreground a range of communication issues inherent in this form of text-based computer-mediated communication. Conversational coherence (or the lack of it), for example, has received considerable scholarly attention (Berglund, 2009; Lam & Mackiewicz, 2007; Woerner et al., 2007; see also Markman in current volume), as well as the communicative effects of multitasking and multiple concurrent conversations (Cameron & Webster, 2005; Reinsch et al., 2008; Rennecker & Godwin, 2003; Turner & Reinsch, 2007) and the problematic nature of turn-taking (Condon & Cech, 2002; Hancock & Dunham, 2001; Markman, 2005; Simpson, 2005b).

To some extent, all of the above issues are somehow linked to one particular aspect of text-based digital communication, stemming from the technicalities of the medium: the absence of a shared physical environment. This means that the creation of the messages (i.e., writing) and the interpretation of the messages (i.e., reading) take place in two separate physical environments, and interactants therefore miss out on the interpersonal and situational context cues as well as non-verbal signs that would normally aid the creation of coherence, the flow of the interaction, and mutual understanding (Chesin et al., 2011; Choi, 2013; Fagan & Desai, 2003; Thompson & Coovert, 2003; Vroman & Kovacich, 2002). Computer-mediated discourse research has already pointed out that, in order to compensate for the absence of these cues, digital discourse tends to utilize the resources available: the whole range of characters and affordances made available by the keyboard (punctuation, keyboard symbols, capitalization), orthographic and typographic strategies as well as the verbal signs. In the following, a more detailed account is given about these strategies and their crucial importance in professional digital environments, in particular for the achievement of effective communication and efficient cooperation. First, I discuss briefly what needs to be known about the distinctive discourse of text-based computer-mediated business communication, with special attention to the role of non-verbal signaling in professional communicative environments. Then, I give a brief summary of the current state of scholarship on non-verbal signals in digital discourse, in order to provide a foundation for the analytical framework proposed in the following section.

The language of professional instant messaging

Organizational and management communication literature has previously acknowledged the lack of non-verbal cues and the effects this might have on professional communication, as well as the relatively high "weight" of the written words in text-only CMC (Berry, 2011; Chesin et al., 2011; Fagan & Desai, 2003, Thompson & Coovert, 2003; Vroman & Kovacich, 2002). Thompson and Coovert (2003) observe that:

> Interactional dynamics suffer during CM (computer-mediated) collaborations, because give-and-take is hindered by the concentrated effort required to type and relay information that is easily transmitted via nonverbal and paraverbal nuances. Online collaborators may attempt to communicate such nuances via a variety of techniques, such as complex syntax and redundancy, however, these techniques are generally regarded as *low-quality, time consuming* substitutes (highlights from the ED). (p. 136)

Similarly, Cornelius and Boos (2003) found that the missing non-verbal cues in task-oriented computer-mediated interactions could only be compensated for by *costly* verbal feedback, which, as pointed out by Fagan and Desai (2003), for many people "presents an insurmountable barrier to full and normal communication" (p. 124). To give countenance to these claims, in a recent large-scale report the majority of respondents (94%) claimed that inability to read non-verbal cues was one of the most challenging aspects of working virtually (CW3, Cultural Wizards, 2010).

Despite this apparent link between verbal and non-verbal communication and possible communication issues in professional online environments, approaches that are concerned with language use and discourse have been somewhat neglected in business and organizational literature. Descriptions such as "virtual communication is confusing" (Thompson & Coovert, 2003), "impoverished," "more laborious and more cognitively taxing" than face-to-face communication (Cornelius & Boos, 2003; Purvanova & Bono, 2009) are often made without empirical support provided from systematic analysis of naturally occurring data. The chapter aims to address this particular gap: by offering a linguistic focus, the chapter aims to bridge the gap between organizational disciplines and language-oriented studies, in particular through the exploration and analysis of text-only digital discourse samples. The chapter aims to inform both areas by raising critical awareness of the range of available and used linguistic and discursive devices, and by offering a framework that could contribute to the improvement of communication effectiveness in the workplace.

Non-verbal cues in digital business discourse

To some extent, as I will demonstrate below, the exploration of the linguistic and discursive features in workplace text-only digital communication has already begun. However, the lack of convergence between (computer-mediated) discourse studies and organizational disciplines make these observations fragmented and not easily applicable to professional situations to improve communication effectiveness.

For example, Nardi et al. (2000) have identified variables in internal IM conversations that have an influence on how the formality of workplace interactions are perceived, claiming that the language use in IM plays a major role in it being perceived as an informal channel. They conclude that language phenomena responsible for the casual nature of IM include "relaxed grammar and spelling," and specifically point out the *liberal use of exclamation marks* as a signal for "friendly responsiveness." Emoticons have also been extensively researched, and in professional contexts have been found to achieve a wide range of communicative functions, for example, contributing to the formation of judgments and impressions about colleagues (Byron & Baldridge, 2007), or to the softening and strengthening of possibly face-threatening messages (Skovholt et al., 2014). In external encounters, Fagan and Desai (2003) examined librarian–patron interactions, and identified a wide range of verbal and non-verbal techniques that add an element of informality to librarian IM, consequently encouraging participation. Specifically, they pointed out humor and expression of sympathy as effective interactional techniques, as well as the use of "emoticons, exaggerated typographical features," and mood comments as ways to add interpersonal content. They suggested that, as a way of improving digital communication skills, librarians should read the printouts of each other's conversations to identify "what works and what doesn't" (p. 154). Similarly, in customer service chats, L. Zhang et al. (2011) found that the inclusion of paralinguistic cues – primarily emoticons – helps to establish the connection between service agents and customers, although negatively relating to the perception of reliability.

Although these findings are useful in informing the individual academic disciplines of organizational studies and computer-mediated discourse studies, further work is clearly necessary to combine these results, including identifying the specific communicative functions of the addressed cues and techniques and exploring how these findings could be used to improve communicative effectiveness at work. This chapter aims to serve as a first step in this work, offering a theoretical framework embedded in the sociolinguistic tradition that allows for a more methodical explanation of the various cues reported in previous literature and also offering a method that allows the various functions of these cues to surface. To introduce the framework, therefore, in the next section I give a brief overview of the current state of the field of computer-mediated discourse analysis (CMDA) regarding CMC cue research, and then introduce the concept of contextualization and the method of immersive linguistic analysis for the exploration of text-only interactional data. Next, I demonstrate the use and usefulness of such an approach through the analysis of excerpts from naturally occurring professional IM data, concluding the chapter by showing how this method could be utilized in preparing professionals for online text-only communication.

Non-verbal cue research in computer-mediated communication

Both the popular media and academic research have long been interested in the typical linguistic features of text-only CMC since the communication mode became available to the wider public. In scholarship there has been a wealth of attempts to categorize, analyze, and describe the creative writing and discursive strategies that serve as non-verbal cues in text-based computer-mediated communication genres, the earliest account dating back to 1980 (Carey, 1980). The early studies of non-verbal signals typically took a heuristic approach, addressing the role of these cues in interaction management, impression formation, and clarification of communicative intent (Carey, 1980; Ferrara et al., 1991; Lea & Spears, 1992; MacKinnon, 1992; Reid, 1991; Thurlow, 2001), but they tended not to consider the closer and wider context of use and do not address important questions such as when exactly these linguistic devices are used, and the interactional and discursive functions assigned to them.

More recent studies have set out to systematically describe written non-verbal cues, with the aim of accounting for the whole range of linguistic devices used for non-verbal signaling. For example, Riordan and Kreuz (2010) identified five big groups of cues: capitalization, repeated letters, repeated punctuation, creative punctuation, and emoticons as eminent cues in their examined corpora. Similar, but slightly different, categories were set up by Bieswanger (2013), who examines emoticons, non-standard spelling, and creative use of writing systems, abbreviation, and non-standard punctuation. Haas et al. (2011) take a writing-focused approach to drawing up their taxonomy of instant message features, while Herring (2012) follows the traditional hierarchy of grammatical phenomena as a framework to discuss all features of "electronic language." The acknowledgment of and the need for research into the complexity and highly context-dependent nature of these cues has also been repeatedly expressed in the literature (Bieswanger, 2013; Thompsen & Foulger, 1996), along with calls to further explore instances where, for example, standard writing functions such as non-verbal signaling or the *lack of* certain features or chronemic information have communicative functions (Darics, 2014). As a response to this call, Kalman and Gergle (2010) set out to explore the meaning of a wide range of paralinguistic CMC cues and proved that the interpretation of these cues is always highly context-dependent. Vandergriff (2013) examined the pragmatic functions of CMC cues, demonstrating that such cues are constitutive of online communication and play a crucial role in emotive communication. The present chapter also sets out to follow this line of inquiry. However, instead of making an attempt to systematically describe CMC cues and their possible meanings, the framework proposed below focuses on the whole range of devices that could possibly serve as *contextualization* in written digital discourse.

Contextualization and immersive textual analysis

The notion of *contextualization cues* has been employed in interactional sociolinguistic literature to refer to the verbal and non-verbal signs that "construct the contextual ground for situated interpretations and thereby affecting how particular messages are understood" (Gumperz, 2005, p. 221). The notion was originally developed for the exploration of oral exchanges, because contextualization cues are thought to be ever present in talk, since spoken messages are always accompanied by paralinguistic and non-verbal signals. These cues are "constellations of surface features of message form by which speakers signal and listeners interpret what the activity is, how semantic content is to be understood and how each sentence relates to what precedes or follows" (Gumperz, 1982, p. 131). Contextualization cues relate to contextual presuppositions (tacit awareness of meaningfulness) and allow participants to make situated inferences about the most likely interpretation of an utterance. Speakers can make choices between features at any of a number of levels including, for example, code, dialect or styles switching; prosodic features; lexical and syntactic options and formulaic expressions; and conversational openings, closings, and sequencing strategies as well as non-verbal cues (Gumperz, 1982).

Contextualization in digital discourse

Naturally, cues that relate to auditory or visual signals are not present in text-only CMC because of the technicalities of the medium, but ways of inscribing such information into writing and other means of contextualization have previously been explored in the CMD literature. Loos (1999), for example, attests that typographic manipulation of texts – the use of italics, underlining, and capitalization – function as contextualization to evoke a shared cultural context, which guides behavior and communication between interactants. Georgakopoulou (2011) examined code-switching and code alterations in email interactions, and found that these are frequent strategic activities utilized as contextualization, in her corpus specifically to signal intimacy and participant alignment. G. Zhang (2011) found that, in Chinese recreational forums, as well as written paralinguistic devices, semantic and syntactic features also play a crucial role in "guiding the tone and the expected development of participants' discussions," especially when signaling playfulness or seriousness. Elsewhere (Darics, 2013), I have argued that the orthographic manipulation of words should also be viewed as contextualization rather than as a means of inscribing vocal information into writing, specifically if the aim is to capture the wide range of possible meanings evoked by this cue.

However, in both oral and digital interactions, the examination of contextualization cues can be problematic. The main difficulty in identifying the cues and how these cues contribute to the creation of meaning lies in the fact that they do not have referential (decontextualized) meaning (Auer, 1992, p. 24). Instead, they have a natural meaning base, the utilization or interpretation of which depends greatly on the wider and closer context as well as on the interactants. In order to explore how contextualization cues "nudge the inferential process" (Levinson, 2003) and influence meaning-making, previous scholarship has taken a discursive, interactional approach aiming to shed light on the discursive creation and negotiation of micro-level meanings (Schiffrin, 1996, p. 315). Drawing on this method, analysts investigate the interaction itself and arrive at an interpretation by demonstrating how participants respond to each other's utterances – that is, by using the reactions that an utterance evokes as evidence of whether interpretive conventions were shared (Grainger, 2013; Gumperz, 1981, quoted in Schiffrin, 1996, p. 314). This immersive textual analysis allows researchers to identify the cues that might have a role in the contextualization of the messages as well as their effects on the interpretative process.

Methodological issues

In order to improve communication effectiveness, particularly in the digital realm, communicators have to be (critically) aware of the range of linguistic, paralinguistic, and discursive strategies available to them to get their meaning across, as well as the wide range of roles, functions, and meanings these strategies can take on. As I have shown above, the concept of contextualization offers a theoretical approach that can account for both the range of cues and their effects in interaction. However, I have also shown that contextualization cues are complex, subtle, and often ambiguous, and their effects during interaction can only be uncovered through close linguistic analyses. To conduct such analyses typically requires training in linguistics, some oversight of anthropology or sociology, and a familiarity with the methodology of qualitative, immersive textual analysis. Perhaps, these requirements account for the fact that this framework has not been extensively utilized for the training and improvement of communicative competence (see, e.g., Schiffrin, 1996).

The method proposed here bridges this gap, enabling non-expert audiences to zoom in on the surface features of text and explore contextualization in digital communication without the need for formal training in the previously mentioned academic disciplines. The method, however, could well be utilized as a research tool to expose and examine the range of cues that could function as contextualization in digital discourse.

The deanex method

In the previous section, I noted that contextualization can occur at any level of linguistic production, and I demonstrated that contextualization and meaning-making can be surfaced through immersive qualitative analysis of naturally occurring data. In what follows, I demonstrate that, by drawing on the conceptual framework of contextualization and applying elements of conversation analysis, it is possible to expose the cues that could function as contextualization and explore their meaning in the given context. The deanex method, this chapter advocates, consists of three stages, and is based on deconstruction–analysis–explanation of natural language examples. To demonstrate the method I use two samples of naturally occurring workplace-based instant message conversations, collected as a part of a bigger corpus of naturally occurring interactions in a virtual team (Darics, 2012). For the purpose of the demonstration very short samples have been chosen, in order to enable us to focus on the process of the analysis and a particular cue type. As will be shown later, the method can also be applied to extended data samples as well as multimodal data.

The "ellipsis mark" example

Deconstruction

The first stage of analysis is called **deconstruction**.[1] This refers to the process in which the analyst zooms in to the surface of the text in order to identify the particular verbal or non-verbal cue (or cues) that might have a role in the contextualization of the messages. In some cases these cues can be very complex and extensive (for example, the tone of a whole message). However, in other cases, they might be as small as a single mark of punctuation. The chosen excerpt exemplifies the latter, focusing on two sets of ellipsis marks in line (2).

Excerpt 1
1. Kaithlin | 16:29 | victor wants a favour
2. Jones | 16:30 | i don't normally do that sort of thing... i have a strict list of clientelle...

Analysis

The second stage – **the analysis** – is the process during which the function or the role of the cue in question is exposed by contrasting the original version of the interaction with a manipulated version. For non-expert audiences the rewriting of the message without the cues in question or replacing the cues with an alternative might offer the possibility of contrasting and comparing the two versions, exposing the possible meanings and functions the cues in question fulfill. In the example below, I have removed the two sets of ellipsis marks in line (2) and replaced the first set by hitting RETURN, to indicate a sentence-final punctuation (Table 12.1).[2]

This stage draws attention to a hidden layer of meaning and function of the ellipsis marks during the interaction, enabling the analysts to

Table 12.1 Manipulation of the ellipsis marks

Excerpt 1	Manipulated version
1. Kaithlin | 16:29 | Victor wants a favour	1. Kaithlin | 16:29 | Victor wants a favour
2. Jones | 16:30 | I don't normally do that sort of thing… I have a strict list of clientelle…	2. Jones | 16:30 | I don't normally do that sort of thing
	3. Jones | 16:30 | I have a strict list of clientelle

compare the original text with a text that lacks the marks in question. As well as the actual manipulation of the surface features, this stage serves as an exposure for the cues and their role in the interaction.

Ellipsis marks have received considerable attention both in scholarship and in popular literature, because of their history in other non-computer-mediated written genres, where they are used mainly to signal the omission of words or phrases or to denote hesitation. In computer-mediated genres, they have been found to take on floor management functions to facilitate coherence, signaling the turn-final position (Berglund, 2009; Fagan & Desai, 2003) and also denoting hesitation/pauses (Hård af Segerstad, 2002; Simpson, 2005). A recent analysis by Mak (2014), however, suggests that ellipsis marks take on a much wider range of communicative functions, and – unlike hesitation in speech – should be viewed as intentional and self-motivated signs that require conscious input by the keyboard. The above extract and its manipulated version prove the validity of these claims, exposing how the ellipsis marks in question accomplish important interactional work in the possibly highly face-threatening situation created by a refusal in a professional business context. During the final stage of the deanex method, it is specifically this interactional work that is exposed and the contextualization function of the ellipsis mark explained.

Explanation

The third stage is the **explanation**, during which the focus is on the evaluation of the differences between the two versions of data. During this stage an attempt is made to account for the relational or task-related communicative functions and the contextualizing nature of the analyzed cues.

In the example above, the main role of the ellipsis mark is neither to facilitate interaction management nor to signal pause but to attenuate the force of refusal. As we can see in Excerpt 1, Kaithlin presents a request to Jones in line (1). Jones' reply in line (2) is potentially not preferred by his partner and could be interpreted either as an indirect refusal or an expression of unwillingness to comply. Jones first provides an explanation, which could be interpreted as a way of distancing the refusal from himself and portraying his actions as prototypical. The second part of his message then provides further explanation for the implied refusal. Both sentences are followed by an ellipsis mark, the significance of which is best understood in comparison with the version not containing the marks in question. While Jones' utterances in the manipulated version read definitely and directly, not displaying any concern for the maintenance of a friendly, collegial relationship with his colleague, in the original version the ellipsis marks attenuate the directness of the refusal. The mitigating nature of the ellipsis mark lies in its ability to signal hints. This means that face-threatening acts are not directly communicated but are inferred by the addressee (on hints in the workplace, cf. Holmes & Stubbe, 2003, pp. 50–2).

For non-specialists, such observations suffice to appreciate the complexity of the written language and cues, and to develop a critical awareness of the range of meanings and possible communicative functions of the various cues and discourse strategies, thus contributing to the improvement of digital communicative competency. When the three-stage deanex method is used for the academic analysis of contextualization in digital discourse, further observations – drawing on previously well-established analytical frameworks such as linguistic politeness and conversation analysis – can also be added. For instance, in the case above, it can be noted that, if we consider the function of hesitation in spoken interactions, the use of ellipsis marks to contextualize hedging is not surprising: as well as signaling intent to hold the floor when the speaker wants to indicate that he or she needs time to think about his or her next utterance or find his or her next focus (Locher, 2004), hesitation has also been found to serve as a device to mitigate a directive intent (Holmes & Stubbe, 2003), a hedging device to signal topic change, or a device to express deferential politeness, in the case of an apology, for instance (Darics, 2010). In text-based digital discourse, ellipsis marks can also take on the breadth of functions of hesitation in speech: as we saw in the example, the aposiopetic function in particular offered a way for non-speakers to finish sentences, thus working as an implication rather than a direct utterance about the task to be done.

The ALL CAPS example

Writing a word or message in capital letters has traditionally been viewed as shouting (Danet et al., 1997; Hård af Segerstad, 2002; Postmes et al., 2000) and has become stigmatized in CMC, especially workplace CMD (see netiquettes on IM, for example, McKillop, 2006). Linguistic research, however, has asserted that capitalization is in fact a creative linguistic strategy that is used to emphasize content or evoke prosody, intonation, or stress (Carey, 1980; Riordan & Kreuz, 2010; Thurlow, 2001; Vandergriff, 2013). The following example demonstrates that, applying the deanex method, it is possible to move beyond popular claims about capitalization and expose the complex contextualization accomplished by this technique.

Deconstruction

Excerpt 2
1. Kaithlin | 12:21 | Hey G
2. George | 12:21 | helloooo
3. Kaithlin | 12:21 | did we get the dates
4. George | 12:22 | Yes I sent to you and Jack I think... let me check
5. Kaithlin | 12:22 | I AM SURE YOU DID
6. Kaithlin | 12:22 | sorry found it
7. George | 12:22 | cool thought I was losing my mind:-)

Excerpt 2 above contains a range of cues that could serve as contextualization by adding to or refining the communicative goals of the verbal message: the informal greeting in line (1), the relaxed spelling in line (2), the lack of proper punctuation in line (3), the ellipsis mark in line (4), the capitalization of the entire utterance in line (5), the relaxed style and emoticon in line (7), or even the timing – the very close succession of the messages in the interaction. In this example, I will focus on line (5), the usage of ALL CAPS.

Analysis

During the second stage, a manipulated version of the original interaction is created and the two versions compared. In doing so we aim to expose how Kaithlin's strategy of capitalization enables the reader to infer the most likely interpretation of the message "I am sure you did" (Table 12.2).

Explanation

Comparing the two versions, it is obvious that the usage of capital letters enables George to narrow down the range of possible interpretations of the verbal message. As written in the manipulated version, "I am sure you did" carries no indication as to whether it should be read

Table 12.2   Manipulation of ALL CAPS

Excerpt 2	Manipulated version
1. Kaithlin | 12:21 | Hey G	1. Kaithlin | 12:21 | Hey G
2. George | 12:21 | helloooo	2. George | 12:21 | helloooo
3. Kaithlin | 12:21 | did we get the dates	3. Kaithlin | 12:21 | did we get the dates
4. George | 12:22 | Yes I sent to you and Jack I think... let me check	4. George | 12:22 | Yes I sent to you and Jack I think... let me check
5. Kaithlin | 12:22 | I AM SURE YOU DID	5. Kaithlin | 12:22 | I am sure you did
6. Kaithlin | 12:22 | sorry found it	6. Kaithlin | 12:22 | sorry found it
7. George | 12:22 | cool thought I was losing my mind:-)	7. George | 12:22 | cool thought I was losing my mind:-)

as a reassuring, positive message or perhaps as an ironic comment hinting the opposite of the literal meaning. The usage of entirely capital letters thus functions as added emotional content, reassuring George of Kaithlin's trust in George's task completion. In line (3) Kaithlin's request or checking of the task could be interpreted as a sign of her dominance in the interaction, which consequently entitles her to do the "checking." The capital letters in line (5) therefore mitigate the force of this imposition, emphasizing the solidarity and common ground between her and her conversational partner.

This observation is particularly important if we consider that, in the situation above, Kaithlin and George are on the same level of organizational hierarchy. In professional encounters where participants are equal colleagues, careful consideration is typically paid to politeness issues and relational work, particularly if one conversational partner wants the other partner to cooperate (Holmes & Stubbe, 2003). The application of the three stages of the deanex method (Table 12.3) sheds light on the fact that in text-based digital interactions capitalization not only adds vocal or other types of emphasis to written text but, by expressing positive emotional attitude, also contributes to the relational work invested in the interaction in order to maintain a familiar and equal working relationship.

Further applications and limitations

The previous examples have shown that by looking at various cues closely within their close textual contexts in a conversation, it is possible to expose their interactional functions. Specifically, I demonstrated the roles of ellipsis marks and capitalization in the achievement of relational goals: the work they accomplish during a conversation as

Table 12.3   The three stages

Deanex method
1. Deconstruction The identification of linguistic and non-verbal cues that might function as contextualization in the digital text; elements that affect the verbal meaning of the messages.
2. Analysis The manipulation of the identified cue, for example contrasting a version of the text WITH the cue with a version without, or replacing the cue.
3. Explanation The explanation of what the cue in question does in the text – how it changes the communicative function in terms of the content and the communication of interpersonal intent, or the communication of identity.

a means of mitigating the force of a refusal or as a means of adding emotional emphasis. The application of the deanex method, however, is also possible in instances where analysts have no access to an entire interaction, for instance, in the case of stand-alone emails, online reviews, or website communication. In these cases it is also possible to identify discourse strategies and verbal or non-verbal cues that contextualize messages or take on specific communicative functions. The interaction in these cases, however, takes place between the message and the reader-analyst, who interprets the message generally and the identified cues specifically (Figure 12.1).

For example, in the case of pop-up communication from Twitter, the deanex method can be applied to expose the meaning and function of "hmm" in the message. Following the creation of a manipulated version (for example, by removing or replacing the non-lexical token "hmm"), the reader-analyst compares how the two versions affect his or her own interpretation, thus exposing the difference caused by the inclusion of the non-lexical token. The deanex method can also provide indirect insights into multimodal communicative episodes, when, for instance, an image, or the size and typeface of a message is manipulated.

One possible limitation of the deanex method is if the targeted cues are complex and not easily identifiable. So far the examples listed in this chapter have been relatively easy to find in the written messages, but complex cues, such as "style" or "tone" are harder for deanex to expose. For instance, in email communication, how the written words are chosen, expressed, and organized plays a crucial role in the contextualization of

Figure 12.1 A Twitter message

messages (Chen, 2006). Other problematic cues include the *lack* of cues, as in the conventional use of spelling or grammar, or cues not present in the script, such as chronemic cues (Darics, 2014). Although it is possible to apply the three stages of the deanex method in these instances, the exercise might require a substantial rewriting of the original message and would thus require longer preparation, as in the examples cited before. Naturally, as a result of an extensive rewriting, there is a higher risk of the distortion of the sense-making or inductive reasoning process, therefore this exercise has to be used with caution for scientific analysis. However, the comparison enabled by the manipulation of the data and the exposure of the communicative and contextualizing functions of the complex cues could still be highly beneficial for students or trainees, raising critical awareness of the range of possible cues and consequently improving their digital communication competency.

It is also important to note that while the close, immersive analysis of deanex allows for the exploration of textual and (meta)discursive functions, further and much more detailed insights could be gained if the method is complemented by other, qualitative approaches. Barton and Lee (2013), for example, attest that interviews and logbooks could provide invaluable information about the lives of IM users and shed light on whether their "IM text-making might have been mediated by other online practices" (p. 169). Similarly, Gimenez (2014) argues that it is necessary to adopt a multidimensional analytical approach, which draws on the examination of a variety of networked data sets, such as naturally occurring data, narratives, documents, and artifacts, in order to capture the complexity of online professional communication. These methods could thus be used along with deanex as multi-method approaches in research, but also for training and instruction to enable a reflection on professional practice.

Conclusion

Real-time or near-real-time text-based digital conversations have become critical for today's organizations and businesses: communication technology is used by companies to facilitate internal communication between team members who do not share the same physical environment, typically for quick discussion and information exchange but also as a means of creating a notion of a shared working environment. Externally, communication technology is increasingly utilized for customer support services (e.g., Fagan & Desai, 2003; L. Zhang et al., 2011) or professional–client interactions, for instance, in healthcare (Stommel & Houwen, 2013). As a result of advances in communication technologies and the ability of customers to initiate conversation and voice their critical opinions, there is also a pressing need for companies to engage in interactions via various social media platforms (Lillqvist & Louhiala-Salminen, 2014; Vásquez, 2014).

These mediated interactions have now become critical aspects of business success because of their real economic impact and financial consequences. Within a workplace or work team, the effectiveness of digital interactions and the resulting outcomes are thought to be "dependent on the resolution of miscommunication and conflict, the development of adequate and competent roles within the team for working together, and facilitating good communication between team members" (Berry, 2011, p. 202). In external communications, interactions with consumers have considerable effects on impression formation, consumer satisfaction and trust, consequently affecting sales and brand loyalty (Lillqvist & Louhiala-Salminen, 2014; Vásquez, 2014). It is not surprising, therefore, that researchers have set out to explore how exactly communication happens online, emphasizing the crucially important role of language and discourse during the complex, digitally mediated meaning-making processes. This shift of focus towards the "discursive details" (Lillqvist &

Louhiala-Salminen, 2014) answers the call of Potter and Balthazar, who urge the research community "to develop additional theoretical perspectives as well as additional methodologies and research approaches in order to get a deeper insight into computer mediated workplace interactions" (Potter & Balthazar, 2002).

This chapter contributes to this development by offering an analytical framework that draws on the findings of interactional sociolinguistics and on the methodology of conversation analysis. The method is based on a three-stage process, comprising the "deconstruction" of digital utterances and the identification of elements that could contribute to the contextualization of messages; the "analysis" of the identified phenomena by creating a manipulated version of the data and contrasting it with the original version; and the "explanation" of the communicative roles and the contextualization that takes place in the specific context of usage. In this chapter I have used two extracts from workplace IM conversations to demonstrate how the method can be used to identify the subtle and complex communicative functions of written non-verbal strategies. The examples specifically focused on the usage of ellipsis and capital letters. However, it has also been pointed out that the method is applicable to the whole spectrum of possible contextualization cues.

As well as functioning as a research tool for the identification of contextualization in digital discourse, it has been proposed that the method also be used as a training tool for professionals and other non-academic audiences for the improvement of computer-mediated communication effectiveness. In spoken interactions, it has been found that contextualization can only be learnt by rich exposure to a communicative tradition and a deep immersion in social networks (Levinson, 2003). In the case of digital texts, the deanex method enables the speeding up of this process through exposure of a wide range of contextualization cues and their possible roles in task-related or relational communication.

It has to be noted, however, that by focusing on surface-level phenomena that inscribe an additional layer of meaning into digital texts, the embedded nature of language in social practices should not be neglected. In her recent book on corporate discourse, Breeze (2013) draws attention to the "continuum extending from the surface of the text, through the roles that this text performs in social contexts, to the structures and ideas that configure whole societies" as well as a "two-way influence along this line." To account for this continuum and the social embeddedness of digital workplace discourse, further research could explore the use of contextualization cues by users of various cultural backgrounds and in multicultural interactions (e.g., Mak, 2014), the role of contextualization in the interactional creation of professional identities and communication power (Skovholt, in current volume) or gender (see, e.g., L. Zhang et al., 2011). By enabling the analyst to adopt a microanalytic discursive approach, the deanex method highlights aspects of interaction that would pass unnoticed, therefore contributing to a more complete understanding of how linguistic and discursive choices shape meaning as well as interpersonal relations, and consequently how they affect the effectiveness of internal and external professional communication.

Notes

1. I have chosen this name partly due to the literal sense of the word denoting the deconstruction of discourse to the smallest elements, but also partly to evoke a basic stance of Deconstruction (Derrida, 1982) about signs and terms.
2. Both sets of ellipsis marks could have been replaced by full stops to indicate sentence-final punctuation. However, in instant messaging, the full stop to signal the end is often omitted (cf. Haas et al., 2011, p. 385)

References

Auer, P. (1992). Introduction: John Gumperz' approach to contextualization. In P. Auer, & A. Di Luzio (Eds), *The Contextualization of Language* (pp. 1–37). Amsterdam: John Benjamins.
Barton, D., & Lee, C. (2013). *Language Online*. Abingdon: Routledge.
Berglund, T. Ö. (2009). Disrupted turn adjacency and coherence maintenance in instant messaging conversations. *Language@internet*, (6). Retrieved October 30, 2010 from: http://www.languageatinternet.org/articles/2009/2106/?search term=berglund.
Berry, G. R. (2011). Enhancing effectiveness on virtual teams: Understanding why traditional team skills are insufficient. *Journal of Business Communication, 48* (2), 186–206. doi: 10.1177/0021943610397270.
Bieswanger, M. (2013). Micro-linguistic structural features of computer-mediated communication. In S. C. Herring, D. Stein, & T. Virtanen (Eds), *Pragmatics of Computer-Mediated Communication* (pp. 463–485). Berlin: Mouton De Gruyter.
Breeze, R. (2013). *Corporate Discourse*. London and New York: Bloomsbury.
Byron, K., & Baldridge, D. C. (2007). E-mail recipients' impressions of senders' likability: The interactive effect of nonverbal cues and recipients' personality. *Journal of Business Communication, 44* (2), 137–160.
Cameron, A. F., & Webster, J. (2005). Unintended consequences of emerging communication technologies: Instant messaging in the workplace. *Computers in Human Behavior, 21* (1), 85–103.
Carey, J. (1980). Paralanguage in computer-mediated communication. Paper presented at the *Proceedings of the 18th Annual Meeting on Association for Computational Linguistics*, Philadelphia, pp. 67–69.

Chen, C. E. (2006). The development of e-mail literacy: From writing to peers to writing to authority figures. *Language Learning & Technology, 10* (2), 35–55.

Chesin, A., Rafaeli, A., & Bos, N. (2011). Anger and happiness in virtual teams: Emotional influence of text and behavior on other's affect in the absence of non-verbal cues. *Organizational Behaviour and Human Decision Processes, 16* (1), 2–16. doi: 10.1016/j.obhdp.2011.06.002.

Choi, S. (2013, 18 December). Does punctuation influence social customer service? Retrieved from: http://www.sparkcentral.com/blog/punctuation-influence-social-customer-service/.

Condon, S. L., & Cech, C. G. (2002). Profiling turns in interaction: Discourse structure and function. Paper presented at the *Proceedings of the 34th Annual Hawaii International Conference on System Sciences 2001.* 10–20.

Cornelius, C., & Boos, M. (2003). Enhancing mutual understanding in synchronous computer-mediated communication by training. *Communication Research, 30* (2), 147–177.

CW3 Cultural Wizards. (2010). The challenges of working in virtual teams. Retrieved on 12/09/2012 from http://rw-3.com/VTSReportv7.pdf

Danet, B., Ruedenberg-Wright, L., & Rosenbaum-Tamari, Y. (1997). "HMMM ... WHERE'S THAT SMOKE COMING FROM?" Writing, play and performance on internet relay chat. *Journal of Computer-Mediated Communication, 2* (4), doi: 10.1111/j.1083-6101.1997.tb00195.x.

Darics, E. (2010). Relational work in synchronous text-based CMC of virtual teams. In R. Taiwo (Ed.), *Handbook of Research on Discourse Behavior and Digital Communication: Language Structures and Social Interaction* (pp. 830–851). Hershey, PA: IGI Global.

Darics, E. (2012). Instant messaging in work-based virtual teams: The analysis of non-verbal communication used for the contextualisation of transactional and relational communicative goals. Unpublished PhD, University of Loughborough, Loughborough.

Darics, E. (2013). Non-verbal signalling in digital discourse: The case of letter repetition. *Discourse, Context & Media, 2* (3), 141–148. doi: http://dx.doi.org/10.1016/j.dcm.2013.07.002.

Darics, E. (2014). The blurring boundaries between synchronicity and asynchronicity: New communicative situations in work-related instant messaging. *Journal of Business Communication,* 1–22. doi: 10.1177/2329488414525440.

Derrida, J. (1982). *Positions.* London: The Athlone Press.

Fagan, J. C., & Desai, C. M. (2003). Communication strategies for instant messaging and chat reference services. *The Reference Librarian, 38* (79–80), 121–155.

Ferrara, K., Brunner, H., & Whittemore, G. (1991). Interactive written discourse as an emergent register. *Written Communication, 8* (1), 8–34.

Garrett, R. K., & Danziger, J. N. (2008). IM = interruption management? Instant messaging and disruption in the workplace. Journal of Computer-Mediated Communication, *13* (1), 23–42. doi: 10.1111/j.1083-6101.2007.00384.x.

Georgakopoulou, A. (2011). On for drinkies?': E-mail cues of participant alignments. *Language@internet, 8* (4), 06/03/2013.

Gimenez, J. (2014). Reflections of professional practice: Using electronic discourse analysis networks (EDANs) to examine embedded business emails. In F. Sudweeks & H. L. Lim (Eds), *Innovative Methods and Technologies for Electronic*

Discourse Analysis (pp. 327–345). Hershey, PA: IGI Global. doi: 10.4018/978-1-4666-4426-7.ch015.

Grainger, K. (2013). Of babies and bath water: Is there any place for Austin and Grice in interpersonal pragmatics? *Journal of Pragmatics, 58,* 27–38. doi: http://dx.doi.org/10.1016/j.pragma.2013.08.008.

Gumperz, J. J. (1981). Conversational inference and classroom learning. In J. Green, & C. Wallat (Eds.), *Ethnography and language in educational settings* (pp. 3–23). Norwood, NJ: Ablex.

Gumperz, J. J. (1982). *Discourse strategies.* Cambridge: Cambridge University Press.

Gumperz, J. J. (2005). Interactional sociolinguistics: A personal perspective. In D. Tannen, D. Schiffrin, & H. Hamilton (Eds), *The Handbook of Discourse Analysis* (4th edition, pp. 215–228). Oxford: Blackwell.

Haas, C., Takayoshi, P., Carr, B., Hudson, K., & Pollock, R. (2011). Young people's everyday literacies: The language features of instant messaging. *Research in the Teaching of English, 45* (4), 378–404.

Hancock, J. T., & Dunham, P. J. (2001). Language use in computer-mediated communication: The role of coordination devices. *Discourse Processes, 31* (1), 91–110.

Hård af Segerstad, Y. (2002). *Use and adaptation of written language to the conditions of computer-mediated communication.* Unpublished PhD, thesis, Göteborg University, Sweden. Retrieved from: http://www.ling.gu.se/~ylvah/dokument/ylva_diss.pdf.

Herring, S. C. (2012). Grammar and electronic communication. In C. A. Chapelle (Ed.), *Encyclopedia of Applied Linguistics.* Oxford: Wiley-Blackwell. doi: 10.1002/9781405198431.wbeal0466.

Holmes, J., & Stubbe, M. (2003). *Power and Politeness in the Workplace.* Harlow: Longman.

Isaacs, E., Walendowski, A., Whittaker, S., Schiano, D. J., & Kamm, C. (2002). The character, functions, and styles of instant messaging in the workplace. *Proceedings of the 2002 ACM Conference on Computer Supported Cooperative Work,* pp. 11–20.

Kalman, Y. M., & Gergle, D. (2010). CMC cues enrich lean online communication: The case of letter and punctuation mark repetitions. Unpublished manuscript. Retrieved October 17, 2011 from: http://www.kalmans.com/MCIS2010Cues.pdf.

Koester, A. (2006). *Investigating Workplace Discourse.* London: Routledge.

Lam, C., & Mackiewicz, J. (2007). A case study of coherence in workplace instant messaging. *Professional Communication Conference, 2007. IPCC 2007. IEEE International,* pp. 1–6. doi: 10.1109/IPCC.2007.4464067.

Lea, M., & Spears, R. (1992). Paralanguage and social perception in computer-mediated communication. *Journal of Organizational Computing and Electronic Commerce, 2* (3–4), 321–341.

Levinson, S. C. (2003). Contextualizing "contextualization cues". In S. L. Eerdmans, C. L. Prevignano, & P. J. Thibault (Eds), *Language and Interaction: Discussions with John J. Gumperz* (pp. 31–40). Amsterdam and Philadelphia: John Benjamins.

Lillqvist, E., & Louhiala-Salminen, L. (2014). Facing Facebook: Impression management strategies in company–consumer interactions. *Journal of Business and Technical Communication, 28* (1), 3–30. doi: 10.1177/1050651913502359.

Locher, M. A. (2004). *Power and Politeness in Action: Disagreements in Oral Communication*. Berlin: Mouton de Gruyter.

Loos, E. (1999). Intertextual networks in organizations: The use of written and oral business discourse in relation to context. In F. Bargiela-Chiappini & C. Nickerson (Eds), *Writing Business: Genres, Media and Discourses* (pp. 315–332). New York: Pearson Education.

MacKinnon, R. C. (1992). *Searching for the Leviathan in Usenet*. Unpublished MS, San Jose State University.

Makarem, S. C., Mudambi, S. M., & Podoshen, J. S. (2009). Satisfaction in technology-enabled service encounters. *Journal of Services Marketing, 23* (3), 134–144.

Mak, B. C. N. (2014). Instant messaging in office hours: Use of ellipsis dots at work and Hong Kong culture. *International Journal of Language Studies, 8* (2), 25–50.

Markman, K. M. (2005). To send or not to send: Turn construction in computer-mediated chat. *Proceedings of the Twelfth Annual Symposium about Language and Society*, Austin. 115–124.

McKillop, R. (2006). *How to be polite while you're online (practicing good netiquette)*. Retrieved October 9, 2012 from: http://www.simplehelp.net/ 2006/08/14/how-to-be-polite-while-youre-online-practicing-good-netiquette/.

Nardi, B. A., Whittaker, S., & Bradner, E. (2000). Interaction and outeraction: Instant messaging in action. *Proceedings of the 2000 ACM Conference on Computer Supported Cooperative Work*, pp. 79–88.

Pazos, P., Chung, J. M., & Micari, M. (2013). Instant messaging as a task-support tool in information technology organizations. *Journal of Business Communication, 50* (1), 68–86. doi: 10.1177/0021943612465181.

Pearce, G., Thøgersen-Ntoumani, C., & Duda, J. L. (2013). The development of synchronous text-based instant messaging as an online interviewing tool. *International Journal of Social Research Methodology, 17* (6), 1–16. doi: 10.1080/13645579.2013.827819.

Postmes, T., Spears, R., & Lea, M. (2000). The formation of group norms in computer-mediated communication. *Human Communication Research, 26* (3), 341–371.

Potter, R. E., & Balthazard, P. A. (2002). Virtual team interaction styles: Assessment and effects. *International Journal of Human Computer Studies, 56* (4), 423–443.

Purvanova, R. K., & Bono, J. E. (2009). Transformational leadership in context: Face-to-face and virtual teams. *The Leadership Quarterly, 20* (3), 343–357.

Radicati, S., & Levenstein, J. (2013). *Email Statistics Report, 2013–2017*. Palo Alto, CA: The Radicati Group, Inc.

Reid, E. (1991). *Electropolis: Communication and community on Internet relay chat*. Unpublished manuscript. Retrieved September 24, 2006 from: http:// www.irchelp.org/irchelp/communication-research/academic/academic-reid-e-electropolis-1991.html.

Reinsch, N. L., Turner, J. W., & Tinsley, C. H. (2008). Multicommunicating: A practice whose time has come? *The Academy of Management Review, 33* (2), 391–403.

Rennecker, J., & Godwin, L. (2003). Theorizing the unintended consequences of instant messaging for worker productivity. *Sprouts: Working Papers on Information Environments, Systems and Organizations, 3* (3), 137–168.

Riordan, M. A., & Kreuz, R. J. (2010). Cues in computer-mediated communication: A corpus analysis. *Computers in Human Behavior, 26*, 1806–1817. doi:10.1016/j.chb.2010.07.008.

Schiffrin, D. (1996). Interactional sociolinguistics. In S. Sandra L. McKay & N. H. Hornberger (Eds), *Sociolinguistics and Language Teaching* (pp. 307–328). Cambridge: Cambridge University Press.

Simpson, J. (2005). Meaning-making online: Discourse and CMC in a language learning community. In A. M. Vilas, P. B. Gonzales, G. J. Mesa, & G. J. A. Mesa (Eds), *Recent Research Developments in Learning Technologies* (pp. 175–179). Badajoz: Formatex.

Simpson, J. (2005b). Conversational floors in synchronous text-based CMC discourse. *Discourse Studies, 7* (3), 337–361.

Skovholt, K., Grønning, A., & Kankaanranta, A. (2014). The communicative functions of emoticons in workplace e-mails::-). *Journal of Computer Mediated Communication, 19* (4), 780–797. doi: 10.1111/jcc4.12063.

Stommel, W., & Houwen, F. V. D. (2013). Formulations in 'Trouble' chat sessions. *Language@internet, 10* (3), May 2, 2014. doi: urn:nbn:de:0009-7-36966.

Thompsen, P. A., & Foulger, D. A. (1996). Effects of pictographs and quoting on flaming in electronic mail. *Computers in Human Behavior, 12* (2), 225–243. doi: 10.1016/0747-5632(96)00004-0.

Thompson, L. F., & Coovert, M. D. (2003). Teamwork online: The effects of computer conferencing on perceived confusion, satisfaction and postdiscussion accuracy. *Group Dynamics: Theory, Research, and Practice, 7* (2), 135–151. doi: 10.1037/1089-2699.7.2.135.

Thurlow, C. (2001). The internet and language. In R. Mesthrie (Ed.), *Concise Encyclopedia of Sociolinguistics* (pp. 287–289). Amsterdam: Elsevier.

Turner, J. W., & Reinsch, N. L. (2007). The business communicator as presence allocator: Multicommunicating, equivocality, and status at work. *Journal of Business Communication, 44* (1), 36. doi: 10.1177/0021943606295779.

Vandergriff, I. (2013). Emotive communication online: A contextual analysis of computer-mediated communication (CMC) cues. *Journal of Pragmatics, 51,* 1–12. doi: http://dx.doi.org/10.1016/j.pragma.2013.02.008.

Vásquez, C. (2014). Hotels' responses to online reviews: Managing consumer dissatisfaction. *Discourse, Context and Media, 6,* 54–64. doi:10.1016/j.dcm.2014.08.004.

Vroman, K., & Kovacich, J. (2002). Computer-mediated interdisciplinary teams: Theory and reality. *Journal of Interprofessional Care, 16* (2), 159–170. doi: 10.1080/13561820220124175.

Woerner, S. L., Yates, J. A., & Orlikowski, W. J. (2007). Conversational coherence in instant messaging and getting work done. *40th Annual Hawaii International Conference on System Sciences, 2007. HICSS 2007,* pp. 77–87.

Zhang, G. (2011). Age, culture, and communication: Contextualization and framing in a playful online forum. *Proceedings of the American Society for Information Science and Technology,* New Orleans, USA, *48* (1), 1–9. doi: 10.1002/meet.2011.14504801029.

Zhang, L., Erickson, L. B., & Webb, H. C. (2011). *Effects of "emotional text" on online customer service chat.* Paper presented at the 16th Graduate Students Research Conference in Hospitality and Tourism, University of Massachusetts, Amherst. Retrieved January 19, 2015 from http://scholarworks.umass.edu/gradconf_hospitality/2011/Presentation/42/

Index

GPSR Compliance
The European Union's (EU) General Product Safety Regulation (GPSR) is a set of rules that requires consumer products to be safe and our obligations to ensure this.

If you have any concerns about our products, you can contact us on

ProductSafety@springernature.com

In case Publisher is established outside the EU, the EU authorized representative is:

Springer Nature Customer Service Center GmbH
Europaplatz 3
69115 Heidelberg, Germany